tempered radicals

Tempered radicals

How People Use Difference to Inspire Change at Work

Debra E. Meyerson

Harvard Business School Press
Boston, Massachusetts

Text design by Joyce C. Weston
Printed in the United States of America
05 04 03 02 01   5 4 3 2 1

Requests for permission to use or reproduce material from this
book should be directed to permissions@hbsp.edu, or mailed to
Permissions, Harvard Business School Publishing,
60 Harvard Way, Boston, Massachusetts 02163.

Library of Congress Cataloging-in-Publication Data
Meyerson, Debra.
Tempered radicals : how people use difference to inspire
change at work / Debra E. Meyerson.
p. cm.
Includes index.
ISBN: 0-87584-905-9 (alk. paper)
1. Organizational change. 2. Corporate culture. I. Title.
HD58.8 .M493 2001
658.4'06--dc21
2001024505

The paper used in this publication meets the requirements
of the American National Standard for Permanence of Paper
for Publications and Documents in Libraries and Archives
Z39.48-1992.

To the memory of my dedicated and loving father,
Aubrey Jay Meyerson (1931–1995),
who showed me how to take risks
and live life fully.

And to my mother,
Marcia Meyerson,
who throughout my life has
provided the love and safety
to let me do so.

Each time a man stands up for an idea, or acts to improve the lot of others, or strikes out against injustice, he sends forth a tiny ripple of hope, and crossing each other from a million different centers of energy and daring, those ripples build a current that can sweep down the mightiest walls of oppression and resistance.

Few are willing to brave the disapproval of their fellows, the censure of their colleagues, the wrath of their society. Moral courage is a rarer commodity than bravery in battle or greater intelligence. Yet it is the one essential, vital quality for those who seek to change a world that yields most painfully to change.

— *Robert Kennedy*

Contents

Preface

"TEMPERED RADICALS" are people who want to succeed in their organizations yet want to live by their values or identities, even if they are somehow at odds with the dominant culture of their organizations. Tempered radicals want to fit in *and* they want to retain what makes them different. They want to rock the boat, and they want to stay in it.

I have been amazed by the wide range of people who identify with this description. Since the original article Maureen Scully and I published in 1995, a later feature, and dozens of talks and classes I have delivered on the topic, I have heard from hundreds of people—many of whom would never consider themselves "radical"—who recognize their own experiences in descriptions of "tempered radicals."[1] Some see in these portraits a new way to "be" in organizations in which they do not completely fit. Others take comfort in knowing that they are not alone in their struggles, and still others are reassured in seeing that their everyday efforts to resist the majority culture and uphold personal values and commitments might actually be making a difference for others.

The people who identify with this portrait include women and men who work in a variety of professions—from business to education, from nursing to politics, from architecture to the military—at different levels of seniority—from the very "top" to the very "bottom"—of their organizations. These men and women of all races, religions, ethnic origins, ages, and sexual orientations from every corner of the globe describe how they must walk a fine line in their efforts to fit in without selling their souls. Some want to effect change but know they must tread cautiously so as not to jeopardize their organizational credibility.

The people who see themselves as tempered radicals feel somehow different from the traditional majority in their organizations—women and men concerned about social justice or environmentalism in profit-motivated corporations; people who want to be active parents or citizens in all-consuming, high-tech companies; women who don't want to act like men in male-dominated institutions; people of color who want to expand the boundaries of inclusion in predominantly white organizations; people who believe in humanist ideals in economically driven professions; and so forth. These people want to fit in and succeed. But they also want to speak their own truths and many want to effect change.

I have written this book to reveal the spectrum of approaches people use to walk the fine line between difference and fit, and to use their differences to inspire positive changes in their organizations. Unfortunately, many people never find a way to sustain this balance, so they have fundamentally disempowering experiences of being "different." They respond to ongoing pressure to conform to the majority in ways that hurt themselves and limit the possibility for broader learning and change. While some people silence their differences purposefully and feel that the benefits of fitting into the majority are worth the personal compromises, many others conform simply because they see no other choice, so they surrender a part of themselves in order to survive. Others opt to leave the organization, feeling that they have no way to "be" within the status quo. Still others flame out; they stridently challenge the status quo in a manner that is sufficiently antagonistic that they confirm what they believed—that they do not belong.

These responses can entail a good deal of pain. I have witnessed the loss people suffer in the course of compromising their sense of self and silencing their commitments to fit in. I have heard the resignation some express as they leave organizations because they cannot find a way to be true to their values and identities and still survive. And I have seen the antagonism others express through increasingly radical and self-defeating acts.

But these are not the only options for those who want to fit in and also want to express their differences. A wide middle ground stretches between the extremes of conformity and pure radicalism. In this book I lay out a continuum of responses—from tempered and quiet efforts to hold onto and express one's different self to more public and deliberate efforts to effect change. This continuum represents the range of responses and strategies that I have called tempered radicalism.

MY INTEREST in this topic grew out of my personal experience and my own sense of misalignment. In the early 1980s, Maureen Scully and I were doctoral students together at Stanford's Graduate

School of Business. As women concerned with justice, inequities, and the constraints placed on men and women in traditional organizations, we were not the ideal students in our graduate program. Like other doctoral programs based in business schools, our program was designed to train its students to become educators of the next generation of elite corporate leaders.

Put simply, we were "poor fits" in our profession. Our values and interests were at odds with those dominant in our profession, yet we were both committed to succeeding within the profession and trying to change it. We did not have to look far in our profession to find others who shared our sense of misalignment. Linda Smircich, a well-established scholar, publicly struggled with a similar tension in a paper she presented, "Can a radical humanist find happiness in a business school?"[2] The dilemmas she articulated fueled our concerns. It was also no coincidence that both of us were advisees of Professor Joanne Martin, a surviving feminist and the first tenured woman at Stanford's Business School. Behind the closed doors of her office, she shared with us some of the dilemmas she faced in balancing the demands of the male-dominated culture of the business school with her own progressive ideals and the needs of her family. We watched her navigate between her commitment to maintain her credibility within the mainstream of the profession and at the same time advance a social agenda that involved opening opportunities for women and minorities and breaking down boundaries within the profession. Her career entailed an ongoing "swim against the tide."[3] Both of us directly benefited from and were deeply moved by her struggles.

Maureen and I shared our feelings of professional misalignment in a general sense, but also in the context of specific choices we faced. When we proposed working on topics that reflected our interests, such as the challenges faced by "feminist executives," we were strongly advised by faculty against taking up such a radical and risky topic at this formative stage in our careers. We needed to build our credibility, they cautioned, and association with such a radical topic could tarnish our reputations. This advice left us wondering whether we would ever legitimately be able to pursue our interests and stay true to our values within the mainstream institutions of our field.

Maureen and I followed the advice we were given and put our original concerns about "feminist executives" on hold long enough to land faculty positions in business schools. But our ideologies and scholarly agendas continued to feel at odds with what was valued in our profession. Each of us felt a deep ambivalence toward our profession, and my own ambivalence grew as I began teaching business students and executives, submitting papers to professional journals, and taking on an increasing range of professional responsibilities.

Along with my sense of misalignment, however, I began also to feel a growing sense of opportunity. I came to accept my ambivalence as sustainable and even advantageous. I thought, "If I can influence a few managers to think differently about hidden biases at work, if I can contribute slightly to broadening the scope of what my profession sees as a contribution, if I can prod the minds of a few students to think about how they use their power and privilege, or if I can challenge the rigid linear career ladder within academia, I would be acting on my values and possibly making a small difference inside and outside of my profession."[4]

Maureen and I eventually returned to our original interest in feminist executives and expanded it to include others who feel in some way at odds with their institutions and want to effect change. We coined the term "tempered radical" to capture the competing pulls faced by these individuals and the delicate balance between conformity and rebellion that they must sustain.

My interest in writing this book was kindled by people's interest and questions following that article and subsequent presentations. I wanted to explore further the experiences of people who are different from the majority culture and who hold commitments to effect change within organizations that leave little room for such differences. I wanted to understand more fully the range of strategies people use to act on and proactively uphold their competing values and commitments. And, most important, I also wanted to learn more about how tempered radicals' efforts contribute to learning and adaptation beyond the individuals themselves.

The Research

In a sense, my research for this book started fifteen years ago with the work Maureen and I did for our original article. During that project, we conducted over thirty interviews and dozens of observations of tempered radicals in different occupations, ranging from academics to corporate ethics officers, neurosurgeons to college admissions officers, corporate executives to secretaries.

For the specific purpose of this book, I conducted semistructured interviews with 102 people in two primary business organizations and an additional 80 interviews in a third company. (See appendix A for further details on the sample and appendix B for details on my interview methodology.) In addition, I conducted 56 additional interviews with individuals who self-identified as change agents. This included six students who had just completed a master's degree program in business and social responsibility and were now working to put these ideals into practice.[5] This portion of the sample also included people with a wide variety of change agendas in a number of different occupations: doctors, nurses, lawyers, architects, social workers, teachers, engineers, academics, public health professionals, organizational development professionals, admissions officers, secretaries, consultants, investment bankers, entrepreneurs, chief executives, managers, public officials, journalists, and a female admiral in the U.S. Navy.

I chose my two primary research sites—Western Financial and Atlas Tech (both pseudonyms)—for the purpose of contrast. I believed that these organizations would have drastically different cultures that would produce distinct experiences and challenges for tempered radicals.

Western is a traditional financial institution located in the northwestern United States. I chose Western partly because the CEO, who was expected to retire soon, had made several public statements about the importance of diversity and had allocated significant resources to create corporate diversity programs and to recruit women and people of color. Some people reported that he wanted diversity to be part of his legacy. I wanted to see to what extent this commitment affected people's day-to-day experiences.

In many ways, the organization exemplified a bureaucratic institution: roles and ranks were clear, lines of authority were well defined, and career paths were well demarcated. Its formal structure was reflected also in its traditional culture. All officers and managers had regular offices, the sizes of which varied predictably by people's rank.

People dressed in formal business attire, though at the time of my study, they were beginning to experiment with "casual Fridays," which was seen as a bold intervention. People were expected to work hard at Western, and there appeared to be little informal "hanging out" during regular work hours. At the time of my study, Western's management refused to recognize and sanction identity-based employee groups (e.g., gay and lesbian groups, women's groups), thinking they were too similar to unions, which Western had a long history of opposing. At Western, I interviewed fifty-eight men and women, all but thirteen of whom held the rank of assistant vice president or higher (see appendix A).

The culture at Atlas appears as the polar opposite. Based in the heart of Silicon Valley and founded in the late 1970s, Atlas is now a mature, publicly traded global corporation that designs, manufactures, and sells computer components throughout the world. In contrast to Western's culture, Atlas's culture is the epitome of high-tech informal. I regularly witnessed jokes about running into the CEO in the corporate cafeteria and rhetoric about flattening the hierarchy. Most employees worked in cubicles designed to open up communication and "flatten the hierarchy." People dressed informally—some employees regularly wore T-shirts and shorts, no doubt a remnant of the company's strong engineering origins. People worked hard at Atlas, and some casually mentioned their recent "all-nighters," but they also seemed to take pride in the fact that they "played hard" as well. Employees regularly spoke of the importance of fitting into the "Atlas way," and virtually everyone I interviewed interpreted this in the same way—as confident, hard-working, smart, and outspoken. The CEO of Atlas emphasized diversity, and Atlas had an office of "multiculturalism" staffed by four full-time employees, including the leader of the office, a director-level professional who reported to the senior vice president of human resources. Atlas's management fully sanctioned and supported employee groups based on cultural identities. At the time of my study, they sponsored eleven groups. At Atlas, I interviewed forty-four workers at the entry, mid-, and senior levels of management.

I also conducted extensive research at Shop.co (also a pseudonym), a global publicly traded retail organization, which at the time had operations in forty-five countries; I studied only its corporate headquarters in England. This research was initially designed for a different project, but it turned out to be highly relevant. Though Shop.co was two decades old, it still operated in the entrepreneurial spirit of its founder. The organization had little formal structure: roles were fluid, boundaries of authority were unclear, and career trajectories were idiosyncratic. Its entrepreneurial legacy was also reflected in its informal, youthful, and creative culture, which could best be characterized by an "in-your-face" irreverence characteristic of the founding group. Shop.co was known also for its progressive values and stand on social issues. At Shop.co, I interviewed eighty people, many of them multiple times, at all levels—from the CEO to workers on the shop floor. I also conducted extensive observations over a period of three years.

In some ways, the cultures of these three global corporations could not be more different. Western epitomized a formal, bureaucratic institution; Atlas was a mature, but highly informal innovation-driven high-tech organization; and Shop.co was a progressive, hip, retail organization that shunned any suggestion of systems and bureaucratization. While clearly different, these organizations also shared some very important similarities. In each case, senior executives espoused the importance of diversity, and each organization had initiatives to work on this issue. The demographics at the top levels of management were comparable.[6] All three had a very potent and clearly dominant culture, the norms of which were strictly enforced. And the ways the dominant culture of each organization asserted itself and the manner in which power operated were remarkably similar. In each culture clear criteria distinguished insiders from outsiders, and strong norms for action and interaction enforced these distinctions. In general, the forces of the dominant cultures and, most important, the consequences for individuals who did not fit in or who challenged cultural norms were surprisingly similar.

Accordingly, and to my surprise, the struggles and activities of tempered radicals in these three organizations were comparable. I had expected my research sites to illuminate how different organizational contexts shape the experiences of tempered radicals. But since the differences across sites proved to be relatively insignificant, I focus on situational distinctions. The fact that I observed such similar workings of power and protest across these seemingly distinct contexts speaks to the pervasiveness of these dynamics.[7]

The Book

While my general framework is based on inferences from my entire sample, I selected eight people as principal protagonists: Martha Wiley, Sheila Johnson, Peter Grant, and Tom Novak from Western; John Ziwak, Isabel Nuñez, and Jennifer Jackson from Atlas; and Joanie Mason from Shop.co. (All names from these three companies are pseudonyms.) These eight people surfaced as the most consistently representative of the issues I explore, and their examples effectively illustrate the strategies I lay out. In addition, collectively they represent a diverse pool whose "differences" stem from a wide variety of factors, including race, gender, sexual orientation, values, and beliefs. These people appear throughout the book.

To supplement the experiences of these protagonists, I also draw on examples from secondary characters, who appear only once or twice in the book. Most of them come from one of the three main organizations I studied, but I occasionally bring in outside examples. My objective has been to provide the most illustrative and diverse set of examples.

I WRITE this book for the many different types of people who might be tempered radicals even if they don't know it yet. I have organized the book to illustrate the range of ways that tempered radicals effect change. Some bring about change by holding strong to their values and identities and expressing parts of themselves that are at odds with the majority. Whether or not they mean to effect change, simple expressions of "self" that challenge conventional expectations, such as dress codes or norms of professionalism, can provoke meaningful adaptation in the organization. Other tempered radicals make an impact more deliberately and strategically.

Part 1 of the book sets the stage. In chapter 1, I introduce tempered radicals more completely and describe the tensions they experience, explore the range of action strategies they use to respond to these tensions, and outline my general theories of change, the "self," and the relationship between the two. Since tempered radicals all feel somehow different from the dominant culture, I explore distinct sources and experiences of difference in chapter 2.

In part 2 of the book—chapters 3 through 7—I describe a continuum of responses, ranging from quiet modes of resistance to more direct and deliberate strategies of change and protest. This spectrum represents different strategies of action, not types of tempered radicals. In part 3 of the book, I explore the challenges faced by tempered radicals, and the opportunities those challenges represent for organizations and society. Chapter 8 in this section focuses on the difficulties associated with acting as a tempered radical and the conditions that make it more and less challenging to take this stance. Chapter 9 concludes by summarizing the organizational implications of tempered radicals' acts and showing how and why these acts represent a crucial form of leadership, what I call "everyday leadership."

THIS BOOK provides a portrait of the experience of people who make up contemporary organizations, each of whom, in many contexts, must struggle to bring his or her whole "self" to work. I describe how tempered radicals effect change while staying credible, how they sustain their dual commitments and identities, and the everyday, sometimes mundane, processes by which they slowly and incrementally make a difference. I hope that those who hope for a different kind of organization will come away with a new way to think about their struggles and a new set of strategies with which to act. And I hope that, after reading this, people who identify with the tensions I describe will feel less alone and more convinced that through persistent, everyday actions, they can make a difference for others.

Acknowledgments

I AM BLESSED with a long list of people whose talent, ideas, and support made this book possible. My deepest gratitude goes to all of these individuals.

Maureen Scully was my collaborator in the original work on tempered radicalism, and several of the ideas I present originated in this collaboration. Though Maureen decided to focus on another body of research, she generously gave her support and friendship throughout this project. This book was also informed by our joint collaboration with Ella Bell and Stella Nkomo on tempered radicalism as it relates to black and white professional women, and I owe my thanks to them as well.

Professor Joanne Martin, my mentor and advisor at Stanford's Graduate School of Business, played a pivotal role in shaping our initial interest and questions. Her experiences as a feminist in a business school, a woman in a predominantly male institution, and a parent in a profession that demanded all-out commitment became grist for our mill. Joanne generously shared her experiences as we developed nascent theory about the phenomena she came to personify. During this early work, and for almost fifteen years since, Joanne's professional support, intellectual guidance, and friendship have enriched both my work and my life.

My colleague Deborah Kolb provided ongoing support, encouragement, and insightful feedback. Her review of an earlier draft and her subsequent willingness to work through some of the challenges posed by early reviews were enormously helpful. Deborah's recent work from her book *The Shadow Negotiation* (with Judith Williams) has directly informed my thinking. I am also grateful to Jane Dutton for her thoughtful and detailed comments on an earlier draft. The care she took with the manuscript is testimony to Jane's insight and professionalism and her deep concern for the topics I address. Her own work has also influenced my thinking. Two anonymous reviewers also provided careful and insightful feedback for which I am grateful. In addition, I owe thanks to Robert Sutton, my colleague at Stanford, who, always with great humor, tolerated my regular "out-of-context" queries on various logistical details about book writing.

I owe tremendous gratitude to Professor Karl Weick, the scholar, for his groundbreaking work on organizational change, sense-making, small wins, and improvisation that provide the conceptual foundation upon which so many of my ideas are built. Perhaps more important, I am indebted to Karl Weick, the man, for his care and kindness over the years, and the generosity with which he provided me with examples, references, and guidance during the four years I was a junior faculty member at the University of Michigan and occupied the office next to his. His work has played an enormous role in shaping my understanding of the social world, and I only hope that I've applied his concepts in the spirit he intended. Of course, I take full responsibility for the ideas I present here.

I could not have done the work behind this book had many other colleagues not provided access in various ways. I am particularly indebted to Patricia Callahan, Santiago Rodriguez, Anita Roddick, Judy Marshall, Nancy Hopkins, Lotte Bailyn, Cate Muther, and Jacqui MacDonald, who provided their own insights and/or helped me secure research sites. I am also, of course, indebted to the hundreds of men and women who generously gave their time and shared their experiences with me, and the dozens of students, executives, and workshop participants who enriched my thinking by working and experimenting with the concepts of tempered radicalism.

I am also blessed with several friends who showered me with their support and interest, many of whom willingly engaged in debates over my topic and title and patiently allowed far too many dinner conversations to be dominated with these debates. These people include Tony Stayner, Beth Cross, Robin Ely, Su Moon Paik, Ann Mathieson, Patty Jackson, Patty Collier, Linda Schuck, Lisa Kelley, Nancy Katz, my brother, Aaron, and my sister-in-law, Lizzie. Liz Bradley has been a particularly important source of support throughout this long process, poring over multiple versions of chapter 1, providing important input, and generally being there when I needed support.

I also owe an enormous debt to the pathbreaking work of Learning as Leadership (LAL), and, in particular, the insights of Claire Nuer, the organization's late founder. I have been studying and thinking about the strategies of tempered radicalism for almost fifteen years. Nevertheless, the two LAL seminars I attended in 1999, and subsequent

Acknowledgments

conversations with Lara Nuer and Marc Andre Olivier, two of those who have carried on this work, have influenced my thinking and my life enormously.

I am also grateful to the wonderful group of professionals at Harvard Business School Press, many of whom I had the pleasure of working with directly, others indirectly. I thank Janet Coleman, no longer with the Press, who saw promise in these ideas long ago, and Marjorie Williams, who continued to check in with me years before I was ready to write. Marjorie's editorial hand early in the process was tremendously helpful. Nikki Sabin gracefully took over this project with her gentle guidance and demonstrated a dedication beyond the call of duty. Melinda Merino inherited the project during its final phase and engaged in the work with an enthusiasm and expertise as if she'd been on it all along. Her contributions, even at this late stage, have been enormous. I am grateful to the many others at HBS Press, including Carol Franco, Sylvia Weedman, Jane Judge Bonassar, Sue Miller, and Gayle Treadwell, who have shown a level of patience and commitment to this project that most authors can only wish for. To all of these professionals and others, I thank you. I am also indebted to Amanita Rosenbush for her editorial assistance, her late-night efforts, and her growing enthusiasm for the ideas she had a hand in shaping. I thank Katie Haskin, who provided administrative support and eleventh-hour help with references.

I could not have written this book had it not been for the dedication and reliability of Denise Angelone, who for the past eight years has been a part of our family, has provided care for my three children, and has kept our home going. During my final push she pitched in willingly and cheerfully. Knowing that your children are in loving hands when you are not with them provides peace of mind that cannot be underestimated. With all my heart, I thank Denise.

To my three wonderful children, Danny, Adam, and Sarah, who put up with parents who were sleep-deprived for far too long, I owe a huge thank you. Danny, who at 11 casually and lovingly observed during my final phase of revision that "we had gotten along better when the book was in review," showed understanding far beyond what one might reasonably expect from someone his age. Adam, 9, barely uttered disappointment when I asked him to wait several months until A.B. (after book) to plan his birthday party. Thanks to Adam's good humor and patience, A.B. has become a family refrain. Sarah, at 5, kept me going and smiling with her daily 12:38 P.M. post-kindergarten visits to my home office and her cheerful reports about Smokey the classroom rabbit. No parent could be more blessed than I.

And finally, I owe my deepest gratitude to my husband and partner, Steven Zuckerman, for his nurturing support, his unwavering belief in me, and his love. During a time that he was also completely overwhelmed at work, he suggested I go away for a week to write without distraction, and he'd pick up the slack at home. As icing on this wonderful cake, Steve spent many a late-night hour poring over my manuscript with pen in hand. During a time when he had no time at all to give, he still found it and gave it lovingly. As a colleague recently commented, Steve is a rare and precious man.

To all these people, I express my sincerest appreciation.

PART

1

Tempered radicals

I long to accomplish a great and noble task, but it is my chief duty to accomplish humble tasks as though they were great and noble. The world is moved along, not only by the mighty shoves of its heroes, but also by the aggregate of the tiny pushes of each honest worker.

— *Helen Keller*

Who Tempered Radicals Are
and What They Do

tempered \'tem-perd\ adj 1 a : having the elements mixed in sat-
isfying proportions: TEMPERATE b : qualified, lessened, or diluted by
the mixture or influence of an additional ingredient: MODERATED

radical \ra-di-kel\ adj 1 : of, relating to, or proceeding from a root
. . . 2 : of or relating to the origin: FUNDAMENTAL 3 a : marked by
a considerable departure from the usual or traditional: EXTREME
4 b : tending or disposed to make extreme changes in existing
views, habits, conditions, or institutions[1]

MARTHA WILEY sits in her tenth-floor office in a prestigious high-
rise building in downtown Seattle. Decorated with earth-tone sofa and
chair, overgrown ivies, and floor-to-ceiling ficus tree, her office looks
as if she has inhabited it for years. Traditional management books line
her bookshelves, interrupted only by a few recognizable volumes on
women and management, a stone abstract carving of a woman and
child, and a half-dozen silver-framed pictures of her two children and
husband. Neatly stacked piles of paper cover her desk, suggesting that
an orderly and busy executive sits behind it. Only running shoes and
sweats in the corner disrupt the traditional mood of this office.

At 44, Martha has spent the past ten years working her way up to
her current position as senior vice president and highest-ranking
woman in the real estate division of Western Financial. She shows no sign

of slowing down. From the time Martha walked into her office at 7:00 A.M. until this last meeting of the day at 5:30 P.M., she has sprinted from one meeting to the next, stopping only for a one-hour midday work-out. This last meeting, before she rushes home to relieve her nanny, was requested by one of her most valued employees to talk about "the future." Her employee nervously explains that since returning from maternity leave with her second child, she has found it increasingly difficult to be in the office five long days each week. She needs to find an alternative way to continue performing her job.

After thirty minutes, the two women agree to a plan: the employee will work two days from home and three days in the office, and every other week she will take one day off. Martha's only request is that the employee remain flexible and be willing to come into the office when it is absolutely necessary for her work.

Martha is pleased that she can meet this employee's needs. In fact, she has actively looked for opportunities to initiate changes that accommodate working parents and that make her department more hospitable to women and people of color. A full 30 percent of her staff now have some sort of flexible work arrangement, despite a lack of formal policy to guide these initiatives. Martha has little doubt that her experiments in work arrangements, even though she has kept them quiet, have been slowly paving the way for broader changes at Western. She had heard that word of her successes was spreading, and that it was only a matter of time before the institution caught up to her lead. (Eventually, the organization did initiate some policies that have given employees more flexibility in arranging their work schedules.)

This example is typical of Martha's approach to change at Western. Though her agenda for change is bold—she wants nothing less than to make the workplace more just and humane—her method of change is modest and incremental. Martha constantly negotiates the path between her desire to succeed within the system and her commitment to challenge and change it; she navigates the tension between her desire to fit in and her commitment to act on personal values that often set her apart. As a result, she continues to find ways to rock the boat, but not so hard that she falls out of it.

All types of organizations—from global corporations to small neighborhood schools—have Marthas. They occupy all sorts of jobs and stand up for a variety of ideals. They engage in small local battles rather than wage dramatic wars, at times operating so quietly that they may not surface on the cultural radar as rebels or change agents. But these men and women of all colors and creeds are slowly and steadily pushing back on conventions, creating opportunities for learning, and inspiring change within their organizations.

Sometimes these individuals pave alternative roads just by quietly speaking up for their personal truths or by refusing to silence aspects of themselves that make them different from the majority. Other times they act more deliberately to change the way the organization does things. They are not heroic leaders of revolutionary change; rather, they are cautious and committed catalysts who keep going and who slowly make a difference. They are "tempered radicals."[2]

Competing Pulls

Tempered radicals are people who operate on a fault line. They are organizational insiders who contribute and succeed in their jobs. At the same time, they are treated as outsiders because they represent ideals or agendas that are somehow at odds with the dominant culture.[3]

People operate as tempered radicals for all sorts of reasons. To varying extents, they feel misaligned with the dominant culture because their social identities—race, gender, sexual orientation, age, for example—or their values and beliefs mark them as different from the organizational majority. A tempered radical may, for example, be an African American woman trying to make her company more hospitable to others like herself. Or he may be a white man who holds beliefs about the importance of humane and family-friendly working conditions—or someone concerned for social justice, human creativity, environmental sustainability, or fair global trade practices that differ from the dominant culture's values and interests.

In all cases they struggle between their desire to act on their "different" selves and the need to fit into the dominant culture. Tempered radicals at once uphold their aspiration to be accepted insiders and their commitment to change the very system that often casts them as outsiders. As Sharon Sutton, an African American architect, has explained, "We use our right hand to pry open the box so that more of us can get into it while using our left hand to be rid of the very box we are trying to get into."[4]

Tempered radicals are therefore constantly pulled in opposing directions: toward conformity and toward rebellion. And this tension almost always makes them feel ambivalent toward their organizations.* This ambivalence is not uncommon. Psychologists have found that people regularly feel ambivalent about their social relations, particularly toward institutions and people who constrain their freedom. Children, for example, regularly hold strong opposing feelings, such as love and hate, towards their parents.[5] Sociologists have observed a comparable response in employees toward their organizations. They frequently counter organizational attempts to induce conformity and define their identities with efforts to express their individuality.[6] People who differ from the majority are the most likely targets of organizational pressures toward conformity, and at the same time they have the greatest reason to resist them.

A Range of Responses

If ambivalence is the psychological reaction to being pulled in opposing directions, how does it lead people to behave? Some people make a clear choice, relieving their ambivalence by moving clearly in one direction or the other.[7] Others become paralyzed and ultimately so frustrated that escaping the situation is their only relief. Some people flame out in anger. They grow to feel unjustly marginalized and focus on how to avenge perceived wrongs. They feel victimized by their situation and ultimately come to be at the mercy of their own rage. While the pain and anger are often justified, they can become debilitating.

Tempered radicals set themselves apart by successfully navigating a middle ground. They recognize modest and doable choices in between, such as choosing their battles, creating pockets of learning, and making way for small wins.

---

*Though this is a pervasive state, it is nonetheless a simplification that people are pulled only in two directions. The nature of the "self" is complex and people are pulled in multiple directions. Here, I emphasize this general stance that results from two types of pulls that are at odds with each other. Later, we discuss the specific content of the pulls toward difference and ways people respond to them.

Tempered radicals also become angry, but they mitigate their anger and use it to fuel their actions. In the world of physics, when something is "tempered" it is toughened by alternately heating and cooling. Tempered steel, for example, becomes stronger and more useful through such a process. In a similar way, successfully navigating the seemingly incongruous extremes of challenging and upholding the status quo can help build the strength and organizational significance of tempered radicals.[8]

Note, though, that *tempered* radicals are not radicals. The distinction is important. The word *radical* has several meanings: "of, relating to, or proceeding from a root," or fundamental, as well as "marked by a considerable departure from the usual or traditional," or extreme.[9] Tempered radicals may believe in questioning fundamental principles (e.g., how to allocate resources) or root assumptions, but they do not advocate extreme measures. They work *within* systems, not against them.

Martha, for example, could stridently protest her firm's employment policies or could take a job within an activist organization and advocate for legalistic remedies to the inequities she perceives. But she has chosen the tempered path, in part because she believes that she can personally make more of a difference by working within the system. Her success has created a platform from which to make changes—often seemingly small and almost invisible—which over time have the potential to affect many people.

Martha also has chosen her course because she likes it. She is quick to admit that she loves her job, takes pride and pleasure in moving up the corporate ladder, and enjoys the status and spoils of her success. She likes living in a comfortable home and taking summer vacations in Europe. While Martha clearly enjoys the privileges that come with success, she believes that the criteria by which the system distributes these privileges need to be changed. Does this belief make her a hypocrite? Or does it simply speak to a duality she and other tempered radicals constantly straddle?

A Spectrum of Strategies

Martha makes choices every day, some conscious, some not, in order to strike a balance. She is committed to chipping away at her "radical" agenda, but not so boldly as to threaten her own legitimacy and organizational success. What is the right balance to strike? More generally, how do tempered radicals navigate the often murky organizational waters to pursue their ideals while fitting in enough to succeed? How do they successfully rock the organizational boat without falling out?

These questions drove my research and form the heart of this book. Not surprisingly, there is no single formula for finding a successful course. Rather, tempered radicals draw on a wide variety of strategies to put their ideals into practice, some more forceful and open, others subtler and less threatening. By choosing among these strategies, each tempered radical creates the balance that is appropriate for him or her in a given situation.

Figure 1-1 presents a spectrum of strategies. It is anchored on the left side by a collection of strategies I have labeled "resisting quietly and staying true to one's 'self,'" which includes acts that quietly express people's "different" selves and acts that are so subtle that they are often not visible to those they would threaten. The other end of the spectrum, "organizing collective action," reflects actions people take to get others involved in deliberate efforts to advance change. Martha's initiatives around flexible work arrangements and similar strategies fall in the category of "leveraging small wins," between the two endpoints.[10]

The spectrum varies along two primary dimensions. First, it speaks to the immediate scope of impact of a tempered radical's actions. At the far left, only the individual actor and a few people in his or her immediate presence are likely to be directly affected by the action. At the opposite end of the spectrum, tempered radicals' actions are meant to provoke broader learning and change. At the far left, the action is invisible or nearly so and therefore provokes little opposition; at the far right, the action is very public and is more likely to encounter resistance.

Figure 1-1: How Tempered Radicals Make a Difference

Resisting quietly and staying true to one's "self"	Turning personal threats into opportunities	Broadening the impact through negotiation	Leveraging small wins	Organizing collective action

The second overlapping dimension is the intent underlying a person's actions. At the left, people primarily strive to preserve their "different" selves. Many of these people who operate quietly are not trying to drive broad-based change; they simply want to be themselves and act on their values within an environment where that may feel difficult. Others who resist quietly do intend to provoke some change, but they do it from so far behind the scenes that the actions are not visible. At the right end of the spectrum, people are motivated by their desire to advance broader organizational learning and change. In reality, of course, no one person sits on a specific point on the spectrum, and the strategies themselves blur and overlap. I've distinguished them for the purpose of contrast, rather than to suggest that they reflect distinct responses. A few examples may help bring this spectrum to life.

Sheila Johnson is a black woman from a working-class family. She has worked her way up to senior vice president in the private equity division at Western Financial. Even though she is one of only a handful of black women in Western's professional ranks, she thought that she would have a reasonable chance of succeeding here because of Western's stated commitment to "diversity." Sheila has tried over the years to keep a low profile, but when she has a chance to help other minorities, or when she feels she must speak up, she usually does so.

Sheila recalls a period when her division's human resource manager complained about the inability to find and hire "qualified minorities" at every level. She knew that standard recruiting procedures at elite college and graduate schools did not constitute the kind of pipeline that would bring in enough diverse candidates to change the face of Western. So she took it upon herself to post descriptions of entry-level jobs throughout minority communities. She did not call attention to her intervention—she didn't ask for permission or insist that the practice become recruiting policy. But through her quiet efforts, she helped create a more diverse pool of candidates, many of whom were hired into entry-level jobs.

Sheila could have broadened the impact of her actions by talking openly about them to enable others to recognize why their standard recruiting practices had failed to fill the bill. Had she made this link clear, she would have pushed others to learn from her actions, which might have led to additional adaptations. Although taking these additional steps could have broadened the impact of her actions, Sheila probably would have had to overcome opposition and assume a potentially greater risk. Because she undertook her actions so quietly, and outside the scope of the organization, I see her behind-the-scenes efforts as an example of "quiet resistance."

John Ziwak is a tempered radical of a different sort. On the surface, he seems to have little in common with Sheila. John has enjoyed all the privileges of growing up in a white middle-class family. He attended an elite university, went to business school at a branch of the University of California, and landed a plum job at a local high-technology company. Six years later, now married with two children, John accepted his current post as manager of business development at Atlas Tech. Although he wants to continue to rise within Atlas, he has no intention of shirking his duties as parent and partner. He can't. His wife also works in a demanding career, and they have always shared responsibilities—and plan to continue.

But it isn't that easy. John, like his wife, faces ongoing pressure from his organization to choose between his commitment to his work and his commitment to his family. John doesn't think that this choice is reasonable; he doesn't believe that he should have to give up his duties at home to prove his commitment and to succeed at Atlas. So in both big and small ways he resists pressure to make such choices and, when appropriate, he challenges prevailing expectations.

One morning John's boss told him that he needed to get on that night's red-eye flight to New York to meet with an important candidate for acquisition. His wife was already out of town and he did not want to ask the babysitter to stay overnight, so he told his boss that he couldn't go: "I told him that I was sorry I would miss this meeting because I would have brought a lot to the discussion." At the same time, John made sure to point out that he usually can travel, but that he needs some advance notice owing to his wife's travel schedule. John hoped that his boss would understand the broader implications of his resistance—that only a subset of employees can be available on such short notice and that the boss's expectations penalize those who can't pick up and go at the last minute. Whether the boss understood the bigger issue or not, he did begin to give John advance notice about travel whenever possible.

John's act was not dramatic or proactive. A normal reaction in a normal encounter between himself and his boss, it illustrates the strategy

I have called "turning threats into opportunities." In this instance, John turned an immediate threat to his personal values and priorities—a request to meet organizational expectations that clash with personal values—into an opportunity for learning. Though John cannot tell how much his boss actually learned, he thinks he made at least a start.

The actions taken by John, Sheila, and Martha fall at different points on the spectrum shown in figure 1-1. On another day, any one of them might take another action that might fall elsewhere on the spectrum, depending on the opportunity, the situation, the importance of the issue to them, and—as Sheila admitted—"how much sleep [I] had on a given day." Though the actions of some tempered radicals tend toward one end of the spectrum versus the other, most take different actions at different times. It is important to understand that *the spectrum represents different strategies for acting, not different types of people.*

The spectrum does not imply that the quiet responses on the left are in any way less important than those on the right. As we will see, a lifetime of quiet resistance can require enormous patience, conviction, and fortitude. And sometimes persistent behind-the-scenes actions cumulate over time for lasting change or set the context for more public and revolutionary acts.

Guiding Models

Tempered radicals face two primary sets of challenges: those related to the preservation of their "selves" and those that involve advancing an agenda for change from within. Given the centrality of these themes, I want to make explicit my assumptions about how organizations change, the nature of the "self," and how the two are connected through action. These ideas are supported by my own research and guided by the research of others.

How Organizations Change

My "theory" of change begins with the notion that organizations are always changing, continually adapting in response to an ongoing flow of inputs and activities.[11] Since most changes are small, incremental adaptations scattered throughout organizations, it may be difficult to recognize this movement as *change,* except retrospectively when small effects have had time to accumulate. In addition, because this process is diffuse, specific *causes* of change are often difficult to pinpoint. Indeed, the change process looks more like random events and chaos than it does rational cause-effect sequences.

Here's an example of the difficulty of pointing to the source of change: Four years after my first interview at Western, a senior human resources officer explained that during the previous five years, the culture had shifted dramatically to be more hospitable to working parents. Whereas once a 5:30 P.M. staff meeting would have been the norm, now it would be seen as completely inappropriate to schedule meetings that late. She was at a loss to point to the specific cause of this shift. The change evolved, she concluded, because many employees, over a period of years, pushed back on the old expectations and set examples for new ones.

This image of change as a continuous and fragmented process bears little resemblance to portraits of episodic and revolutionary change processes you read in many best-selling management texts. These more dramatic pictures of transformation see organizational change occurring not continuously, but periodically as a result of specific trigger events, such as crises, technological innovations, top-down strategic mandates, or bottom-up revolutions. These moments of large-scale transformation are the "figure" against the "ground" of periods of stability.[12] While I do not deny the significance of the occasional crisis, technological innovation, or dramatic intervention, there is significant evidence that such events do not drive much of the adaptation that occurs in organizations.[13]

Many mundane processes that play a part in incremental adaptation disappear as organizational noise if we think of organizational change strictly as episodic and revolutionary. If, however, we look at change as emergent and ongoing, little prods like Sheila's recruiting efforts, which redirect organizational momentum slightly, suddenly appear as significant catalysts of adaptation. So too are small, local accommodations that accumulate into something bigger, such as Martha's flexible work initiative. Interpretation and learning are also pivotal components of this adaptive change process. As people understand things differently, they act differently, and different actions inspire more change.

This view of organizational and social change makes room for lots of normal people to effect change in the course of their everyday actions and interactions. It is an inclusive model that sees people on the margin as well as at the center making a difference in a wide variety of ways. Change agents are not just those characterized by bold visions and strategic savvy, but also those characterized by patience, persistence, and resourcefulness. In this model, change agents are sensitive improvisers who are able to recognize and act on opportunities as they arise.

This view of change and change agents is less dramatic, less inspiring, and less breathless than portraits of grand transformation and revolutionary leaders. It is also more inclusive, more realistic, and more hopeful for most people who care to make a difference in their worlds. I believe it is also more reflective of how most real and lasting change occurs.

The "Self"

My assumptions about the "self" also follow from theories that emphasize fluidity. I begin with the notion that who we are—our "selves"—is at the same time stable and mutable.[14] Some aspects of our core identities remain relatively stable, and other, more mercurial aspects are highly sensitive to social cues.[15] For example, some people may want to downplay a part of their identities, but if colleagues see and reinforce those aspects of their identities, they will be compelled to acknowledge these aspects of themselves more explicitly.[16] High-level women who want to ignore their gender identity, for example, are often forced by others who interact with them *as women* to acknowledge and address this aspect of themselves. The reverse is also true. Say an individual defines his religion as a core part of his identity. If, however, others challenge or criticize him when he acts on his faith by, say, reading the Bible in public or praying in a group setting or even talking about being a regular churchgoer, he may be less inclined to express that part of his "self" explicitly in the future. In this context, he may completely suppress it.

Thus the "self" is not immune to external cues; it is built and sustained in relationships with others. Accordingly, both sides of a tempered radical's competing "selves" develop in interactions with others. Since work life tends to be full of relationships that enforce the part of the "self" that identifies with the majority culture, the social cues that lure the "self" toward conformity are strong. It is crucial, then, for people to interact with people inside and outside their organizations who affirm the nonconforming parts of their "selves." These relationships help keep their threatened identities alive.

Action, the "Self," and Change

So what is the connection between people's "selves" and the outcomes of organizational learning and change? One piece, as I mentioned earlier, is that asserting the nonconforming aspects of oneself can pave the way for learning and change by questioning current practice and expectations and providing an alternative.

This dynamic can also be self-reinforcing. When people act in ways that outwardly express a valued part of their selves, they make that part of their selves "real." The act of putting this part of themselves out in the world for affirmation and challenge often reminds them, and others, that they will not silence these valued parts of their selves and that they will not allow the dominant culture to define who they are. Not only is action driven by people's valued selves, but it helps construct and fortify those selves.

Actions produce other consequences as well. When people act on their different selves, they make it possible for others who share their social identities and values to find each other. When environmentalists do something *as environmentalists,* for instance, they become visible to other environmentalists. Gay people report that once they come out of the closet, they suddenly discover dozens of other coworkers who are gay. In this way, people's actions have the unintended effect of creating relationships with similar others, thus making the context more friendly.

Actions can also bolster people's sense of efficacy, proving to themselves and to others that they can make a difference, even if the direct consequences of their actions are small.[17] When people believe they can make a difference, they are more likely to search for opportunities to act, which makes it more likely that they will locate opportunities. When people recognize opportunities for action, their environment will seem less threatening and more amenable to action.[18]

This self-fulfilling cycle suggests the crucial importance of *action* as a starting point and trigger for a wide range of outcomes. Actions help

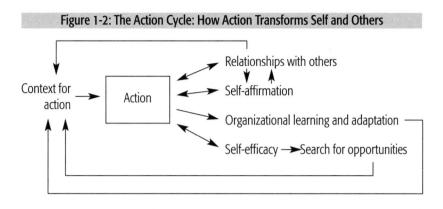

Figure 1-2: The Action Cycle: How Action Transforms Self and Others

develop sustaining relationships with similar others, affirm threatened "selves," generate organizational learning and change, fuel a sense of efficacy, and heighten attention to opportunities. The first and last of these create a context more amenable to action.[19] (See figure 1-2.) While most people talk about action being driven by people who see themselves as change agents, I've observed how the reverse is true— and very powerful; actions transform people from the stance of passive bystander or victim to that of constructive agent.

Why People Act as Tempered Radicals

Why do people bother to navigate such a difficult maze of conformity and rebellion? Why might you want to do so? Given the multitude of organizational processes that steer people toward conformity, wouldn't it be easier to go along, at least until you have "enough" power to make "real" change without jeopardizing your job? Challenging the status quo can be very risky, which puts an extra burden on tempered radicals to perform well in their jobs. Wouldn't it be simpler to find an organization where all parts of your core "self" are valued, where you don't face extra pressures? It certainly is not easy to act in ways that keep these competing selves alive, nor is it comfortable psychologically to remain in an ongoing state of ambivalence. So why do people take this path?

The most straightforward answer is that they don't like the alternatives. While the lures toward conformity can be overwhelming in some contexts, for some people this route is unacceptably demoralizing and draining. If they conform completely, they essentially silence a core part of their selves. Some people feel that they are "selling out" on their values and turning their backs on their communities. This route can also enervate people, as they come to see themselves as victims of their situations. For many of the tempered radicals I interviewed, complete conformity was not an option.

A person could also stay consistently true to his or her self, and simply start fresh when the friction gets too great to bear or when he or she is forced from the organization. But most people have neither the desire nor the luxury to risk the alienation (and displacement) that would likely result. Those who end in this direction don't survive in conventional organizations; they are often the ones better suited to the role of pure radical, advocating from outside the organization, from a position closer to their ideals.

With these alternatives, we might ask the opposite question: Why aren't more people tempered radicals? The obvious answer, as I mentioned earlier, is that it creates a difficult ambivalence to tolerate and manage. And for many, the rewards of conformity—combined with the risk of exclusion—are too great to pass up. While this simple answer is undoubtedly true, I suggest that in fact *many people are tempered radicals and just don't realize it*. They struggle silently with their ambivalence, reluctant to acknowledge it and uncertain how they might make it work better for themselves and constructively for their organizations.

Fortunately, when people do act on their convictions, they set in motion a powerful cycle (see figure 1-2) and make a start at managing the ambiguity of their situations. Even small acts can have far-reaching effects, affirming an actor's sense of self, fueling their sense of efficacy, and making a difference for others.

Tempered Radicals as Everyday Leaders

Few of the tempered radicals mentioned in these pages see themselves as heroes or champions of organizational revolutions. They often are not the CEOs, presidents, or senior professionals in their organizations, and yet they sometimes play a role in organizational adaptation as crucial as that of their colleagues with more authority. They have become the "everyday leaders" in their organizations, often unrecognized but nevertheless essential agents of organizational learning and change.

When these individuals push back on conventional expectations, challenge assumptions about what is "normal," and revise work practices to meet unaddressed needs, they push others to learn and force systems to adapt to impending challenges. Martha's initiatives, for example, have responded to the needs of certain employees who cannot continue to work effectively in traditional, full-time work arrangements. As word of her successes has spread, the organization has been challenged to confront this issue in a more systemic way. John's push back on his boss' expectations about travel brought into focus entrenched practices and assumptions that inadvertently penalized certain groups of employees and made them less effective at work. Sheila's efforts to hire from the community addressed an immediate recruiting challenge her group was facing. Had she intervened more visibly, she could have pointed to the limitations of the organizationally endorsed approach to recruiting. To different extents, each of these relatively small actions took steps toward surfacing and addressing an important adaptive challenge facing the system.[20]

Tempered radicals also provoke learning and adaptation through the perspective they bring as people who are not fully assimilated into the system. Tempered radicals are more likely to think "out of the box" because they are not fully in the box. As "outsiders within," they have both a critical and a creative edge.[21] They speak new "truths."

For example, someone concerned about environmental sustainability probably has a different view of time than others, seeing the long-term effects of current actions. That person thus brings an entirely new set of perspectives, asks different questions, and might pose different solutions to problems such as urban growth and development. In the film industry, we have the example of Robert Redford, who is both an insider and yet a self-appointed outsider, an atypical member of the film community. His innovations in independent filmmaking, born as an alternative to Hollywood, have been an influential force for creativity *inside* Hollywood. His stance as an "outsider within" gives him a critical edge that both questions "normal" ways of doing things in his profession and offers new possibilities. Redford is, in many ways, a quintessential tempered radical, and whether he intends to be or not, a leader within his industry.

Conclusion

Tempered-radical-as-leader is a more inclusive, realistic, and inspiring way to think about leadership—and life—than are images of leadership found in fairy tales and the popular business press. To gauge the efficacy of one's efforts against portraits of leaders as lone crusaders at the helm of dramatic transformation is to resign oneself to falling short, to feeling that one's efforts have not made a *real* difference. The depiction of tempered-radical-as-leader provides more compelling metrics and ideals. It allows that through a wide range of ways people make a difference for others, create new truths, and live lives of integrity, meaning, and purpose.

Tempered radicals exist at all levels in all kinds of organizations. Not only do they exist, but they persist and, to varying extents, succeed. Even if they don't feel "radical" or have an explicit agenda for change, countless people act as tempered radicals, at least over some portions of their careers and under certain circumstances. They know that the challenges they pose may bring some risk to their careers, yet many feel that going along in silence can bring even greater costs to their souls.

While John Ziwak, Martha Wiley, and Sheila Johnson face similar challenges, their experiences as tempered radicals, particularly their experiences of being "different," are not the same at all. Most of this book focuses on common tensions and action strategies for people who differ from the norm in any multitude of ways. But before we move on to that focus, we'll explore how different kinds of tempered radicals experience their differences.

Different Ways of
Being "Different"

In the politics of human life, consistency is not a virtue. . . . to be consistent means "standing still or not moving."

— *Saul Alinsky,* Rules for Radicals

JOANIE MASON sits at her small desk at Shop.co in one of many offices that line the perimeter of the company's global headquarters. Her office would be just as nondescript as all the other executives', except that she has adorned hers with a four-foot-by-six-foot yellow and green woven wall hanging, odd-shaped percussion instruments in each corner, and multicolored baskets displayed prominently on her bookshelves. Joanie acquired these and other crafts in her travels to economically depressed villages in every corner of the globe, villages she cultivated as trading partners for Shop.co. Some of these crafts are gifts of gratitude, given by members of villages who viewed these partnerships as routes to their communities' economic sustainability.

Working with communities to create viable projects for "fair trade" has been the easier part of her job. The more difficult part has been implementing her agenda *within* Shop.co. The materials and products she sources are more costly because they come only from sources that pay fair wages and are generally not produced or shipped in bulk. So when it is time to get her colleagues to support her program, they often balk. Joanie did not anticipate running into this clash in values and priorities at Shop.co:

I thought this was an organization committed to doing things differently, that sourcing products as I do was an explicit priority. I had the expectation that I would fit in and that my personal values would be the same as the values that guide this organization. But so often the [organization's] rhetoric hasn't matched reality and I have had to fight this uphill battle to put my values and vision for social change into practice.

Joanie's situation is unusual among tempered radicals because her formal job gives her a mandate to do work consistent with her personal values. Nevertheless, her actual experience within Shop.co is not so aligned. Joanie's experience of "difference," like that of many other tempered radicals, is rooted in a clash between her values and beliefs and those that guide organizational practice.

Tempered radicals share the defining experience of being "different" from the majority, but what their identities mean to them and how they experience their "difference"—not just how they appear to differ from the majority—varies from person to person.[1] In my research, I have identified three primary ways people experience "difference" from the majority:

• Those who have different social identities from the majority and see those differences as setting them apart and excluding them from the mainstream

• Those who have different social identities and see those differences as merely cultural and not a basis for exclusion

• Those who have not cultural but philosophical differences, which conflict with the prevailing values, beliefs, and agendas operating in their organizations.

When I use the term *social identity,* I'm referring to how a person defines his or her "self" as a member of a larger enduring social group based on, say, ethnicity, race, gender, sexual orientation, or religion.[2]

In the first group's view, their social identities mark them as different and as partial outsiders within their institutions. For example, for Sheila Johnson, her racial identity not only marks her as demographically different from the majority, but also makes her a target for systemic exclusion. The people in the second group experience their social identities as a source of difference, but not as a basis of differential *treatment*. For example, an Asian man at Western feels that, because of his cultural identity, he follows slightly different norms at work, but he does not feel this has any bearing on how he is evaluated or on his access to opportunities. Finally, the third group includes people whose "difference" arises from values and beliefs that depart from the organizational norm.

Whereas the third group is probably the most straightforward—Joanie at Shop.co is a great example—the first and second groups are a bit more complex because they appear very similar but in fact are very different. For example, two white women may both identify as women and may both feel "different" from their male coworkers. But one woman may view gender as a basis of exclusion (and inclusion), while the other woman may see gender more neutrally: as a source of different styles and tastes. She might like to wear brighter colors, for example, or think of herself as more sympathetic than men in her organization. This second woman, though she feels "different," does not associate it with patterns of access and power or differential treatment in the workplace.

These distinctions between the first two categories matter. Whether one experiences one's (or others') social identity as a neutral distinction or a source of systemic differential treatment shapes one's likely responses to the "difference." When one sees "difference" strictly as an interesting distinction, one is less likely to see a need for change in the broader system. On the other hand, one who sees links between identity-based differences and patterns of differential treatment will see a need for change and more likely act to challenge these patterns. Not surprisingly, people in the second group, who do not link difference to systemic patterns, tend not to behave as tempered radicals. Still, we consider their experiences for the purpose of contrast and because some of their small assertions of self can plant seeds for change, even if inadvertently.

A few caveats here: Because it is often hard to isolate the source of a person's difference, the categories help point up contrasts—I do not mean to imply that people are "frozen" in a certain category, or that they always experience their "selves" the same way, or that other

---

What Is "Difference"?

For a person to feel or be treated as different, he or she must be different *from* something. The experience of difference presumes some criteria of normality, and only against these criteria can people be judged as different. Yet what is "normal" is hardly an objective reality.[4]

Take one of my favorite examples: Visualize a world built by and for people under five feet tall. Buildings, cars, clothes, and furniture are all created with short people in mind. The people who thrive in this world are the ones who are short. They hold the most important positions while the tall people take the support jobs. To gain acceptance, tall people must adjust to the world they live in. They must stoop in the doorways, squat in the chairs, and walk hunched over so as not to stand out. This struggle further highlights their difference from the norm.[5]

This example points to the arbitrary nature of what we consider "normal" as opposed to "different." Nothing is fundamental or natural about who and what are considered "normal" in organizations either. Rather, "normality" and difference are socially constructed standards.[6] Yet because we also consider as *neutral* that which we consider *normal*—in other words, unbiased and universal—we rarely question how our standards came to be or on what set of assumptions we predicated those standards in the first place.

---

people's responses do not affect them.[3] I also want to make clear that in reality these categories overlap. Martha Wiley, from the last chapter, identifies as a woman in a predominantly male culture, and she experiences her gender identity as a source of differential treatment. This understanding contributes to how she acts. But she also holds strong values about justice and inclusiveness, which fuel her desire to create a more humane and equitable workplace for everyone, and she is concerned as much about the treatment of racial minorities as she is about the treatment of women. These concerns flow partly from her experience as a woman in a male-dominated organization.

I want to emphasize that I am not suggesting that only women take up concerns related to gender based on their identity, or that only gay men and women take up an agenda related to sexual orientation. Indeed, anyone can fight for justice and diversity—one need not have experienced discrimination to value and act on behalf of these ideals.

Social Identity as a Source of Difference and Differential Treatment

A significant number of the people I have studied have become tempered radicals because of social identities that differentiate them from the majority. Many of them understand their social identity partly in terms of its political significance—as a marker that serves to marginalize them within their workplaces. Although a number of social identities—physical disability, social class, age, religion—can be sources of differential treatment, in my research I have focused on three: race and ethnicity, sexual orientation, and gender.

Before looking at each of these identities in depth, I want to acknowledge that my categories oversimplify reality. People have multiple social identities, and it's hard to isolate which ones shape a person's perceptions. A black woman's experience of her identity as a *woman* in a predominantly white male organization, for example, is inseparable from her experience of being a *black woman* in that setting. For the purpose of this discussion, I have isolated the identities that seem most salient for people.

Race and Ethnicity

The black people in my studies have consistently experienced their racial identity as a source of "difference." Even as they struggle to gain acceptance as insiders, they have always been conscious of being treated as outsiders. For some, this outsider-insider stance has translated into an enduring sense of ambivalence.

Peter Grant, an African American who spent thirty years working his way up to a senior executive position, has become well known at Western, in the financial community at large, and in the black professional community. After all these years, when he attends executive gatherings he feels he is still treated as if he doesn't belong:

Being the only one is something I'm aware of because the people around me are obviously aware of it. They reflect it back onto me. They look at me, and its clear they are trying to figure out why I am there.

Peter explained to me that he finally reached a point where he stopped caring what white people think; he decided he wouldn't expend any more energy trying to fit in to make them comfortable: "It's their problem if they're not comfortable [with me]." But when I turned the tape recorder off during our interview, the first thing he asked was whether he made me uncomfortable. His self-consciousness with me seemed to belie his conviction that he is no longer concerned about social acceptance. I suspect that this seeming insincerity reflects a deeply ambivalent attitude toward the majority. It is as if he says he no longer needs to worry about inclusion and social acceptance within the majority culture *while* he worries about it a great deal.

This "double-consciousness," as W. E. B. DuBois termed it, is nothing new to Peter.[7] As a young boy Peter cultivated the capacity to function as a black boy in a predominantly white world; doing so meant staying aware of the rules of his own culture and his own personal needs as well as the rules of the white culture. As he grew up, he was able to come to terms with his position between the white and black communities: "The fact that I'm comfortable [economically] and that I conjugate my verbs doesn't mean that I wear a mask or that I'm any less black. . . . I wanted to get the grade. I wanted to be an astronaut. So what was my choice?" Straddling the outsider-insider border demanded a dual consciousness, as well as behaviors that responded to these competing pulls.[8]

In my research, ambivalence also surfaced in people's seemingly conflicting beliefs about their chances in life. On the one hand, many black professionals I interviewed suggested that they believe that hard work *has* paid off for them; on the other hand, despite their apparent success within predominantly white organizations, they still feel that hard work won't necessarily pay off, and that they are still outsiders looking into the mainstream culture. As a result, Sheila Johnson at Western holds conflicting beliefs about her own situation and feels torn about what to tell aspiring minority professionals. She explained:

> I can be out there saying, "You can get promoted, you can move up, you can do the same type of thing that I've done." And I ask myself, "Can they really do it? Does everyone have that opportunity?" You go out and actually tell these kids that they have these same opportunities, that if they just work hard and get the education they too can get promoted. . . . And I ask myself, "Is that really true?"[9]

Peter's ambivalence differs slightly from Sheila's, but both Peter and Sheila are responding to their fundamental experience: having to function as insiders while cast as outsiders because of their racial identity.

While my research has shown that black professionals are the most consistently conscious of the ways their racial identities make them outsiders, members of other ethnic and racial minority groups often revealed comparable sentiments.[10] For example, a Latino product manager at Atlas described his experience like this:

> As a Hispanic from Spanish Harlem in New York, the effort involved in achieving professional and academic success while maintaining a commitment to my ethnic community is tremendous. Aside from the energy needed for my professional success, I need extra energy to signal that I'm not culturally lost. Just about every minority friend I know who has done reasonably well has this same feeling of ambivalence and faces the same pressure to play the role and not sell his soul.

Like Peter, Sheila, and other ethnic minorities, this man feels that his ethnic identity differentiates him from what is deemed "normal" and marks him as a cultural outsider. People who make this association between their race or ethnicity and broader patterns of inclusion and exclusion often feel that it is up to them not only to break through as insiders, but also to broaden the parameters of inclusion for others behind them.

Sexual Orientation

Gay and lesbian employees who work in predominantly heterosexual settings tend to experience their sexual identity as a source of difference and as a marker that marginalizes them within their institutions.

Tom Novak, a well-respected vice president in the public relations group at Western, has for many years been open about being gay. As a new hire at Western, he was determined to be more open about his sexual identity, but early on he found it tricky to determine how, when, and with whom it was safe to "come out of the closet." Tom attributes his increased openness and activist behavior to a shift in how he came to understand his sexual orientation, and thus his "difference," in the context of a predominantly heterosexual institution:

I realized that I was in the closet because of my own biases and stereotypes of lesbians and gays. Slowly, I started to shift some of the blame for my sense of shame and low self-esteem from myself to society and to institutions that help perpetuate homophobia and heterosexism.

Other gay employees made similar observations. When they shifted their view outward, away from self-shame and toward institutional bias, they became more activist. For some, this shift also corresponded to their decision to come out. Jennifer Jackson, a sales manager at Atlas, explained:

At first I felt resentment and then anger at the institutions that kept me and tried to push me back into the closet, that made me feel there was something wrong with me. I think I've turned this anger and resentment into a need to affect change in institutions.

The reverse is also true. Those who internalize shame are less likely to act to change their institutions.[11]

Gender

Some women experience their gender identity as a basis of differential treatment in organizations, particularly as they advance to positions in organizations where there are relatively few women. Their sense of being a partial outsider tends to intensify, and their gender identity becomes increasingly salient as a point of differentiation from their peers. This certainly has been the case for Martha Wiley. The higher she has advanced at Western, the more she has felt different from her peers and the more she has felt that her experience of being an executive is not comparable to that of her male peers. This difference, for Martha, has been a distinct disadvantage. Most of her male colleagues can focus just on being good executives—they don't need to concern themselves with other areas of their lives as she does, because most of them have wives who take care of these other responsibilities. She is sometimes at pains to point out to her colleagues how her life differs from theirs and what this means:

Every once in a while I would have to remind them, "I *am* the wife, and the mother too. I don't have a wife at home. It's me." My point to them was that I can't stay until all hours meeting and socializing. It's clear my life is different. I never used to think about being a woman. But now it is impossible for me not to see how this creates a different kind of experience for me here.

Independent of anyone's intent to treat her differently—and she believes that none of her colleagues *mean* to treat her differently—Martha's experience of being an executive has been fundamentally different from that of most of her male colleagues. She feels that now this difference puts her at a disadvantage:

It's the first time I've ever felt that working harder and smarter isn't going to do it for me. People tell me to lighten up. But I also know if I lighten up, I'm going to be seen as a lightweight. It's hard to find the right way to be.

It's a similar story for Isabel Nuñez, 44, a Latina marketing executive who has worked her way up through the product marketing groups at Atlas. Her male colleagues advised her to change her management style, telling her she was too open and collaborative. "They said it would be hard for me to survive at this level because these characteristics would be perceived as a weakness. They were not considered leadership qualities." After she toughened her management style to compensate for her more collaborative inclinations, she was told that she was "too confrontational."

Isabel felt caught between a rock and a hard place.[12] If she acted in ways that were characteristically feminine, others viewed her as lacking initiative and confidence and judged her too weak to be a leader. Yet if she followed prescribed recipes for success by being more assertive and taking more risks, others saw her as too combative and self-promoting (for a woman). Isabel became more and more convinced that her gender—and, more specifically, deeply rooted expectations about how women, particularly Latina women, are and are not supposed to behave—had everything to do with how her coworkers were perceiving and evaluating her.[13]

Although Isabel feels that her struggle to find an acceptable way to behave is partly personal, she also believes that this struggle is not just about her. Systemic processes have made it difficult for her—as a Latina woman—to find a credible management style. Gender stereotypes create expectations for how women and men are supposed to behave that create a mismatch between qualities associated with leadership and qualities associated with women.[14]

Both Isabel and Martha have experienced their gender identities as a source of difference and as a basis of systemic disadvantage within their predominantly male workplaces. They attribute many of the struggles they face as women to these built-in biases within their institutions, not to their own personal difference or deficiencies.[15] Accordingly, they focus their energy toward trying to challenge and change these systems even as they work to succeed within them.

This is true for others who feel marginalized by their social identities. Tom feels similarly about the tensions he faces because he is gay. He doesn't believe that most of his colleagues are homophobic (though he knows some are)—rather, he thinks institutions enforce implicit norms of heterosexuality that make gay people seem deviant. As Tom works to fit in at Western, he also works to challenge some of the subtle practices that marginalize gays. By the same token, Sheila and Peter understand that the tensions they feel in their organizations are a product of a wide variety of institutional practices that set apart and exclude people based on their racial and ethnic identities. Accordingly, they constantly seek ways to challenge and change, or simply get around, these systems.

As we will see in the next chapter, one thing that helps bolster these individuals' activism and affirm their threatened identities is to develop strong relationships with people who share their marginalized identities. Ties with people inside or outside the organization can be crucial in these ways.

Social Identity as a Source of Cultural and Stylistic Difference

On the surface, it would appear that the bind Leanne Wilson faces as a woman in a predominantly male organization is comparable to Isabel's, but their experiences of their gender identity, and thus their understandings of the tensions they confront, are not at all similar.

Leanne Wilson, a white woman, is director of the public relations group at Atlas. Both at a previous company and at Atlas, she was promoted rapidly. Her style of managing is to make decisions by building consensus in her team and to push and coach her subordinates to help them develop their skills. This developmental, collaborative style plays on her natural skills and inclinations as a manager, and it has always served her well.

The more Leanne has advanced, however, the more she has begun to notice discrepancies between her own management style and that of her peers. She feels growing pressure to change her behaviors. People at her management level build credibility by acting as experts, by being "decisive," and, as one of her colleagues said, by being "hungry for the next opportunity." To fit in, she can emulate her peers, but she prefers not to. She wants to find a way of managing that feels authentic but also allows her to acquire the reputation she needs to move up in the company.

Like Isabel, Leanne understands the tension she faces as a product of gender—as a woman she prefers one style and her male peers prefer another, so she has to adjust to fit in. In contrast to Isabel, however, Leanne experiences this tension as a dilemma about her own authenticity. From her perspective, the bind she faces is rooted in how men and women are socialized to behave, not in gender expectations built into the system. Since she is the one who is "different," Leanne feels it is up to her to find a style that can work for her and enable her to fit in.

This way of understanding one's difference—as a matter of cultural or stylistic distinctions—surfaced among at least as many white women as did the alternative I described earlier. It was also the most prevalent way Asian Americans and Asian minorities experienced their identities. To the extent that the Asian Americans I interviewed registered race or ethnicity as a basis of difference, most of them understand it as a neutral cultural marker—"I observe some customs and you observe others." Some of the Latino men and women also experience their ethnic identities in this way—purely as a matter of cultural distinction, an indicator of unique customs, histories, foods, language, and ties to a cultural community. These individuals do not see connections between their ethnic/racial identity and how they are treated in organizations, what is expected of them, or how they interact with majority members.

When people understand their experiences in this light, they are more likely to view their differences as a personal dilemma and are more likely to expend their energy looking for ways to fit in, rather than working toward changing the criteria of fit in their organizations.

Recent immigrants are particularly likely to take this stance toward assimiliation.[16] They become their own targets for change.

Moreover, as people see their issues as theirs alone, they do not seek out natural allies for support. Leanne has kept her struggle to herself, which has prevented her from sharing her experiences with other women, such as Isabel. Her isolation has prevented her from seeing patterns and developing an alternative perspective on her situation, which may suggest new ways to address it. At the very least, talking to others might help her see that she is not alone, and that she is not necessarily to blame for many of her struggles.

Values and Beliefs as a Source of Difference and Conflict

Tempered radicals whose personal values clash with the majority encompass a wide range of people. My research has focused exclusively on people whose principles are more progressive (versus more conservative) than the dominant value system. Many of these people have clear agendas for change linked to their values—for example, relating to fair trade practices, social justice, environmental sustainability, human creativity, and healthy families, to name just a few. As is the case for Joanie Mason at Shop.co, the clash in values often plays out as conflicts between progressive, socially driven concerns and their organization's economically driven practices. Although these interests and their underlying values need not conflict, in practice they too often do.

John Ziwak (from the previous chapter) experiences his difference in this way. His values with respect to his family and his commitment to parenting put him at odds with institutional beliefs about what makes an ideal, committed executive. As we saw, John responds to this conflict by looking for ways to push back on prevailing expectations and practices.

Roger Saillant is a senior executive at Visteon Corp., a company that develops integrated automotive technology systems. He is passionate about the importance of environmental sustainability and wants to give high priority to research and development projects that advance this agenda. He must constantly balance his commitment to this agenda with his company's short-term economic priorities. Thus, for example, when he advocates putting resources behind "green" technologies, he often relies on long-term financial arguments to help make his case. His capacity to balance the immediate priorities of the business with agendas that he "knows are right" has been the mark of his career, and at times he has gone way out on a limb to do so. Roger knows that some of his colleagues see him as "outlandish." He also knows that "they trust me to get the job done."

To rely on a famous example, Robert Redford's values and vision deviate sharply from the film industry standard, and yet he continues to find plenty of work as producer, director, and "leading man." According to an article in the *New York Times Magazine*, Redford "continues to work in the studio system he abhors. A case in point is Redford's dogged determination to perpetuate the independent movement while making 'naked schlockfest' movies such as *Indecent Proposal*."[17] This blatant contradiction, the article claims, seems to be something akin to "bipolar disorder."

Redford has no "disorder." He holds values and an alternative vision of filmmaking that differ dramatically from those that prevail in Hollywood. Yet he advocates and pursues them while also participating in the mainstream of his industry. Accordingly, he is decidedly both an insider and outsider in Hollywood. As the magazine article pointed out,

> With one foot securely planted on each bank of the entertainment river, Redford has watched the water rise and the channel widen. . . . Unlike most stars, Redford doesn't believe in selling out in increments. In return for the independence he craves, he's willing to deal directly with the devil.[18]

Redford explains his "bipolar" behavior in terms of his desire to change the Hollywood formula by broadening the array of films available to the public. As a result, he has infused creativity into the industry as a whole—both in the nontraditional "independent" film industry and in the core of the Hollywood machine.

Several common qualities characterize people whose differences are driven by the conflict between their personal values, beliefs, agendas and those dominant in their organization (or industry). First, many of these individuals frequently do not naturally interact with people who share their values within their organizations. Joanie, for example, often feels like she is fighting a lone battle and sometimes wonders why she bothers. Her connections with people in the human rights community outside of Shop.co, particularly with people who are more radical than she is, have become increasingly important to her. These relationships fortify her commitments and remind her why she bothers. This description holds for others as well. Without sustaining relationships, people in this group find it very difficult to maintain their values and agendas amid organizational pressure to put them on hold.

My second observation about individuals in this group is that they tend *not* to interpret their differences as personally problematic—as something deviant about themselves. Though they may feel psychologically torn about their roles, they recognize that the tension is rooted in something bigger than themselves.

Finally, most of these tempered radicals have explicit agendas for change and are unapologetic about their desire to advance them. Joanie clearly knows that to put her values into practice, she would have to change some of the organization's work practices. Similarly, John Ziwak believes that the culture at Atlas, not his own values and work habits, needs to change.

Conclusion

I've described three ways people experience differently from the majority: those who perceive systemic bias against their social identity groups; those who see their social identities as the source of stylistic and cultural preferences; and those whose values, beliefs, and agendas differ from those of the majority.

What's significant about people in the first group—who work to succeed as insiders but feel cast as outsiders by their race or ethnicity, sexual orientation, and/or gender—is that this felt tension translates into two related challenges. Many people in this category experience the tension as both a challenge to stay true to their identities and beliefs and as a challenge to effect change, working to be included at the same time as they challenge the system of inclusion. As a result, people like Tom Novak, Sheila Johnson, Martha Wiley, Isabel Nuñez, and Peter Grant draw on the entire spectrum of responses—from those aimed at self-preservation to those directed toward institutional change.

Men and women who fall in the second group, who experience their difference purely as cultural or stylistic variation, see the tensions they experience as a personal struggle to fit in. These people have little intent to effect change beyond their personal behaviors or patterns of interaction. Their behaviors tend to be directed inward toward personal change—to figure out how to fit in while still holding onto pieces of their nonconforming selves.

Finally, the men and women I observed who fell into the third category—whose differences are rooted in value clashes—tend to embrace social change agendas tied directly to their personal values and beliefs. They resist the dominant culture and sometimes pursue a social change agenda. The challenge facing most of them centers around the struggle of finding ways to put their agenda in place and effect change while maintaining their legitimacy. Many of their behaviors are directed outward, intended to bring about change beyond their individual circumstances. Thus, responses that are driven directly by their values tend toward the more deliberate change approaches shown in figure 1-1.

In the pages that follow we explore in depth the wide variety of action strategies used by some of the tempered radicals we have already met and others. In chapter 3, we start with the quietest forms of responses.

PART

2

how tempered radicals make a difference

We must be the change we seek in the world.

— *Gandhi*

Resisting Quietly and
Staying True to One's "Self"

*Whether adversity be a stumbling block, discipline, or blessing
depends altogether on the use made of it.*

— *Anonymous*

MARTINA HOLBRINA, a first-generation American of Mexican
descent, grew up in a working-class, predominantly Caucasian community. From early on, her mother taught her the importance of deferring to the traditions of the community, speaking without an accent,
and generally "fitting in." But Martina also learned the importance of
retaining and taking pride in her Chicana identity, even if she did not
express this part of herself at work. To this day, as a university administrator, she lives this legacy, and separates the self she displays in public from the self she values.

John Ziwak displays his personal values in big and small ways, right
down to the oversized cartoon on his cubicle wall of a child trying to
adopt his nanny as his parent because his own parents are working
all the time. On the one hand, the cartoon is simply a quiet way of
voicing his own concerns. But the humor also points to the personal
and social cost of "normal" work schedules.

Peter Grant has spent the past three decades working his way up
to a position at Western that very few people of color have achieved
in financial institutions. Along the way, many of his black friends from
his youth accused him of selling out for the spoils of success. Peter

knows differently. Over the years he has worked persistently to advance opportunities for ethnic and racial minorities both within Western and outside of it through ongoing efforts in hiring, mentoring, and networking. He has undertaken many of these efforts behind the scenes so as not to encounter resistance. Only over the last few years has he more publicly challenged biased practices. It has pained him that people outside Western have not been able to see his efforts, but he understands that his success, together with his quiet approach to change, could give others the mistaken impression that he is not committed to pursuing an agenda beyond his own success.

These three examples reflect the three forms of responses we explore in this chapter: psychological resistance that manifests itself primarily in thoughts; self-expressions that display an aspect of one's "different" self; and behind-the-scenes actions that are deliberate acts that resist the status quo but are too quiet to stir concern.

My placement of these quiet responses on one end of the spectrum may suggest that an individual who relies on these subtler approaches is somehow "less" a tempered radical than someone who tends toward more public and risky strategies. All types of efforts, including quiet forms of resistance, can *and often do* contribute to learning and adaptation, even though history's depiction of social change does not give much credit to the role of these more mundane behind-the-scenes actions. Take Rosa Parks.[1] Most people learn about Parks in school as "the black woman who refused to go to the back of the bus to give up her seat in the white section." History books cast her as "the mother of the civil rights movement," and they depict her refusal to take a back seat as *the* single act that ignited the year-long Montgomery bus boycott. Missing from this account, however, is the long list of often frustrating and behind-the-scenes actions that set the stage for this dramatic act—the resisting, planning, recruiting, networking, and organizing that took place more quietly everyday. Most reports miss the fact that many people, and Parks herself, had worked for civil rights for twelve years outside the public eye, slowly building the platform for her dramatic refusal to comply. My point is not to diminish the significance of her brave and catalytic act, but rather to give credit also to the immense number of humble and quiet efforts, including her own, that preceded and set the stage for it.[2]

Let's look now at the three forms of quiet resistance in detail.

Psychological Resistance

The psychological capacity to withstand the dominant culture's definition of oneself—and to hold fast to one's own self-definition may be essential to everyone; it is particularly crucial to those whom the dominant culture demeans and excludes.[3] This psychological resistance says to the dominant culture, "You cannot define who I am or convince me that I do not belong."

Martina Holbrina has been pressured all her life to assimilate; early on, she learned how to fit in. But she also learned that to wholly accept the dominant culture's definition of her would be psychologically devastating:

> The easiest thing to do and the thing most people would be comfortable with is if I did assimilate and acted like you. But I am not like you. I don't want to be. *That is not who I am*, so I have to struggle to hold onto my culture. I've got to hold onto my heritage. I've got to be proud of the accomplishments that my people have made because your people never will be. I can't give that up.

Even if this resistance occurs primarily in Martina's head, it reflects an affirmative stance to protect her self-definition. And while this form of resistance is typically driven by a personal desire to hold onto a threatened identity, it can have broader political implications.[4] Whenever people refuse to participate in their own subordination, they resist the way power asserts itself in organizations and society. Majority groups maintain their own power and the status quo partly by perpetuating beliefs about certain groups of people—defining who they are and how they behave—that justify excluding them.

This is how negative stereotypes—"tree-hugging" environmentalists," "indecisive" women, "intellectually inferior" black people—are born and perpetuated. These generalizations provide the majority with alleged rationale for continuing to marginalize people who belong to targeted groups. Stereotyping is particularly pernicious because of the psychological damage it does. All too often, stereotypes can become self-fulfilling prophecies, convincing the target that the damaging definition of his or her "self" is true. That's why it is so important for people to learn to resist these definitions.

A classic study of high-achievement college students demonstrates dramatically the devastating social consequences of accepted negative stereotypes.[5] Stanford social psychologist Claude Steele and his colleagues wanted to explain why black students who were every bit as academically qualified as white students were performing far worse as a group, as measured by grades and attrition rates. He found that when the black students were challenged academically, as most incoming students are during their first few semesters, they tended to call up culturally prominent negative stereotypes that portray them as unqualified and inferior students. In effect, these students came to believe that poor performance would "prove" those stereotypes correct, and this possibility loomed as a threat to their identities. The threat was so stressful in some circumstances that it actually distracted them enough to undermine their academics. White students, in contrast, blamed external factors, such as the academically challenging content of the material, for difficulties they faced. Society had given them no reason to believe they had personal shortcomings. So while white students did not alter their self-perceptions and just tried harder, black students stopped thinking of themselves as academic achievers—they changed their self-images as they stopped trying to excel.[6]

Culturally prominent stereotypes are thus insidious; with these black students it created a cycle leading to real performance gaps and ultimately supporting the stereotypes. Other stereotypes—women aren't good at math, white men can't keep up with black men in sports—perpetuate themselves the same way. And these processes play out in the workplace as well as in school.

Faced with negative beliefs about their identity groups, individuals face an unacceptable choice: internalizing the damaging beliefs or repressing part of themselves and assimilating into the dominant culture. Neither of these routes is self empowering. For this reason, learning to reject negative self-definitions is a crucial psychological step toward resisting one's own subordination and thus toward self-affirmation and self-esteem.

Given the prevalence of threats to people's "different" selves and the ongoing lures toward conformity, *how* do people hold onto their sense of self?

First and foremost, the tempered radicals I have researched build supportive affiliations with people inside and outside their organizations. They interact regularly with people who affirm their identities and create relationships and safe "spaces" that enable them to nurture the parts of their selves that feel threatened within the dominant culture.[7] As one tempered radical explained, "You can't keep sane on your own."

Employee groups, student fraternities and associations, and community groups based on common social identities or values create places where people can express their marginalized identities and learn self-pride. Some employees at Atlas, for example, participate in a large Latino group because it provides them with a community and helps them affirm positive images associated with their ethnic identity. It is no coincidence that a central function of political consciousness-raising groups in various civil rights movements has been to bolster group pride.[8] Slogans such as "black is beautiful" and "gay pride" reflect a refusal to be defined and subordinated by the dominant culture.

People also resist the dominant culture's perception of them and defend against threats to their identity and esteem through various tactics known as psychological "armoring." Though relevant to anyone, armoring has most commonly referred to "behavioral and cognitive skills used by black and other people of color to promote self-caring during direct encounters with racist experiences and/or racist ideologies."[9] One way to wear psychological "armor" is to learn how to channel frustration and rage to avoid being controlled by these emotions. When Peter Grant was very young, for example, his father taught him

---

Maintaining Positive Self-Definitions

1. Building relationships with people inside and outside the organization who share and appreciate marginalized aspects of your identity can help keep threatened identities alive.

2. Developing a discipline to manage heated emotions to fuel your agenda puts you in the driver's seat and keeps you from giving in to the forces that could marginalize.

3. Separating public "front-stage" performance from "backstage" acts to create an appearance of conformity while *acting* on differences to sustain your sense of self.

to rise above the unfair treatment and cruel images he would be subjected to in life. His father told him the choice was simple: Peter could
be a victim of racism and be at the mercy of his own anger or he could
rise above and try to do something about it:

> He would say, "It's racist, and the world is f----- up, but you have
> to do the best you can do anyway. It isn't acceptable to use racism
> as an excuse." My mission all my life as been to do my work, suc-
> ceed, and try to make things a little better for the next group of us.
> My father didn't want me to be a victim. He wanted me to show
> them that we were better than that and that we wouldn't settle for
> what we have been dealt.

Martina Holbrina recalled learning a similar lesson in how she
should behave if she wanted to "armor" herself within her predominantly white community.

> We were the only Mexican family in town. Mama learned very
> quickly that we were completely surrounded and outnumbered. If
> she tried to stand up for herself or her children, she was completely
> crushed. She taught me and my brother that in order to survive, we
> could not confront white people head on. We learned exquisite
> manners, we learned to lie, to smile, to tell people what they wanted
> to hear.

Underneath her feigned deference, Martina maintained a steely commitment to her Chicana identity and community. "Mama showed us
how to pursue our agendas secretly when possible, but [with] no head
on confrontations," she said. Though she complied in the workplace,
she worked as an activist on behalf of the Chicano community outside
of the workplace. These activities helped Martina maintain her pride and
resist internalizing the cultural messages that attempt to squelch her
Chicana self. Like others, Martina protects her threatened self by distinguishing between her "front-stage" and "backstage" performances."[10]
  People also act out their resistance behind the scenes, in a number
of ways that are too subtle or diffuse to come under public scrutiny.
Not only do these acts have the potential to produce real change, but
they can fortify the self. Other acts of resistance, some of which can
be destructive to the organization, are inconspicuous and serve a similar purpose in helping people defend their selves against a dominant

culture that silences them.[11] We will talk more about behind-the-scenes tactics later in this chapter.

Self-Expressions as Resistance

Another way the tempered radicals I have studied fortify their senses of self is through small expressions that display the traits or values that differ from the majority. These expressions—dress, office decor, language, leadership style, for instance—help remind them who they are and what they value. These displays can be simple, spontaneous, and unaffected expressions of self, like the cartoon about a child adopting his nanny that John Ziwak displays in his office. Or they can represent more calculated acts of resistance, like marching in a gay rights parade with the company's banner. Either way, they express and affirm identities, and sometimes they have consequences above and beyond self-affirmation.

Alan Levy, a mid-level professional at Atlas, insists on taking off work to observe important Jewish holidays. Initially, he was the only one in his department who missed work for these occasions, as the Atlas calendar allowed only for the observance of Christian holidays. But by taking these days off, he has signaled that it is legitimate to observe one's religious and cultural traditions and has made it easier for others to take time off for their own holidays. Over time, people in his department came to expect this as the norm. As Alan's colleagues moved or were promoted into other areas of the organization, they modeled the same behavior in their new departments, and others began to follow their leads. After a while, Atlas responded to people's different personal needs by developing an organizational policy that gives people a certain number of "personal days" beyond vacation and sick days, thus validating behavior that once deviated from the norm. The policy implicitly endorses the legitimacy of people's different needs and traditions.

Small actions that demonstrate conformity reinforce the dominant culture; similarly, small actions like Alan's can disrupt the status quo. Mundane patterns of action and thought—how people talk, interact, decorate their offices, dress, spend their time, act on personal traditions, manage subordinates, perform in rituals, and think about themselves and others—are the threads of culture.[12] Thus someone who conforms to prescribed codes of behavior reinforces the dominant culture. In contrast, someone who deviates from "normal" patterns causes cultural disruption.[13] And even if the person's intent is not cultural disruption per se but simply self-expression that requires some level of resistance to norms, his or her everyday acts can be like throwing stones into a river: they create ripples that travel downstream.

The rippling occurs partly through a process Karl Weick calls "deviation amplification," in which a single atypical action sets the stage for others like it to follow.[14] When Alan took days off to observe his religion, people perceived that it is all right to observe non-Christian religious holidays in the workplace. More people followed his lead, and eventually, due to this behavior and others like it, Atlas created a policy.

Alan was not trying to promote organizational change: he was just staying true to his personal identity and to his beliefs as a Jew. But his initial action "enacted" a different context for future actions—it seemed to take on a life of its own, and soon this behavior was normal at Atlas.[15]

Let's now look at what some of these self-expressive behaviors are. It's important to think of them as illustrations of the many ways people express themselves and, in so doing, affirm their threatened identities and resist conventional expectations.

Dress

People dress "the part." Clothes, hairdos, makeup—all play a part in a public display of self. Sociologist Erving Goffman mentions dress as part of people's effort to place themselves in a social system.[16] Others have called it an important indicator of organizational role taking; if we dress "appropriately," it means we have accepted our prescribed role and will perform according to expectations.[17] Dress can thus be an important symbol of conformity.

Dress can just as easily signal resistance to prescribed codes of behavior. Dr. Frances Conley, a renowned neurosurgeon at Stanford Medical School, made national headlines when she accused her male colleagues of persistent discrimination and harassment. This strong public stand was not her first act of resistance against the male bastion of neurosurgery. Long before she hit the national news with her accusations (and subsequent resignation), she resisted in subtler, more personal ways. When I first met Conley, she was uniformed from head to ankle in asexual, drab surgical scrubs.[18] She looked the role of the traditional neurosurgeon. But barely visible under her dull uniform were dainty, white lacy ankle socks. They were her way of saying, "I am a neurosurgeon *and* a woman."

Conley's dress reinforced her sense of self as a woman in a predominantly male context. Her subtle display of femininity, which others certainly noticed, also made it slightly more legitimate to be a woman in this male-dominated profession. Does this mean that others followed her lead and wore lace ankle socks? Probably not. But her gesture created a small opening for others to challenge the macho culture, which others likely acted on in their own ways.

Office Decor

The way a person furnishes his or her place of work can also signify either conformity or resistance.[19] Even the modern cubicle, the epitome of aseptic uniformity, leaves room for individual personality. Our values, identity, and personal lives often come alive in how we decorate our offices, right down to the cartoons and photos we display.

Photographs in particular seem to make a statement about personal lifestyle and priorities. John Ziwak's desk is loaded with family pictures. For some people, like Jennifer Jackson, the display of photos represents a brave choice and a statement of their differences from the majority. At both Western and Atlas, gay and lesbian employees told me that they agonized over whether to place pictures of their partners around their offices. Jennifer decided to place the picture of herself with her partner only after their commitment ceremony, four years into their relationship. It was a simple assertion of who she is and who is important to her in her life, the kind of self-expression heterosexuals don't have to think about. But for Jennifer, it is also a visible reminder of the self that differs from the majority.

The impact of her decision went beyond her, however. Over time her colleagues got used to the picture, and then some became more and more comfortable seeing Jennifer with her partner, not only in the picture but also in person. The pairing of the two women became more "normalized" in their eyes. Thus the small but brave gesture of placing a photo on a desk was a step toward making the workplace slightly more comfortable for her—and probably for other gay employees.

Displaying personal belongings and artifacts is another way to establish identity and values. The workout apparel visibly exhibited in Martha Wiley's office, for example, makes it obvious that she spends part of the day exercising. When her employees see her prominent exercise clothes, they may feel more comfortable stepping out for a workout or taking time for other personal needs.

Among the traditional management books on Martha's shelves are volumes on gender and management. The mere display of these books invites conversation about gender and work-family issues. In a similar way, Joanie Mason's office is filled with artifacts from the villages she cultivates as trading partners for Shop.co. It is difficult to be in her office without talking about her travels and the accomplishments of the "fair trade" program. Each time I visit Joanie, I learn more about what she is trying to do, and what she is up against both at Shop.co and within her trading communities. The displays in her office probably lead others to learn more about Joanie's concerns as well. The point is that simple displays can have an impact beyond the individuals, partly through conversations they trigger.

Leadership Behaviors

In spite of pressures to manage in an authoritarian style and focus strictly on bottom-line concerns, Isabel Nuñez at Atlas continues to work collaboratively with her subordinates and persists in her commitment to consider the "people side of things." Although at first her coworkers were generally wary of her style, colleagues told her that some senior managers were beginning to ask more questions about the "human side of the business." Her colleagues pointed to Isabel as someone who had broadened other executives' perspectives and influenced what they entertained in their decisions.

Frances Conley did the same. Whereas most surgical teams have a rigid, top-down hierarchy with the surgeon dictating at the top, she ran her team with a considerably different style. According to some of the nurses, when Conley asked for input from others on her surgical team, treated members of the team with respect, and displayed compassion toward patients on her rounds, she demonstrated an alternative way to lead a surgical team and *be* a surgeon. After she had been working in the hospital awhile, nurses and residents began to have different ideas about how surgical teams should function and how surgeons should treat staff. Thanks to Conley's example, some of the residents might run their surgical teams in a less authoritarian way. Her way of leading teams not only helped fortify her own sense of self and resist dominant expectations, but also served as a model of an alternative to the patriarchal, authoritarian style expected of surgeons.[20]

Rituals

All cultures—whether societal, organizational, or professional—have rituals, which serve to express and reinforce significant cultural values.[21] Graduation ceremonies, bar exams, religious events, and annual company picnics all qualify as rituals. They usually occur at some regular interval, they are usually very structured, and they often call for people to play particular roles and follow a specified format or script. Rituals are upheld over time by people who conform to these scripts and changed over time by people who deviate from them.

Sometimes an adaptation in an accepted ritual begins as a simple expression of self. Take, for example, a well-known psychology professor's adaptation of the ritual of the academic talk. In an academic talk, an expert—usually a professor—conveys his or her expertise by delivering an impersonal and objective account of a research project. The ritual of the academic talk allows for no personal or emotional connection with the topic. On one occasion, however, the professor decided to do things differently. She began her talk, which was about individuals' capacity to think creatively during a crisis, by explaining how her own personal crisis brought her to the topic. This "expert" brought something into the ritual that is "normally" omitted from it: her feelings and personal experience.[22]

This may sound like no big deal, but it represented a significant departure from how this ritual is *supposed* to be performed. Some fellow faculty members were bothered by the deviation. Others were energized by it. Some of the students were intrigued by the implicit invitation to engage the material with their hearts as well as their minds, and were inspired by her example. By deviating from the prescribed behavior, then, the professor disrupted institutional norms and opened the way for alternative methods of interacting and learning within the profession. Her small departure from the norm created new possibilities for her colleagues and students.

Rituals offer people a way to make statements about their identities or their culture. Particularly when people have had to suppress elements of their personal or cultural identities to fit in at work, they can find it liberating to participate openly in rituals that *publicly* celebrate the part of their selves that they've had to silence. And sometimes participating in rituals outside the workplace can have as much organizational impact as actions taken at rituals inside the organization.

Jennifer Jackson marched in a band in a gay and lesbian parade, carrying the Atlas flag. "For me," she told me, "marching in the band declared, 'I'm proud of who I am.'" She also felt that displaying her sexual identity in such a public ritual made it more acceptable for other gays and lesbians, both at her company and outside it, to do the same. She went on,

> When they see me, they can see someone who doesn't look like the stereotypical bull dyke. I look like their daughters, like someone who is straight. I hold a regular job and have similar life ambitions, but I am openly out and I walk with pride in the parade. We are doing something important here. We are changing people's perceptions of who we are.

Jennifer believes that her participation in the parade helped boost her pride, and also that it may have changed people's misperceptions of gay people as "not normal."

Time-related Behaviors

As we have seen, people's personal values often conflict with the expectations and values enforced by their work cultures, and these conflicts sometimes play out in the context of how people do and do not spend their time. Martha Wiley's visible adherence to a regular mid-day workout routine sometimes creates scheduling difficulties. But whereas colleagues initially did not consider her routine "normal," they began to do so as others in her group began to follow her lead.

John Ziwak tries to build his values into his day-to-day behaviors. He tries to leave work by 6:00 P.M., rarely schedules meetings that run later, and generally refuses to take calls at home between 6:30 P.M. and 9:00 P.M. so he can spend uninterrupted time with his family. He makes an issue of it only if something regularly gets in the way of keeping this schedule at work.

Though John consistently works late at night and early in the morning to meet his performance expectations, his schedule constraints initially caused concern. But people respected his performance and his boss certainly did not want to lose him.

Eventually, people in John's group adjusted to his schedule. Conference calls and meetings that involved him were no longer scheduled after 5:00 P.M. Then, his group decided that all meetings should end by 5:30, and soon an informal rule evolved against calling people at home at night unless it was really essential. Productivity does not seem to suffer, and many of his colleagues seem to appreciate these shifts. What began as John's simple adherence to his personal values and priorities has created significant shifts in time-related behavior and has ultimately worked to the benefit of many.

A senior human resource official at Western pointed to a similar evolution in patterns related to time in several departments, initially in those with a high proportion of working mothers in managerial roles. In these departments it became the norm for people to leave work by 5:30 because a number of employees simply had to head for home by then. These behaviors evolved into a pattern that shifted people's expectations about time.

Language

Using language and jargon that express a "different" identity or set of values is a form of self-expression; it also can be an important mechanism of resistance that provokes questioning, learning, and adaptation. Joanie Mason's talk of human rights and fair-trade practices at Shop.co has brought into the discourse a set of concerns that challenges prevailing assumptions and priorities. At times her colleagues have discounted her concerns, but her language has kept people aware of a broader range of issues to consider.

Isabel Nuñez does not try to mask her Spanish accent and is not sure she can even if she wants to. Though her accent sets her apart from her peers, it also helps remind her and others about a part of her "self" that is important to her. Sometimes she speaks Spanish with other Latino managers, and often she speaks to some of the cafeteria workers in their native language, even when she is with other executives. Isabel is happy to make this connection and to express this part of herself. She isn't sure she accomplishes anything, but she likes to remind other executives—who sometimes forget—that there are differences among them.

What people talk about in formal and informal conversations, how they talk, and with whom they talk clearly matter. We'll look more at the role of language and narratives in chapter 6.

Self-Expressions as Cultural Disruptions

Self-expressions vary in their potential impact and risk. The more an act deviates from established role expectations or challenges accepted criteria that separate cultural insiders from outsiders, the more disruptive the act will be and the greater its potential to make an impact beyond the individual. Displaying a picture of a gay partner on one's desk is much less "deviant" and disruptive in the creative culture of, say, an advertising agency or a ballet company than it would be at a conservative bank. Frances Conley's act of wearing lace ankle socks was powerful not in itself, but because it implicitly challenged the criteria for inclusion in a "masculine" profession; it would not have been such a statement in an industry with more women in positions of power. Conley's quiet "transgression" demonstrates that the criteria that mark inclusion and exclusion, like other aspects of culture, are socially fabricated and can be socially torn apart.

Behind-the-Scenes Resistance

In the prior two sections of this chapter, I discussed quiet forms of resistance that are primarily motivated by people's desire to hold onto and express their threatened selves. We've seen how even these personally motivated behaviors can sometimes result in meaningful change beyond the individual. This section addresses quiet actions that reinforce the self but are driven more by a conscious agenda to initiate change. Tempered radicals who take this approach comply with prevailing expectations to project an image of loyalty, but they find ways outside public view to act on their values and identities. Very quietly, they rock the boat.

The behind-the-scenes efforts I observed do not provoke concern and sometimes they remain invisible even to those who they are meant to help. For this reason, tempered radicals who act primarily backstage are sometimes mistaken for conformists and do not get the credit they deserve for their efforts.

In fact, people who do this "backstage" work often have enormous fortitude and personal conviction. Peter Grant is an example. He is able to persist quietly only because of his commitment to hang in for the long-term vision of change and his appreciation for how long real change takes. He claims that his only hope for making lasting change is to chip away slowly and steadily at the practices and beliefs that exclude people like him, not to win a particular battle or to prove his colleagues wrong. He also knows that he must keep going without any promise of concrete outcomes or even recognition for his efforts, even from those who benefit from them.

Indeed, for Peter and others in his circumstances, lashing out or publicly challenging a practice sometimes represents the path of least emotional resistance. Many times, Peter has chosen to bite his tongue in the face of glaringly hypocritical comments made by colleagues who never miss an opportunity to tell him how "lucky" he is to have gotten where he is. In these instances, it takes every ounce of discipline to contain his anger:

> The senior guys tell me that the job is too big for me, that I might make some mistakes. "You moved awfully quickly," they said. Well, hell, I didn't move awfully fast. I sat around for 9,000 years dealing with all their backbiting and slander. And now I have to make them comfortable with me, assure them I'm not going to erupt? I'm sure one of them is afraid that I'm going to blow off in rage. I just take this as motivation to work harder and do what needs to be done here.

Given the fortitude and commitment required and the amount he has quietly accomplished for others, it is easy to see why Peter is so pained by others' accusations that he has sold out. As we shall see, efforts like Peter's can make a tremendous difference to individuals and ultimately to organizations.

While behind-the-scenes actions can take a number forms, I've found that the most prevalent forms tend to fall into three categories: taking extra-organizational action, helping others, and channeling information, resources, and opportunities.

Taking Extra-organizational Action

Some tempered radicals decide that they are better off enacting their values and beliefs or helping their cultural communities by taking action outside their work organizations. Jake Sansome, an ex-lawyer who works in John Ziwak's department (business development) at Atlas has always been a civil rights activist. Though it has often pained him to be silent about the many injustices and inequities he has seen at Atlas, he decided that he did not want to risk his credibility or spend his energy taking up these causes within the organization. He reserves most of his energy to fight injustices outside Atlas by working as a volunteer in a nonprofit legal rights center in a local minority community. This work has helped him express and keep alive core values and commitments, which he does not regularly express openly at work.

Sheila Johnson also has done work outside Western that has kept her connected to her racial identity and roots in the community. She regularly speaks at local high schools to help encourage young minorities, and she has been a mentor to two African American students, whom she meets with regularly. Sheila also accepts most invitations to speak to community and professional groups about issues related to race in business. (Because she is such a visible success within a prominent institution, she receives many such invitations.) Some of Sheila's outside activities, such as posting jobs in the community, have had a direct impact within Western. Taking all these actions that are "invisible" to her work colleagues has allowed her to make a difference in her community and has helped her feel connected to a part of herself that she could easily lose at Western.

Many other men and women have talked to me about taking part in extraorganizational activities that put their values and change agendas into practice—whether they engage in environmental volunteerism or inner-city tutoring of disadvantaged youth. Joanie Mason at Shop.co looks to broaden her impact outside her own company by helping people who are trying to put fair-trade programs in place in their own organizations.

Helping Others within the Organization

Another effective and quiet way to act on values and identities is to help other people within one's organization, particularly those who face comparable challenges. Roger Saillant, the executive at Visteon, for example, has looked for ways to mentor and help people who share his concerns about environmental sustainability. By helping them succeed, he has in effect been extending the concern about the environment within the organization.

Martha Wiley has looked for opportunities for the women and minorities in her department to take on added responsibilities and surpass people's expectations of them. One summer, for instance, Martha hired an African American intern from a local college. After watching him work, she knew he had great potential, so she continued to give him challenging assignments. Soon he was managing clients on his own, and every time he took on new responsibilities, he proved how superbly competent he was. Week after week she handed him challenges, and when she couldn't find anything more in her own department to challenge him, she found a job for him elsewhere in the organization that would enable him to grow. Not only did her efforts make a huge difference in this young man's life, but they had a genuine impact on others at Western, who secretly believed that this man and other entry-level minorities might not be up for the really challenging jobs.

Behind-the-scenes helping can sometimes involve taking on significant responsibilities above and beyond regular work duties. For example, some might do relatively invisible tasks like speaking to recruits or new hires on behalf of one's identity group, assuming extra mentoring responsibilities, or simply talking with junior people who need encouragement and support. More visible responsibilities of this sort include serving on extra committees, being the representative woman or minority on a task force, or being the "female" or minority voice in the community. Isabel Nuñez had to resign from two nonprofit boards because her extra work *within* Atlas became so consuming. She was serving on multiple committees within Atlas to represent both women and Latinos, and she was the informal advisor to dozens of women within the company. This work—sometimes called the "shadow job"—requires substantial time and energy, yet it rarely "counts" when it comes time for evaluation and promotion.[23]

As we have seen, psychological survival and persistence in contexts in which one feels like an outsider can require enormous fortitude that may sometimes be hard to muster. Tempered radicals therefore help others by encouraging them to stay in the game, even when it looks hopeless. Peter Grant routinely gives pep talks to other minorities when they become frustrated and angry. He helps them armor themselves to prepare for their inevitable frustrations and, at the same time, he encourages them to see that they have a choice about how to respond to the pressures they face: "I tell them, they can give up and move on, or they can stick it out and be patient and have some amount of tenacity and keep pushing [to change things]."

Channeling Information, Opportunities, and Resources

Organizational insiders have always relied on informal networks to learn about opportunities, compare salary packages, champion each others' successes, and generally help others within their network. Networks help ensure that opportunities for high-visibility jobs, resources, and information continue to be channeled to the same people—but they can perpetuate exclusion by withholding that information from others.[24] Thus efforts to channel valuable information and resources to those who might not otherwise be privy to them can be a powerful way to make a difference.

As he gained more seniority at Western, Tom Novak saw the importance of sharing information and resources with other gay employees through informal networks. He watched his fellow executives compare notes and share information. He saw how one of his female colleagues settled for a relatively small compensation package because she had no basis of comparison, while her male counterparts actively compared their packages to negotiate more effectively. He saw how other executives tapped people from their networks for particularly promising assignments. Tom became committed to creating this kind of information sharing among the gay employees; once he did, many of his gay colleagues began to come to him as the network "hub." Similarly, ethnic and racial minorities at Western saw Peter Grant as their networking conduit.

Information channeling can go the other way as well. People outside traditional networks are not as visible to senior decision makers as network insiders are. They need someone to channel information *about* them to those on the inside. As a woman, Martha Wiley had

---

Designing Behind-the-Scenes Actions to Make a Difference

1. Whatever the activities are—hiring, helping, channeling, etc.—when driven by your "different" values, beliefs, or identities, they also affirm these parts of your self.

2. Actions designed to create connections with others with similar values, beliefs, and identities, will further the impact of your efforts and help affirm your sense of self.

3. Activities will be most effective if they have the potential to accumulate or to ripple into additional changes. They need not be immediately obvious as change-inducing, and they need not directly threaten the status quo.

---

been excluded from informal networks, and she understands how essential and difficult it is for outsiders to be noticed by insiders. Now, as a senior executive, she deliberately channels information about the accomplishments of other women, minority employees, and people with disabilities to senior executives who might otherwise not notice these employees. As she explained it,

> I often have the ear of senior management, so when I know of somebody in another department who's doing a good job on a project, if it's a woman or a minority or someone with a disability, I take it upon myself to say something casually to other managers. Somehow, I'll make sure the names of these individuals are made known. I'll drop a line like, "Gosh, did you hear what Jackie Jones did?" I seed executives with information and they don't even realize I'm doing it.

Martha's method doesn't make visible waves about bias and discrimination. Yet she has been able to make a difference for people on the margin by quietly channeling information about their accomplishments and potential.[25]

Conclusion

Resistance can take many forms. Individuals who want to express their "different" self and act on their ideals but do not want to risk being seen as a rebel might be wise to follow a course of quiet resistance. All the forms of resistance I've described enable people to act on their values, beliefs, and identities and defend against the forces in the system that tend to render those parts marginal. Though the direct impact of these efforts may be limited in scope, as some of the examples illustrate, they sometimes can accumulate and amplify far beyond one's immediate intent. While wearing her "psychological armor," Martina Holbrina maintains her commitment to the Chicano community and works for change outside the workplace. Alan Levy's quiet insistence on observing Jewish holidays made it a bit safer for others to observe their own traditions. Sheila Johnson maintains her racial identity *and* works for change in her community and workplace by engaging in a wide variety of behind-the-scenes mentoring and support activities.

In the next chapter, we move to more visible and more challenging acts, which turn demeaning or threatening interactions into opportunities to challenge expectations and generate learning. The strategies we discuss in chapter 4 are ways to respond immediately and constructively in the context of an interaction.

Turning Personal Threats into Opportunities

The ultimate measure of a man is not where he stands in moments of comfort and convenience, but where he stands during challenge and controversy.

— *Martin Luther King, Jr.*

TOM NOVAK did not consider himself an outspoken activist. Yet he tried to live his life in a way that felt true to his identity, and that meant being open about his sexual orientation, though he admitted that he enjoyed the legitimacy that came from being able to look just like his straight male colleagues at Western. Over the years, Tom gained the respect and trust of many of his fellow executives, and some even engaged him in conversations about the experiences of gay people at Western and the "gay lifestyle." One day he was in a colleague's office when the executive said, "I can appreciate that some people choose this lifestyle. I just don't understand why gay people have to announce their sexual orientation in the workplace. Why do they have to flaunt it in people's faces?"

The comment caught Tom off guard; he was both hurt and offended. He didn't believe that most gay people "flaunt" their sexuality or have any desire to do so. But he worried that if he expressed his outright disagreement in the heat of the moment, their conversation would be unproductive. So he was inclined to stay silent, at least for the time being. But then a picture on his colleague's desk caught his eye.

I pointed to the picture of his wife and children and said, "Why are you announcing your sexuality? If you go in my office you won't see a photo of me and my partner. It seems that you're the one announcing your sexuality, not me."

Tom could see immediately that his colleague got his point. He responded with a simple "touché."

Tom's effective use of light-hearted irony pointed out how a person's own perception of what is "normal" can so dramatically color a perception of who is "flaunting" what.

In the course of everyday interactions people regularly face choices like Tom's: to remain silent or speak up, to ignore an offensive comment or challenge it, to comply with stereotypical expectations or challenge them, to "pass" as an insider or stand out as an outsider. Whether it is in the context of informal conversations, formal interviews, coffee-break chatter, or formal evaluations, everyday "encounters" such as Tom's present opportunities to express conformity or resistance. In this context, we'll use Erving Goffman's definition of *encounters* as face-to-face, focused interactions that have clear beginnings and ends.[1] We'll focus on encounters in which individuals consciously or unconsciously choose between going along with or challenging prevailing cultural dynamics including dynamics that, intentionally or otherwise, threaten their values or identities or in some way demean them.

In some encounters, a person intentionally tries to establish superiority over, or demean, another.[2] Other encounters are benevolent interactions with no intent other than "normal" communication—people saying what they think or acting as they are supposed to act. Whatever the motivation, when people remain silent—whether they are a target or a third-party observer—in response to a demeaning interaction, their silence reinforces existing patterns of power and exclusion.[3]

And people do go silent—often not by conscious choice but because they feel that they have *no choice*. They feel that their survival in the organization requires that they be cautious in a threatening encounter.

It isn't surprising that so many people respond this way. When people feel threatened, they tend to become defensive, their creativity shuts down, and they think they have no options.[4] In many face-to-face interactions, people do not have time to step back and consider anything beyond instinctive responses. And often instincts and fear point to silence. In short, when we do not clearly see that we have reasonable and *doable* options, we can feel victimized by circumstances and helpless to do anything about them.

Yet it is precisely in these moments when we witness or are engaged in threatening interactions that we may face an opportunity to break negative cycles of inaction and consciously pursue constructive alternatives. Indeed, although Tom felt threatened and personally demeaned, he had the presence to see an opportunity for teaching.[5] Many encounters offer such opportunities to those who can recognize them.

The first and most important characteristic of encounters turned into opportunities is that people see that they have a choice in how to respond. The second critical characteristic is that people recognize a variety of productive responses fall between the extremes of silent submission and aggressive confrontation. Being prepared to look for these alternatives in any encounter is critical to making effective choices in the moment.

Recognizing Choice

It can be difficult to see that a response to any particular interaction is a personal choice. When you feel trapped, you feel trapped.

Recognizing choice entails the capacity to see alternative responses. But even before that, there are mindsets that make it easier to see choices and identify alternatives.

• **Viewing interactions as opportunities:** It is easier to see choices when we see difficult interactions as opportunities rather than threats. As Jane Dutton's research has shown, when we frame an event as a potential opportunity for learning, several positive dynamics occur.[6] First, the event seems more controllable, which heightens our sense that responding will be effective. Second, it seems less threatening, so the defensive postures and lack of expansive thinking associated with threats become dampened. The interaction begins to seem more suited to risk taking. Even when this "opportunity framing" begins largely as an illusion, the illusion can create a self-fulfilling positive cycle. With an "opportunity" frame, we ask more questions, search more vigorously for alternatives, and thereby uncover more viable options for acting.

• **Seeing silence as a choice:** In Western society we tend to view silence as the absence of choice—as a nonaction.[7] This perspective naturally leads people who default to silence to feel victimized. It is therefore important to recognize that silence is itself a choice, and sometimes the appropriate one. To be effective, we must know when it is best to push back and when it is best to go along.

• **Considering the complex "self":** Many interactions can feel threatening because they appear to threaten "who we are." But people have multiple selves, and any particular threat is probably aimed at only one aspect of the self. I am not suggesting that the threat may not be real, or that a firm response may not be appropriate, but it is important to remember that we can evaluate other aspects of the situation and choose how best to respond rather than feeling forced to defend a singular "true self."

• **Depersonalizing encounters:** To better recognize choices, it can be helpful to find a place to stand outside of the personal to provide emotional distance from a direct encounter. This distance can be essential to remove the threat long enough to explore alternative responses. (I discuss this process of "stepping back" further in the next chapter.)

Alternative Responses

In certain circumstances, it becomes difficult to see beyond the most extreme responses to threatening encounters: either to stay silent and let it pass or to confront the threat head on and make it a battle. In this section I present six strategies I observed tempered radicals using in response to encounters. Clearly, not all will be relevant to any given situation. The point, however—and it is an important one—is that having these possible strategies in hand gives a person the ability to see alternatives the next time he or she is "in the moment."

The first four strategies draw directly from the work of Deborah Kolb and Judith Williams. In their book *The Shadow Negotiation,* they offer a typology of responses called "responsive turns."[8] The word *turn* reflects an action intended to change the direction in which an encounter is going, much like a turn in the road changes its direction. Encounters are interactions that often reinforce existing power relations and cultural norms. With responsive turns, participants reframe these dynamics. They might restore a power balance in an unbalanced encounter, recast how one individual is being treated by another, or make apparent a dynamic that only some parties see. Responsive turns not only give a person the ability to diffuse a threatening situation, but they also can challenge the cultural and political dynamics expressed and reinforced in these everyday interactions. Thinking of the responses below as ways to "turn" threatening and demeaning interactions helps further a sense of choice and efficacy.

• **Interrupting momentum:** This strategy can be appropriate when you see that an interaction is beginning to take what you see as a threatening or destructive direction. For example, a female executive with responsibilities at home, whose colleagues are exploring evening venues for a necessary meeting, might quickly offer an alternative time during work hours before her colleagues lock in on an evening proposal. She might create this turn without even identifying the evening proposal as problematic.

• **Naming the issue:** Turning an interaction by naming what is going on may not change the outcome, but it makes the underlying dynamic or consequences more visible. In the preceding example, the woman might agree to the meeting but mention that it is a surprising intrusion into her family life. This naming of the issue might make people more aware of the problem and perhaps make her colleagues less apt to propose a similar meeting without explicitly considering the consequences for everyone.

• **Correcting assumptions or actions:** This approach requires some willingness to be a bit more confrontational, as it involves making explicit what you believe is taking place and pointing out that the other person's actions or understandings may be wrong. Take the preceding example again. To correct the assumption, the woman would point out that she has other responsibilities that she can't easily change without notice. She thus implicitly questions her colleagues' assumptions that people can be available at all times for last-minute meetings. Or say a black man is consistently interrupted at meetings. He might simply say, "I wonder why you didn't hear that I was speaking" to correct the dynamic. His statement not only would make the dynamic apparent but would put the infraction squarely on the other party.

• **Diverting the direction:** This turn represents a response that can have a slightly broader impact. It involves taking the encounter in a different direction, often by pointing to the more general pattern it reflects. For example, another meeting participant might specifically state that the participants have been silencing the black man, perhaps unwittingly, and then might go on to point out the larger pattern of discrimination that seems to be recurring in meetings. This approach can be particularly powerful when someone besides the primary target of the threat initiates this kind of turn.

• **Using humor:** Humor can provide a buoyant, nonconfrontational way to sharpen the focus on an issue that is causing tension.[9] It can be particularly effective at leveling a power dynamic while making light of it. In the case of the evening meeting example, a reply of "Oh, well, good thing my kids ate a big lunch" could clearly point out the underlying issues in this situation, but in a way that doesn't invite a reply or escalate into a difficult debate.

• **Delaying a response:** Any of these strategies can be part of a response delivered in the moment or held for a later time and place. Although delaying the response may look like silence and acquiescence at the time, it can often be a wise choice because it enables you to think about how to address the issue in a more calm or appropriate setting.

Any one of these responsive turns can be appropriate in any kind of encounter. And, as we will see in the example, they are also used differently by third parties who witness an offensive interaction. Indeed, sometimes third parties are much better positioned to apply these turns to challenge existing dynamics and promote learning.

"Responsive Turns": A Summary

Responsive turns help you change the dynamics taking place in an encounter. They represent different levels of challenge and varying potential for creating learning.

1. **Interrupt** an encounter to change its momentum.

2. **Name** an encounter to make its nature and consequences more transparent.

3. **Correct** an encounter to provide an explanation for what is taking place and to rectify understandings and assumptions.

4. **Divert** an encounter to take the interaction in a different direction.

5. **Use humor** to release the tension in a situation.

6. **Delay** to find a better time or place to address the issue.

Courtesy Simon and Schuster. Adapted from Deborah Kolb and Judith Williams, *The Shadow Negotiation* (New York: Simon and Schuster, 2000), p. 109.

Common Opportunities for Choice

Once people are predisposed to choose their responses consciously and have a sense that they can choose from many strategies, they are more likely to manage threatening encounters effectively and turn them into opportunities for pushing back on expectations and learning. Below, I provide examples of encounters and different responses, organized by the kinds of pressures people who differ from the majority frequently face.

Pressure to Conform

An encounter can feel like a test of someone's willingness to go along with the majority and do what it takes to fit in. Sometimes an encounter pressures someone to do something against his or her desires or values: a man might be confronted with pressure to go with his colleagues to a bar or to a strip joint; a woman, to leave her family to play golf with colleagues on a Saturday; an employer, to pay below-living wages to an employee. A person in such an encounter must decide whether to compromise personal values or priorities to fit in and not make waves, or whether to stand up for his or her values and risk social ostracization, exclusion, and humiliation.

Sometimes the choice involves something peripheral to the person's sense of self, but sometimes it cuts right to the core. These "tests" are therefore particularly problematic when going along with the majority requires a person to violate, disguise, or repress a core part of his or her identity. People who are "different" in a meaningful way are subject to these tests all the time.

Tom Novak joined the public relations group at Western partly because his immediate boss had a reputation for being supportive and seemed, from the start, comfortable with his sexual orientation. At one point, however, an interaction with his long-term mentor, a man in a different department who recruited Tom to Western, put Tom in a difficult spot.

Tom's boss invited him to a high-profile charity function sponsored by Western. Tom knew that almost all the senior executives and many important clients—the "who's who" of the community—would be attending. His boss encouraged him to bring his long-term partner, but his mentor, Frank, stopped by Tom's office to advise him to bring a female date instead. Frank told Tom that he was at a pivotal point in his career and that he shouldn't risk "throwing it all away" for one good evening, or to prove a point. As always, Frank was trying to be helpful, to keep his protégé from sabotaging his career. Tom told him he would sleep on his advice.

Tom knew that this was a choice about whether to "pass" himself off as an insider by bringing a female date or to accept the risk of being cast as an outsider. He had no doubt that his career would benefit if he "passed" this test. The temptation to be viewed as a real power player was great, and Tom was afraid that bringing his male partner would jeopardize it all. He also did not want to alienate his mentor.

Nevertheless, Tom knew that the stakes were high in the other direction as well. If he complied and brought a female date, he would be colluding in the very belief system and practices that keep gay people out of the inner circle. It was also an important decision in another way. He knew of other gay men who had agreed to bring female dates and thus had already submitted to the pressure to conform. If he followed suit, he would only be adding to their invisibility. Tom also realized that he was probably in a unique situation because at least he had the support of his immediate boss, if not of his mentor. As he balanced his choices, he knew that he had an opportunity to prove that gay people *do* belong. While he had no choices other than bringing a male date or bringing a female date, he knew that he could choose what, if anything, to say to his mentor.

After a sleepless night, Tom decided that he would escort his own partner to the event. The timing was right to take the risk. That weekend, at the party, his boss immediately took him and his partner by the arm and introduced them around the room, making it clear that she was on Tom's side. Tom hoped Frank would understand his decision, but he decided not to confront him directly. In effect, Tom's action *interrupted* the forces at play. He refused to submit to the pressure to be someone he is not to conform to "normal" expectations. Showing up with a same-sex partner scrambled those expectations.

Tom could have taken the opportunity to change how his mentor understood this situation or to foster broader learning. After all, Frank did mean to help him. Tom could have *named* his mentor's bias and *corrected* his assumptions about who one must be to be a serious "player" at the bank. He could have pointed out that by taking a female he would be colluding in promoting certain expectations about heterosexuality. In short, Tom could have used this encounter to challenge prevailing norms more explicitly.

On the other hand, he could have done much less. The easy choice would have been to take Frank's advice, play it safe, and pass as one of the boys. What he chose to do was to *interrupt* the standard story of heterosexual "normalcy" without standing on a soapbox or directly confronting Frank.

Despite his relatively mild response, looking back at the event, Tom felt his action had an effect beyond himself. At the party, he spotted a few men whom he knew to be gay. They had chosen to "pass" as straight, and his decision to resist conformity pressures did make an impression on them, as Tom thought it might. When some of the gay men saw Tom with his partner, they gave him a warm nod of respect, as if to say, "Thanks for having the guts." Tom had been on the other side enough times to know that the nods meant "It's a bit more okay now, and next time more of us will feel safer to do the same."

In the end, Tom felt his response was neither too risky nor too cautious for that situation. And, while he didn't yet know of all the ramifications of his decision—positive or negative—when he went home that night, he was at peace with it.

Ellen Thomas, a young African American consultant in a technical service business, was faced with a comparable dilemma.[10] Ellen was preparing for her first big presentation to a potential client when Joe, her mentor, stopped by her office for some last-minute coaching. As a parting comment, he said, "Ellen, you should unbraid your hair to appear more professional." She felt stung.

Ellen had worn her hair in long cornrow braids during her job interviews and she chose the company because of its stated commitment to diversity. While she believed Joe probably meant to be helpful, wanting her to "look the part" and succeed, she interpreted Joe's words to mean "look as white as possible." His advice felt like a betrayal and a threat to a core part of her identity. She was too upset to respond immediately, so she *delayed* and simply said, "I'll think about it."

Ellen knew it was a risk to ignore his advice, but her hair was too tied to her sense of self to give in. And pragmatically, unbraiding her hair would require hours of work, hours better spent preparing for her presentation.

By the next day, after cooling off, Ellen was able to see this encounter as a test not just of *her* willingness to conform to fit this definition, but of the *institution's* willingness to adapt to the reality of its diverse workforce. She realized that she had choices. This incident posed an opportunity to challenge Joe's biases and to help him appreciate the connection between this concrete incident and the organization's espoused promise of valuing diversity.

Ellen prepared for her presentation and delivered it with unimpeachable authority. She wore her hair in neat cornrow braids and dressed in a new conservative business suit, a gesture she was perfectly comfortable making. She knew she succeeded in conveying expertise; she also hoped that her display signaled to others that professionals come in many different packages.

But for Ellen, unlike Tom, this was not the end of her response. She wanted to make sure her mentor learned something from this, but not in a way that jeopardized their relationship or put him on the defensive. Immediately following her presentation, Ellen thanked Joe for caring enough to give her advice and gently asked him if he knew how his advice about her hair had affected her. As she suspected, he did not, and he asked her to explain. Ellen described why her hair was not just about "style," and why, to her, it was emblematic of her ethnicity. She let him know that she understood that he had not meant to offend her. She then explained that she chose this company because she thought it would accept her *as* a black woman, and that colleagues communicated this acceptance to her in big ways, like giving her the chance to make such a high-profile presentation, but also in small ways, like how they express expectations about fitting in.

In this conversation, Ellen *corrected* her mentor's assumption that her hairstyle is simply a superficial expression of "style" for her. More important, she *diverted* the issue away from hairstyle and appearance to the much broader issues of the existing parameters of "fitting in" and the company's willingness to expand its implicit definitions of professionalism and put into practice, in day-to-day ways, its espoused commitment to diversity. Ellen thus turned what initially felt like a personal threat to her identity into an opportunity for her mentor to learn.

Issues That Others Don't Recognize

In the course of daily interactions, we all face encounters that implicitly ask us to choose between raising a latent issue or ignoring it. These encounters can function as tests of loyalty and commitment.

Martha Wiley at Western was faced with this kind of "test." In the course of normal interactions during a compensation meeting, a recurring bias was evident that nobody else seemed to notice. She had seen this dynamic before, but this time she felt it was so blatant and consequential that she could not let it persist.

In this case, a man and a woman who held comparable jobs were being considered for promotions. Executives sometimes found the man's aggressiveness less than endearing, but they accepted it because he was charming with clients, who loved him. The woman was equally good, equally accomplished, and equally loved by her clients, though far less aggressive. The woman noticed after a while that she wasn't being offered the same opportunities as her male counterpart and decided to talk more about her accomplishments so that colleagues would notice.

During this particular compensation meeting, the participants not only tolerated the man's aggressiveness and self-promotion but discussed how his behavior would make him very successful. In the same meeting, the same people castigated the woman's efforts to shed light on her own accomplishments and labeled her as self-promoting. Martha recalled how she brought the issue to the fore:

> I finally said, "Look, I just find it odd that he is arrogant and all you do is laugh about it and think it's fine. And she, who no one would describe as nearly as arrogant, you say she's self-promoting if she says one word on her own behalf." I said, "I don't understand. Please explain this. They both have the clients loving them. Why does he get such high marks and she is not getting any recognition? She probably works harder."

Martha *named* the issue and then *corrected* the encounter by pointing to the underlying double standards in her colleagues' assessments. She left no room for doubt: "I had to say it. No one wants to address this sort of thing, but in this case, I had to say it."

Martha was usually not this direct in her challenges, and often she chose not to say anything. But as a witness to the interaction, she saw this as a particularly good opportunity to raise awareness among her colleagues about double standards that she herself experienced.

In this instance, Martha thought the connection between her colleagues' behaviors and the patterns of double standards was pretty blatant. But sometimes biases are so deeply embedded in "normal" practice that they are not evident and it seems that you are creating the issue by raising it.[11] In such cases, you risk being seen as a troublemaker or complainer, particularly if you are perceived as one who has been wronged or are otherwise personally implicated in the latent issue. Women who speak up about harassment, for example, are often accused of causing the problem because they provoked the behavior or simply because they have a "chip on their shoulder." In situations in which you are personally invested in an issue it can be very effective for a third party to step in and raise the concerns as a neutral witness.

This was the case during a meeting between the corporate marketing team and business development group at Atlas. Several people were talking at once about a potential acquisition. A few times a new member of the marketing group offered her concerns about distributing the new business's products outside the country. People continued to talk as if she hadn't said anything. Ten minutes after her last attempt to raise the issue, one of her senior colleagues voiced the same concerns. Everyone stopped talking and turned their attention to his issues. All of a sudden these concerns were the focus of the conversation, and the man who voiced them led the discussion. The woman stayed silent.

Jake, one of the managers in business development who preferred not to make waves, just couldn't believe that no one else was aware of what had happened. He had seen it before, but never so blatantly had he witnessed the silencing of a woman—as it happened, an Asian American woman. After a few minutes, he stepped in and said, "I just have to understand something here. Can you explain why this issue is so important and why the one Carol raised ten minutes ago was not worth talking about? I just want to understand this."

Questioning a statement or asking for clarification of a behavior, as Jake did, is one effective way to *name* what is going on. Sometimes calling attention to people's behavior can change it. At least it makes them aware of what is really happening and makes it clear that their actions have consequences for others. Carol could have done the same on her own behalf, but it would have been riskier in most circumstances, and may not have had the same impact.

In this situation, Jake had the advantage of not being seen as personally invested in this incident; thus he was able to play a critical role in turning the encounter and challenging what was going on. The position of third-party bystander can be an incredibly powerful place from which to intervene and make a difference on behalf of others, providing that the intervention does not further silence or subordinate the wronged individuals.

Let's look at another example of raising hidden concerns that challenge the majority's values and direction. An engineering manager at Atlas recalled attending a high-level meeting with production managers to discuss alternatives for subcontracting the manufacturing of components for a new product. Production managers were advocating a plant in Indonesia that they had used before and that they knew to be less expensive than those run by competitors in other areas of the world. They also knew that this plant used particularly exploitative labor practices and had working conditions far below the relatively loose standards advised by the International Labor Organization.

Enthusiasm about using this facility was building. Finally, the engineering manager asked, "How do they do it so cheaply? Shouldn't we be worried about this?" With this question, he implicitly *named* and called attention to a set of issues that were not on the table, issues that most people preferred not to discuss. He felt that this small prod at least stopped the momentum, raised a concern, and pushed others to pause and think about the noneconomic implications of going down this path. In the end, the production managers decided to go with a plant in India that may not be much better. But at least the engineering manager pushed them to consider and own the implications of their decision.

Offensive Actions

During encounters that involve offensive remarks or acts, the offended person and others must choose, often in an instant, whether (and how) to let the comment go or to challenge it.

Isabel Nuñez of Atlas was at an executive off-site retreat. One day, the company president raked a fellow employee over the coals, calling public attention to the person's mistakes in a brutal and humiliating way. Isabel found it very difficult not to intervene. Given the competitive norms of Atlas's culture, there was nothing particularly unusual about the "grilling," but she felt that the president's behavior was unnecessarily damaging to her colleague, and that other ways of interacting would generate more learning and collaboration within the group. In her view, she was witnessing one more instance of what she felt was becoming an increasingly cut-throat culture. This retreat seemed like the right forum for challenging the norms that impaired the collegiality and effectiveness of the executive team, especially since group morale was deteriorating. But in the moment, Isabel didn't see a way to address the issue constructively.

Isabel thought about it, and at the very next meeting, when a comparable dynamic occurred, she was ready. She simply said to her colleagues, "Aren't we on the same team here?" That one statement said it all. Everyone knew what she meant, and the tone of the group interaction turned almost instantaneously. By choosing to appeal to the "team" and not just to defend a single person, Isabel made it easier for her colleagues to respond and hear her comment as a constructive one.

Initially, Isabel chose to *delay*. She certainly was bothered by the demeaning nature of the interaction, but she didn't know how best to turn this into a learning opportunity. Her patience paid off, and she later managed a comparable interaction effectively. Her brief question, which was not particularly threatening, ever so effectively *named* the ruthless dynamic. She probably could have said a lot more, but she felt that her few words were sufficient to provoke meaningful changes. Letting these demoralizing behaviors continue was simply not productive for anyone, and she knew it just didn't have to be that way. By carefully turning a typical encounter, she had taken a small but important step toward changing a corrosive cultural dynamic that served no one.

Another example further illustrates the importance of identifying responses that feel "doable" as well as effective. Kathleen Casey, a vice president at another high-technology company and a trusted adviser of the newly appointed CEO, was attending a companywide meeting that began with a film of the company's history. The film contained several clips of the past CEO and his wife. After the film, the CEO took the podium and began his remarks with some comments about his predecessor and his wife, including a humorous reference to the wife's "great legs."

Kathleen knew that the remarks had offended other women and jeopardized the CEO's standing in their eyes, but no one said anything at the meeting. Kathleen was the one woman who actually knew the man, and she was sure he had made a thoughtless comment, not meaning to portray women in a demeaning way.

The next day, after the dust had settled from the meeting, Kathleen stopped by the CEO's office and simply said, "Nice speech, but you have to lose the legs jokes." She had no desire to embarrass him or to escalate the issue beyond the immediate incident. She knew that she had to say something, but she decided to do so jokingly, so she could point to the problem and simultaneously ease the tension around it. To her, the best approach was *quick, matter-of-fact, uncritical,* and *private*. This felt like a constructive way to present her concerns while ensuring that he would hear them and learn from them.

To some, this kind of response may seem like a cop-out. It certainly was not radical or risky, nothing like standing up publicly at the meeting and asking the CEO to apologize. Yet if she had seen such an openly adversarial gesture as her only option, Kathleen probably would have done nothing. *Delaying* and *using humor* to talk to the man in the privacy of his office felt doable to her and allowed her to act.

Had Kathleen taken a more radical approach, say, by calling him publicly on his underlying assumptions, she would certainly have posed a deeper challenge and possibly provoked broader learning by all the meeting participants—but it also could have backfired. Embarrassment and antagonism can cause people to retreat further into their position and block subsequent learning and change.

Expectations Based on Stereotypes

All the encounters we have covered so far enact power relations, but some types of encounters play this out more explicitly. Encounters that implicitly ask people to comply with expectations based on demeaning stereotypes ask them to participate in their own marginalization. People must then choose whether and how to respond to such requests.

Hong Lei, an Asian American human resource manager at Atlas, recalled an awkward meeting with her boss's boss about her department's recruiting progress. After the meeting, he said to her, "Hong, I just interviewed this Asian woman from UCLA who looked just like you." Though she believed he didn't mean to insult her, Hong was offended by the suggestion that "you all look alike." The gurgling in her gut told her she had a choice to make. She could let it go or come back at him. Lightheartedly she said,

> Oh really? When I first went to work at Stanford, there was a professor who looked just like you. Both of you are white, medium height, with short gray hair. I used to get you confused all the time.

Her colleague immediately understood what she was challenging him on; he replied, "I guess we all look alike to you too? I'll remember that."

Humor allowed Hong to call attention to what her colleague was doing—categorizing and to some extent stereotyping her—and at the same time make light of this dynamic to avoid antagonizing him or escalating the problem. Humor can make a point but avoid provoking embarrassment and defensiveness; the listener can more easily reflect on assumptions and learn from the interaction. Hong's response, a humorous version of *naming*, exposed the dynamic, made light of it, and pointed to its inappropriateness at the same time.

Sheila Johnson at Western found herself up against stereotypical expectations at precisely the time that she was beginning to feel like she was becoming a "real player" among her peers. At the time, Sheila was a vice president, the most senior black woman in the company, and she was making great progress in her career. Eager to keep increasing her professional network and responsibilities, she asked her supervisor what else she could do to expand her opportunities and skills to ready herself for her next promotion. His response caught her off guard. He asked her to plan the department's Christmas party. "I thought, 'How does planning the department Christmas party enhance my career opportunities? I don't see the connection,'" Sheila told me. "I asked him to explain it to me, and he answered, vaguely, that it would help me secure exposure among senior executives."

Sheila would have loved to tell him what he could do with his Christmas party, but she prudently *delayed* responding until she could cool down and come up with a more reasoned response. Fulfilling a traditional feminine support role was not the way she intended to present herself to senior executives, but she knew that refusing this request flat out would also be damaging. How others would think of her, how they would treat her, and even how she would think of herself, she felt were all on the line.

After giving it a great deal of consideration, Sheila came up with a compromise solution that would get the job done and protect her reputation. She would say neither yes nor no to her supervisor's request. She told him that she would be willing to help, but that she would enlist the services of a more junior person in the group to head up the task.

With this response, Sheila *interrupted* her boss's attempt to cast her in a stereotypical feminine support role. Sheila realized she had opted out of an important opportunity to make a much stronger statement because she had not wanted to send the message that she was not a loyal team player or that she was too "uppity" and inflexible to take on this sort of work. Sheila never came out and directly *named* the biased expectations. Nor did she *name* the potential consequences for her in accepting such a task, both what it would do to her image and how it would consume time that could otherwise be spent on more valued tasks. She could have *corrected* her boss by showing how his request put her in a stereotypical feminine support role and by pointing out some of the assumptions that might have led him to make such a request.

Given how Sheila felt about her position at the time, her response was the one that seemed most pragmatic to her. Her reputation and relationship with her supervisor were too tenuous and she was too dependent on him to support her through the next promotion to confront him any more directly.

In a different situation, however, Sheila responded with a *diverting* turn. She was in her office one morning when she overheard one of her colleagues say to four black men who were passing by, "Uh oh. Something is up. Are you guys plotting something?" Although this person periodically came out with thoughtless comments like that, she knew him well enough to know that he was open to learning and didn't really want to offend people. She also knew he trusted her, so it felt safe to push back on his comments in this situation, particularly since she was not even directly involved in the specific interaction.

Immediately after hearing this comment, Sheila walked into her colleague's office, closed his door, and said:

> What is it about four black men going to have lunch that makes you so nervous? I need to understand this. Let's talk about why you would think they are plotting against the organization or why they might be unhappy? Should I assume that when you go drinking with three white buddies you're plotting something?

With these questions, Sheila *diverted* the focus from the four men to her colleague, and why he thought (jokingly or not) there was a problem. She focused on the larger issue of why he perceived they might be threatening—what about the organization may make them dissatisfied, and why he in particular might be concerned? She also pointed out the privilege he took for granted—he had never been seen as suspect when he socialized with a group of white male colleagues—it was a normal state of affairs. With her diversionary turn, Sheila changed the definition of the problem and created an opportunity for learning.

This response was more challenging than the one in the previous example. It was also a very different situation for Sheila. In the first case, she was the direct target of the demeaning remark; in the second instance, she was personally offended but not the direct target. She also had very different relationships with the people making the

---

How Hard Should You Push?

When choosing appropriate responses in encounters, the following factors are important to consider:[12]

Timing: Is this a good time to take a risk and pose a challenge? Is this a good time for others to be receptive to your "turn"?

Stakes: How high are the stakes for the different parties involved in the encounter? Is this a fight worth picking?

Likelihood of success: How promising are the hoped-for results? Will people learn from the turn? Will they make desired changes in their behaviors?

Options: Are there better alternative responses to those that would pose a significant risk? Are there responses that will enable you to take a stand without overly jeopardizing your credibility?

Consequences of failure: What are the worst possible outcomes of the different choices? How bad are they, and how likely are they to occur?

Personal association: Will this be seen as only "your issue"? Are you outside the interaction or the target of it? If you are the target, would a challenging response be more effective if you could locate a third party to intervene on your behalf?

Doability: Does a response feel "doable"? Is there a response that is not overwhelming, that you can implement more effectively?

---

remarks. In the first case, she depended on her boss's approval, but she didn't trust him completely; in the second case, she trusted her colleague and did not directly depend on him in any way.

Conclusion

We can view encounters as micro-events in which larger cultural and political dynamics surface.[13] They can reinforce existing arrangements and present opportunities to promote learning and change.

Given the range of possible ways to respond in these encounters, how does one choose which one will be the most effective? So many factors come into play—who you are, what point in your career you are at, who the offender is, how much you will accomplish by turning the encounter, and so on. It is important to be conscious of these different factors so that when faced with a heated interaction, you can make a clear choice among many options, rather than feel trapped into silence or react in anger.

The six responsive turns—interrupting, naming, correcting, diverting, using humor, and delaying—can be applied not only in the types of face-to-face immediate encounters we looked at in this chapter, but also in the kinds of situations we'll discuss in the chapters that follow. They are used by parties engaged directly in an interaction, as well as by third parties who witness it. The most important point is that being aware of a range of possible responses creates the perception of *choice*. And this, in itself, can create a sense of opportunity and efficacy.

It is also important to recognize that encounters often represent conflicts that are very real, but only some of the participants recognize or acknowledge them.[14] Accordingly, in many interactions, a participant must decide whether to reveal the conflict or to maintain the illusion that no problem exists. Raising a latent conflict can come with the risk of being seen as disloyal or simply as the one who created the issue. It is crucial to make clear that most conflicts are not created by tempered radicals; but tempered radicals are often the ones who speak "truths" and raise issues that have been suppressed.

In this chapter, we looked primarily at direct reactions that took place in the moment or a day or two thereafter. Many of the responses turned threatening encounters into opportunities for learning, but the scope of the learning and the impact was limited primarily to the immediate situation or to parties directly involved in the encounter. In the next chapter, we'll look at situations in which people take time and apply stategies to consider not only the best response to the immediate situation, but also how to respond in a way that turns the situation into an occasion for broader learning. We'll look at different strategies that build on principles of negotiation.

5

Broadening the Impact
through Negotiation

*I believe that courage is all too often mistakenly seen as the
absence of fear. If you descend by rope from a cliff and are not
fearful to some degree, you are either crazy or unaware. Courage
is seeing your fears in a realistic perspective, defining it, considering alternatives, and choosing to function in spite of risks.*

— *Leonard Zunin*

JOANIE MASON'S job at Shop.co involves developing trade relationships with economically disadvantaged communities throughout
the world and cultivating them as supply sources for raw materials
for various product lines. More strenuous than her dealings with these
trading partners has been her bartering within Shop.co. The research
and development (R&D) scientists responsible for inventing product
compounds were consistently balking when Joanie offered raw materials from trading partners to include in their formulations, and the
purchasing group was finding all sorts of reasons to avoid buying supplies from these sources. Their resistance was making it difficult for
her to carry out her agenda.

One afternoon Joanie arranged to meet with the head of R&D to
convince him to use cocoa butter from a South American village in a
particular product formulation. He quickly reiterated that it was a "no
go." As Joanie recalled, "He told me he had a highly reliable source that
won't mess up the quality of his formulation. He informed me that he
has enough work and didn't have time for my 'nice projects.'"

Joanie left that meeting steaming: "How dare he not take me seriously?" She knew that before she took over the "fair trade" program, Alice, the founder, ran it, and R&D had no choice but to cooperate. Joanie did not wield the same influence.

After stewing for a while, Joanie decided to enlist the support of Alice, not to force the issue, but to sit down with the R&D manager to listen to his concerns. Joanie knew that Alice still had a strong working relationship with this man. Only a few minutes into their lunch, the R&D manager revealed to Alice his belief that the fair trade projects had become a lower priority at Shop.co since Alice had turned over the reins to Joanie. Because the communities often did not use sufficient preservatives, the quality and durability of these raw materials were unpredictable, which made developing quality formulations from them frustrating and time consuming. Since it no longer seemed strategically important, he simply did not feel it was worth the trouble.

After learning about these concerns from Alice, Joanie realized that his resistance was not directed at her personally or even at her "do-good" agenda. The manager's resistance was symptomatic of the bigger issue at the company—the projects to promote trade with poor communities were, in many of her colleagues' eyes, no longer central to the organization's product development efforts, and many in the company viewed these projects as an expensive distraction.

With this perspective, Joanie redirected her efforts. Rather than trying to convince the R&D manager to cooperate, she looked for ways to raise the profile of the work that went into developing fair trade products. She asked Alice to visit the R&D lab to reinforce to the scientists the company's commitment to its fair-trade program and to thank them for their contributions to it. She also arranged for the company newsletter to spotlight R&D's previous formulations using materials from fair-trade projects and to highlight more generally what these projects had accomplished for the company and the trading partner communities around the world.

Over time, Joanie cultivated a better working relationship with R&D, and several of the scientists and others throughout the organization became enthusiastic supporters of the fair-trade program. Joanie realized that this was only a small step toward educating people in company about the importance of these projects, but this conflict with R&D had been an occasion to take this step.

In the previous chapter, we discussed a range of responses, but rarely did individuals push the issue beyond the parties involved in the immediate situation. In fact, in some cases, people missed (or chose not to pursue) real opportunities to make a broader impact.

In most of the encounters we've discussed so far, participants either did not have the time or the perspective to step back to consider what they really wanted to make happen, what they were willing to risk, and what larger issues were at stake in their encounters. With a commitment to seeking out the broader issues embedded in these local encounters and some additional strategies, they could have opened further avenues for acting constructively and creating broader learning. Doing so requires a conscious a process for gaining perspective and influence similar to what people do when they are negotiating.

Approaching Difficult Situations as Negotiations

People negotiate constantly—either formally, in job offers, car purchases, and business deals, or informally, such as when deciding where to go for lunch, what time to start a meeting, or even what time kids should go to bed. Most of the situations described in the previous chapter, and throughout this book, do not initially seem like negotiations. They feel more like threats, criticisms, affronts, or outright attacks. But if we view these incidents as negotiations with the potential for give-and-take, and use explicit strategies for negotiating successfully, we can see more options for responding, including those that promote broader learning and change.

To think in terms of negotiation is to think in terms of competing interests, differing positions and concerns, distinct sources of influence, and alternative framing of issues. Negotiating requires discipline and action: people must participate in shaping how problems unfold.

A negotiation perspective emphasizes the following sets of strategic considerations relevant to a variety of situations faced by tempered radicals:

• **Stepping back:** In any negotiation, it is critical to consider the problem from as wide a perspective as possible to uncover all possible points of leverage. Similarly, stepping back from a difficult interaction keeps you from seeing yourself as the center of the problem, which your emotions will encourage you to do, and gives you a fuller range of options.[1] This involves asking: "What are the larger systemic issues at play here?"

• **Looking inward:** Looking inside and exploring personal motives during a negotiation helps you understand what is really important and worth fighting for and what can be forsaken. Similarly, when faced with a threat, asking the question, "What are my real interests, negotiables, non-negotiables, alternatives, and fears?" will help you focus on what you really want, which is the starting point for all action. Ultimately, these insights provide the confidence to take risks, make trade-offs, and stand up for what's most important.

• **Taking stock of the other person's interests:** Understanding the other party's needs and objectives is critical in any negotiation. Doing so gives you the ability to identify ways to meet acceptable common ground; not doing so is what can lead to deadlock. This requires moving outside of gut reactions and assumptions about the other party and asking, "What are the other party's real concerns and fears?" This enables you to assess what you have to bargain with—which gives you leverage for addressing the broader issues.

• **Using third parties:** In a classic negotiation, seeking information, advice, and assistance from friends and colleagues is almost automatic. Unfortunately, in threatening encounters people often isolate themselves. Thus consciously asking "How can third parties support me in this situation?" can point to additional sources of information and influence.

With this framework in hand, let's look again at Joanie's "negotiation." Initially, she was not able to step outside of the immediate tension of her situation. The scientists' reaction put her on the defensive, and she felt their resistance as a personal affront. But Joanie had the good sense to go to the founder, who had hired her and who had run fair-trade projects in the past. This conversation *with a third party* helped her *step outside* of her panic and fears about being seen as an idealistic "do-gooder" and *refocus on her own priorities* and agenda. Also, the founder was able to *gather intelligence* about what was really going on. It was this information that gave Joanie the capacity to influence the immediate situation *and* to see the broader issues. When she learned that the scientists thought the fair-trade projects were not strategically central, she was able to address this concern, both in its immediate form and its more global implications in the company. As part of her broader effort, she helped the scientists recognize the systemic issue, and she went on to use this example to *educate others* about the larger tensions. In this way, she transformed the problem from a local conflict between herself and the R&D department to a debate about conflicting priorities and values in the company.

Creating Learning from a Scheduling Conflict

Here's another example of how a tempered radical used many of these strategies to transform a personal issue into an opportunity for broader learning and change. You'll recall that in chapter 1, we saw John Ziwak refuse to make a last-minute business trip. On the spot, John pushed back slightly, but he did not make a bigger issue of it. John was later faced with a situation with comparable significance, but now he had the advantage of time to step away from the issue to think about what he wanted to accomplish and how he could most effectively accomplish it.

John's business development group at Atlas routinely held quarterly retreats to discuss developments in past acquisitions, future acquisition strategy, and their functioning as a team. In previous years, the retreats were scheduled for the third Thursday and Friday of the quarter. This year, they were scheduled for Fridays and Saturdays. John wasn't sure what led to the change.

No one in his department seemed to mind the change in retreat schedule. They were all extremely busy at work and seemed happy not to have to squeeze two days from their regular work weeks. None of his colleagues except his boss had children yet, and his recently divorced boss had custody of his two children every other weekend.

John had just agreed to coach his older child's baseball team; their last game conflicted with the date of the first retreat.

When John found out about the change, he was very upset. He felt that his boss and colleagues just didn't care about him. How could they be this insensitive and still "not get it?" How many times had they talked about the importance of respecting outside commitments? He had taken this job partly because his boss appeared to share some of his values. Was this a test of his commitment to work?

John knew that before he figured out how to respond, he had to step back from his initial reactions and personal feelings. After thinking about it for a few days, he was able to step away from his anger and hurt and view this small change in schedule not as evidence of colleagues who didn't care, but as the tip of a much bigger iceberg. This scheduling issue, like so many others that had angered him in the past, was symptomatic of corporate assumptions that serious and committed workers should be available for work at all times—assumptions based on the legacy of a workforce that *could* put work above all else.[2] Since most of his colleagues had lives that conformed to this description— they had no outside obligations, or their spouses expected weekend absences—they were just doing what was "normal." For them, this schedule change did not create a particularly problematic disruption.

With this perspective, John could see choices and he could certainly see why his colleagues "didn't get it." Before deciding how to respond, he took a good look at what he wanted to accomplish and what was really important to him. Was this just about changing the days of the retreat? Was he willing to compromise on this if other things changed? Or was he ready to take a hard line and refuse to give up these particular Saturdays with his family? What was non-negotiable here, and on what was he willing to be more flexible? In asking himself these questions, John realized that although Saturdays in general were important, it was only the one Saturday in the spring that conflicted with his commitment to coaching that felt non-negotiable. John realized that the conflict over this one Saturday was so emblematic of the bigger issues for him, that not only did he have to hold strong to this commitment, he would need to explain why. He wanted his colleagues to learn something from this "little" personal dilemma.

Before he approached his boss about his concerns, John realized he would benefit from understanding why the retreat schedule had been changed in the first place. What did his boss have in mind? He didn't want to raise this with his boss directly, because that would inevitably lead directly into a conversation for which he was not yet fully prepared, and he needed this information from his boss to come up with an alternative solution that would address the needs that led to the scheduling change, and the needs of his group in general.

So he asked his boss's assistant why the retreat had been moved. He learned that his boss was concerned about having the entire group out of the office and unavailable for two full days every quarter. This answer was not surprising, but it gave John specific information that would enable him to develop alternative suggestions.

John asked to be put on the agenda for the next staff meeting. He first laid out his immediate concerns about rescheduling the retreat. He explained that he wasn't happy to see the retreats on Saturdays, but that the first Saturday really was an issue for him. He acknowledged that, yes, it was only a kids' baseball game, but he had made a commitment that was important to him. John also offered an alternative plan that he thought would address his boss's concern: to schedule every other retreat from Thursday afternoon through Saturday morning, then hold the others on Thursdays and Fridays in meeting rooms on-site, with extended lunch periods so that workers could return calls and be generally "available."

John's suggestion demonstrated that he was not inflexible—he was willing to give some weekend time to the firm, and he understood his boss's concerns about availability. The staff talked about alternatives to this particular proposal and finally settled on John's plan, with one modification: the Thursday-Friday sessions would be held off-site, though still with an extended break.

After they settled the immediate issue, John said, "Thank you for your willingness to work this out. I think this will be better for everyone. Now I want to have a conversation about the bigger issue." John pointed out how so many of the implicit norms of the department and the organization as a whole—last-minute meetings outside the "regular" schedule, expectations about travel, and the general crisis orientation of their work culture—presume that employees don't have responsibilities outside of work. He acknowledged that everyone has different priorities that create different kinds of constraints, but he recalled hearing every person in the group saying, in one way or another, that they wanted to create more balance in their lives. John also knew that a few of his colleagues—both men and women—were thinking about starting families very soon, and that they worried about how they would be able to keep working at this pace and also be the kind of parents they wanted to be. He asked them to join him in creating solutions that would satisfy the organization's need for productive and committed employees that also would allow them to be reliable in their lives outside of work. Their willingness to work out the retreat schedule and discuss the issues was a great start.

Through talk, John proactively transformed the problem and reframed the meaning of the immediate issue for his boss and colleagues. He made clear that this conflict over the retreat schedule was not just about his willingness to work Saturdays. It was about the implicit assumption that he and everyone else not only could, but that they should.

To accomplish what he did, John needed to step back from the immediate issue and the emotional reaction it triggered for him. Depersonalizing the situation enabled him to see the larger issues being played out in what otherwise might have remained for him and others a strictly personal conflict. He also had to take a good look at what was important to him and, with the help of a third party, figure out how to address the real concerns of his "adversary." With this knowledge, he could view this threat to his personal priorities as a bigger issue he could actually do something about.

Creating Change from Racial Harassment

Let's look at one more example of using negotiation strategies to help transform issues and open avenues for constructive action.

Cathy Jones (a pseudonym) is an attractive, light-skinned black woman who lives in a small town in the English countryside. She works at a small consulting firm in the same town, making her one of very few ethnic minorities who lives and works there. One morning, soon after she purchased a new sports car, the police pulled her over and questioned her about whose vehicle she was driving. Over the course of the next several weeks, the police stopped Cathy multiple times, and each time was as humiliating for her as the last. Increasingly immobilized by her anger, Cathy was thinking about bringing a story about the harassment to the local press and possibly taking legal action against the police.

Cathy showed up to work late one morning, clearly distraught. The police had stopped her yet again. Al, her boss, called her into his office to ask what was wrong. He asked many different questions, and Cathy felt relieved to get it all off her chest. That day, they went to lunch to discuss further what she should do. By the end of the conversation, she was able to step outside of her personal rage and see this as a much more systemic issue. She could see that these incidents were not about her alone—the police were engaging in racial profiling, an institutionalized practice that in effect sanctions racial stereotypes and discrimination.[3]

The conversation was cathartic for Cathy. She now could see that the practice couldn't be allowed to continue, but she also became convinced that her initial impulse to shame the police by going to the press was not the answer. She wanted to find a course of action that would constructively address her deeper concerns about civil rights and race discrimination in the community.

Al thought Cathy would have the best chance of capturing the attention and engaging the police if he were to write an initial letter on her behalf. He was a well-connected white man in the community, and the police would see him as having no particular ax to grind. Al knew writing a letter was not an ideal way to address the issue, but it would add clout and resonance to Cathy's voice and act as a good place to start. Initially, Cathy had her reservations. Would a third party—a white man no less—undermine her own credibility? Cathy was an independent woman and did not like depending on someone else to fight her battles for her. But in this case, she realized that what she really wanted was to stop the harassment and, if possible, do something about the deeper issues. A letter from an "insider" was probably the most effective way to start the ball rolling.

As they had hoped, Al's letter immediately caught the attention of the chief of police. After apologizing directly to her for the harassment, the police chief and Cathy engaged in a long conversation about the culture of the police force. It turned out that he too wanted to change the culture and was having trouble. He wanted her to help him. As Cathy recalled, "I thought I'd be fed up with the guy [police chief], but he turned out to be very open. He showed me all the incidences of harassment. He told me how difficult it was to find minorities from the community to speak with police and work with them to address the problem." The police chief asked her to help him turn these incidences into a learning opportunity for the entire force: "He was incredibly grateful that I was willing to cooperate with their efforts." He formed a regional commission to look at police behavior toward ethnic minorities and learned that the harassment was widespread. "I meet with him every few months. I went to lunch with him the other day and he told me I had changed his whole view of black people." Cathy was later asked to speak to the larger commission and subsequently invited to help develop an educational program for the force. As she reported to me,

> It was like I took small steps in opening a door and talking to a group that I've been seeing as my oppressor. I now see a man who is trying to do his job honestly. He has his own views shaped by his upbringing, but he's changing his views, and my views of them are changing as well.

Cathy knew that in the course of this process, she and the police chief had learned from each other. She hoped that others would learn directly from them but also see their unlikely collaboration as a model of hope and possibility.

Cathy shifted from being an individual victim of police harassment and racism to becoming an effective agent of change.[4] By stepping back from her personal rage and looking carefully at her own goals, she was able to look beyond revenge and restitution to find courses of action pursuant of her deeper desires. Knowing what she wanted allowed her to swallow her pride and ask for help in engaging the police.

The chief of police's openness to learning from her story engaged Cathy further. Though she continued to feel angry and alienated, she chose to be part of the solution. Cathy's clarity of purpose, openness to uncovering her "adversary's" real intent, and increased appreciation for the larger issues at play allowed her to work with her original adversary in ways that previously she could not have imagined. She could see how they too were a product of a systemic problem.

Using Strategies of Negotiation

We turn now to look more deeply at the four negotiating strategies that Joanie, John, and Cathy used to transform their immediate problems into occasions for broader learning and change.

Stepping Back

Stepping back provides a "place to stand" outside the personal experience of an immediate issue.[5] While it is particularly difficult to step back when an issue feels emotionally charged, this is *precisely* the time when it appears to be most important to do so. When people's emotions are heated up, their thinking becomes defensive, less creative, and narrower.[6] Taking an issue too personally blocks people from seeing the broader issues and dealing with them effectively.

When we change where we stand, we shift our understanding of the problem and open options for influencing it. When we are standing too close, we can't see the forest for the trees. Stepping back involves asking, at the core, "Is this just about me, or are there larger issues and interests being played out in this incident?"

John's case is a powerful example of the value of stepping back. He had to remove himself, temporarily, from his feelings of hurt and anger to look at the broader assumptions underlying the change in the retreat schedule. By seeing beyond his personal issues, John was able to transform the problem from a personal scheduling conflict and threat to his personal priorities to an underlying conflict between the organization's assumptions about what makes a committed "good" employee and the day-to-day reality of a good portion of its productive workforce. Similarly, when Cathy stepped away from her own anger, she too could see the larger issues at play, issues she cared about deeply and wanted to help redress.

Stepping back is easier said than done. Remember, most of these incidences feel deeply personal. They hurt, infuriate, and demean. So *how* do we go about depersonalizing a tension that feels so desperately personal? We'll look at two ways: problem externalization and influence mapping.

Family therapists rely on a methodology called "problem externalization" to help develop a broader perspective and to locate new ways to intervene in the general and particular problems. Externalizing a problem entails thinking about problems *as stories*. The objective is to develop a general story for which a specific incident serves as an example.[7] Although it may sound easy on paper, it's often not. One thing that prevents people from developing a general story from the particular is their tendency to read the same plot—with the same ending—into each incident.

Therapists help people construct alternative endings for their stories, or investigate ways a problem could unfold differently. Doing so both removes people from their "typical stories" and opens up options for acting.[8] One strategy is to reach back into the past and try to recall facts or events that contradict the way the general problem typically unfolds. Joanie would not have to look far. She could recall when Shop.co's founder ran "fair trade" and people took the program more seriously. Another strategy is to draw from imagination to conjure up desirable alternative scenarios for the future. Joanie, for example, might imagine that the Shop.co "brand" could be defined by its fair-trade products and practices. Cathy might imagine a community free of institutional racism, where police don't stop and question anyone without cause. Using imagination to uncover desirable alternative outcomes can have a powerful effect on people's capacity to act.[9] Studies show that "positive illusions" create a sense of control, which impels people to act with more purpose, which in turn increases the odds of producing desired outcomes.[10]

A method called "influence mapping" also helps disengage people from their typical stories of a problem. Influence mapping entails recognizing first, how a problem in its general form influences the person, and second, how the person might influence the general problem.[11] The second part of this is more relevant. Cathy could use her experience to evaluate whether she is pushing as hard as she might or missing opportunities to intervene in the racism she faces, not just within the police, but in her community more generally. She can think about what she does to influence white people's perception of race within the workplace. What does she trigger for them and what might she do with clients to create learning in other situations in which institutional racism rears its ugly head? Has she missed opportunities to work with her fellow workers?

The processes of externalizing a problem by working different "stories"

Stepping Back to Separate Self from the Problem

Moving beyond the personal is easier said than done. Answering the following questions can help with the process of problem "externalization":

1. What are alternative outcomes of this problem? What are some examples of preferred outcomes from the past?

2. What has been or could be done by you or others to influence the problem in its general form?

3. What needs to happen for a desirable outcome to materialize in this situation?

---

helps disengage people from heated situations and develop ways to reframe a problem in alternative forms. This not only increases the probability of dealing more effectively with the issue at hand but can also help identify new ways to influence a problem, sometimes in ways that make a broader and more enduring impact.

Looking Inward

Effective negotiation requires people to be clear about what they really want, how much they want it, and, ideally, what they fear. This kind of self-inquiry is, according to Peter Senge, one of the most important practices involved in system learning.[12]

This process entails facing up to tough questions: "What are the broader purposes I want to accomplish?" "What is non-negotiable for me?" "What am I willing to give up?" "What are my underlying fears?" "What are my alternatives?" The answers to these questions are personal and thus vary across different situations. Not everyone in John's situation, for example, would feel as strongly about working Saturdays or missing a single coaching obligation—some people wouldn't tie it so closely to their core values and priorities. Other people have different priorities that are just as sacred to them. When it comes time to evaluate a course of action—what to do, how far to push, what to give up—this kind of self-knowledge is invaluable.

People may reflect on their personal concerns in a casual way all the time, particularly when they are faced with a conflict. But the kind of self-evaluation that appears to matter is neither casual nor easy. It involves discipline: at a minimum, identifying deeper goals, distinguishing between "negotiables" and "non-negotiables," facing up to fears, and identifying alternatives.

Identifying deeper goals. I do not know how the tempered radicals I studied went about clarifying their personal goals. I know, however, that it would be difficult for them to do so if they remained immersed in their immediate situations and caught up in their anxieties, feelings of self-defensiveness, and anger. That is why it is important to step back, away from the heat, to identify what you really care about in a particular situation and in general, and how best to act on those desires.[13] Without this knowledge, impulses tend to take over.

Distinguishing between "negotiables" and "non-negotiables." Identifying your deeper goals and concerns provides the context and rationale for distinguishing between where you can afford to compromise and where, at all costs, you can't. John Ziwak did this when he differentiated between the significance of the Saturday that conflicted with his coaching commitment and the other Saturdays. While he preferred not to work other Saturdays, they were not nearly as significant to him. Similarly, when Ellen Thomas was asked by her mentor to unbraid her hair, she differentiated between the significance of her hairstyle and her clothes. While she didn't enjoy wearing conservative business clothes, they were not as symbolically significant *for her* as her hair.

Just as knowing what is non-negotiable gives you a firm place to stand, knowing what you *will* negotiate gives you room to maneuver. Joanie gained flexibility from being able to distinguish between her non-negotiables and negotiables. She recalled an argument with a senior colleague over the wording of the company's human rights statement. The statement was intended to articulate Shop.co's beliefs about how people should be treated both within and outside the company. A lot of work went into convincing executives to go forward with the statement, and Joanie wanted to get it through to cement publicly the company's commitment to a set of human rights principles. Though she remained firm about the principles in the statement, she was flexible about the specific wording of some of the items in it. This adaptability provided her with the room she needed to overcome resistance and move the statement through the system. In *The Change Masters*, Rosabeth Moss Kanter concludes that people who are most successful at influencing others are those who are clear about what they want but are flexible in how they achieve it.[14]

Isabel Nuñez's effectiveness at Atlas resulted from this sort of flexibility, which came partly from her ability to distinguish between what was negotiable and non-negotiable to her. This played out in her travels abroad, which she did frequently in her previous position. Faced with cultural norms that clashed with her own principles, she had to make choices about when to put her foot down and when to go along:

> Even if it is the custom in Middle Eastern countries, I am not willing to hide my face with a veil or walk several steps behind a man. That is entirely too subservient a symbol, and would undermine my professional authority and identity. But there are certain things I do out of respect for the culture, that don't compromise me as much. I am happy to wear longer skirts than I would normally choose or to wear my hair off my face as is customary for women in some cultures.

Her criterion was simple: she refused to negotiate anything that significantly compromised her core values or identity. Her flexibility in some areas allowed her to stand firm when it really counted.

Isabel's capacity to distinguish between negotiables and non-negotiables also played out around bigger issues. She recalled an instance when she felt ready to walk away from her job if her colleagues turned down a female colleague who was being evaluated for promotion. Isabel knew the woman was qualified, but she had not cultivated an internal network of support. So Isabel went to the mat on it. Around other issues that seem less clear or where less is at stake, she shows much more flexibility, and she tries to parlay this flexibility into increased influence on issues she cares most about.

Recognizing fears. When people don't identify their fears, they become hostage to looming anxieties, rational or not. Some people I observed became so eager just to resolve an issue and get it over with that they made concessions at the expense of their own interests.

I have seen how facing fears gives people the capacity to steer their own fates. They gain confidence to stay focused on what's important, rather than worrying about nameless future events that *might* happen.

Identifying Fears

It can be useful to ask the following kinds of very simple questions to make explicit the ways in which fears may be unwittingly driving behaviors:

1. What might happen if you take this course of action?

2. What are the worst things that could happen?

3. Why are you so afraid of these outcomes?

4. How bad would it be if feared outcomes materialize?

Too often fear drives people, steering them to be compliant, to pursue misplaced interests, or to remain silent.

People who seem willing to push back against conformity pressures and take risks seem to have come to terms with their fears. Some concluded that short of losing their job, they had little to fear. Others concluded that losing their job would not be that bad; what they really feared was loss of credibility or being excluded from an informal network. People can discern their own limits by recognizing the way fears have previously prevented them from engaging fully, kept them silent when they might have spoken up, or caused them to give in prematurely. When people face their fears, they can keep them in check and *choose* how to respond to them. They no longer become hostage to their anxieties. With this knowledge come real confidence and freedom.[15]

Identifying alternatives. Finding alternatives in the context of a conflict is probably the most potent form of influence in a negotiation—and it also helps alleviate fears. When tempered radicals had clear alternatives, they were better equipped to stand firm on their nonnegotiables, and fear could not hold them to a negotiating table. This fundamental principle of negotiation is sometimes called "best alternative to a negotiated agreement," or BATNA for short.[16] Knowing about viable alternatives in advance makes people less dependent on achieving a particular outcome and therefore more independent of the other parties. And independence breeds confidence and strength.

When Martha Wiley challenged discriminatory practices or when she held firm on her stance regarding Western's decision about whether it would continue to support a nonprofit organization with a formal policy that excluded gay volunteers, she had the confidence to stand firm on what she felt were "non-negotiables." She was ready to walk away from her job if Western decided to continue supporting this organization:

> I basically threw my body in front of the truck on this matter. It was terrifying for me. . . . But this was one of those times when I knew I was right and I had to stand up for what was at stake here.

Martha gained confidence to stand up against significant managerial concerns by knowing exactly what she might do if the organization did not live up to her non-negotiable criteria. Though she didn't want to leave Western, she consciously kept track of the number of head-hunter calls she received so she was always aware that she could walk away. This knowledge gave her strength and helped her assess when she could afford to speak up, over which issues, and how much of a risk she could afford to take. She told me,

> Before I confront someone, I reacquaint myself with my experience and accomplishments so I understand what I'm worth. There is no way I'd have the nerve to take the risks if I hadn't first taken stock of my skills and convinced myself that I would have no trouble getting another job.

There is a big difference between caring about a job and being utterly dependent on it. Recognizing your alternatives gives you the confidence to stay focused on what you want and provides the courage to resist giving in to your fears and anxieties.

Taking Stock of Others' Interests

Effective negotiators understand what drives their adversaries. What is important to them? What do they want? What are their underlying needs and fears? Similarly, understanding the priorities, needs, and fears of other actors in a conflict or encounter dramatically improves the chances of creating desirable alternatives. It provides a window into what they may value—and the greater the capacity to satisfy what the other party values, the more influence you have over the problem.

Joanie Mason's breakthrough came from uncovering the real concerns of the R&D staff, and she went through a similar process with

---

Motivations and Common Currencies in Organizations

1. **Inspiration:** Involvement in tasks of significance and centrality, opportunities to excel, and engagement in tasks that are morally "right."

2. **Task-related:** Access to extra resources, assistance, access, cooperation, information that help accomplish tasks.

3. **Position and legitimacy:** Acquisition of titles, advancement, status, recognition, visibility, reputation, sense of importance, and contacts that enhance reputation.

4. **Relationships:** Gaining acceptance, love, support, mentoring, and understanding through valued relationships.

5. **Professional development and pride:** Involvement in challenging tasks, having ownership and autonomy to increase professional skills and independence.

Adapted from Alan Cohen and David Bradford, *Influence without Authority* (New York: Wiley, 1989), 79. Copyright 1989 Alan Cohen and David Bradford. Reprinted by permission of John Wiley & Sons, Inc.

Shop.co's purchasing agents. In this instance, too, Joanie feared that they had a knee-jerk reaction to her "do-good" projects, which called on the purchasing agents to handle complicated and expensive purchases. Eventually, she went to talk with one of the managers in the purchasing department to convince him to cooperate, but what she learned in that simple conversation pointed to a different resolution. The purchasers' concerns actually centered on the way the staff were evaluated. They were appraised and compensated based on their ability to purchase supplies at prices that matched or beat posted market prices.

Once Joanie found out about this built-in disincentive to purchase fair-trade products, which were always going to be more expensive, she could work directly on the problem—the metric on which the purchasing staff were evaluated. With some difficulty, she was able to establish a sliding metric—when purchasers acquired products related to fair-trade programs, they would be measured by the variance between purchase price and a standard fair-trade price, not the "market price." This would prevent them from being harshly evaluated for purchasing the more expensive fair-trade products. Joanie's "personal" struggle with the purchasing head had not been a personal issue at all, but rather the manifestation of a systemic issue—pitting the company's incentive system against its articulated values and commitment to support fair trade.

Once the motivations of other parties—their priorities, needs, and fears—become apparent, it is helpful to think about what one might do to satisfy them. It can be useful to think of these interests as "currencies" with which to bargain.[17] Their values are not fixed; they float depending on the specific needs, interests, and fears of particular individuals. Joanie's capacity to uncover the real concerns of the R&D and purchasing managers gave her the equivalent of a currency with which she could trade to further her immediate and larger agendas.

Concerns and motivations are limitless, and so are the many forms of "currency" that can be used to satisfy them. See the accompanying box for a list of some motivations and common currencies.

Using Third Parties

Skilled negotiators know how indispensable third parties can be in working through conflicts. In the kinds of issues tempered radicals confront, third parties—friends, allies, colleagues, bosses, subordinates, and so on help in a number of ways, from providing assistance on a specific task to helping frame the meaning of a conflict.

Help with preparation. Because they are outside the immediate encounter and not as susceptible to the blinders of personal involvement and emotion, third parties play a critical role in helping tempered radicals pursue the three strategies previously discussed: stepping back, looking inward, and understanding the concerns of others. Stepping back and looking inward at the same time can be difficult, particularly when a person is consumed by the pain of a conflict. Allies have the distance to help a person step away from the issue and ask the tough questions. Al helped Cathy in this way. She was initially blinded by her anger at the police and desire for revenge. After some conversation and tears, she was able to see that under her impulse was a sense of powerlessness. What she really wanted was to be part of a solution. Staying trapped in a dynamic of revenge would just produce more powerlessness. Al was invaluable in helping her see her way out of this state.

Third parties also help people uncover the concerns and interests of the other parties, much the way they did for Joanie and John. The founder of Joanie's company helped her uncover the issues that were critical to her being able to work with R&D. John's boss's assistant provided him with information that enabled him to develop a workable alternative for scheduling retreats. Allies can also be particularly helpful by providing information about the risks and potential consequences of different courses of action.

Lend legitimacy, clout, and connections. Besides providing information, the right third parties lend legitimacy and clout to your concerns. Perhaps the most important thing Al did for Cathy was lend her his credibility and influence in the community by writing a letter on her behalf.

Tempered radicals do not always have direct access to people who are in positions to further their cause, but a colleague often does. When Joanie realized she needed to change the purchasers' evaluation metric, she needed the approval of the company's chief financial person, whom she did not know well. But Shop.co's founder, who supported Joanie's work, easily provided the link she needed.

Connections to broader networks can also help after a conflict has played out to maximize the diffusion of learning. Stories travel only as far as networks enable them to spread. Cathy had a wide network that included men and women of color as well as white men and women. In addition, her boss, who was connected to important constituencies in the community, was instrumental in helping diffuse stories and thereby expanding the cast of people who might learn from her efforts.

Provide emotional, social, and task support. Allies and friends help lift tempered radicals' spirits, show them they are not alone in their struggles, and provide encouragement and support to keep them going and prevent them from giving up in the face of inevitable setbacks and frustrations. Allies can be instrumental in other ways too, by providing task-related and professional assistance to get things done in a timely way. They can provide resources, technical assistance, feedback, and just plain help getting a job done.

Mediation. Well-positioned third parties also fill the role of mediator, to help break logjams, stop the bickering, put people on their best behavior, and make everyone "play fair." The role of mediator needs to be filled by someone all interested parties trust.[18] Though she called on

them to mediate sparingly, when Joanie came to an impasse with colleagues over an issue she deemed crucial, she would go to one of the
senior executives to help break the impasse. She had to be extremely
judicious in her implicit and explicit threats to appeal to one of these
high-level colleagues, else she might jeopardize her own authority.

Lower anxiety and resistance. Third parties also create safety and
minimize resistance by lowering people's anxiety levels. High levels
of fear and anxiety block the possibility of learning.[19] When the fear
level is down, people can begin to see themselves as part of the solution, they can afford to be more flexible about their assumptions, and
they can envision more daring actions as a response to the conflict.[20]
Had the police not been open to Cathy's overtures initially, a third
party could have lessened their fear by telling them that Cathy did not
want to make trouble.

Help sustain multiple selves. Perhaps most important, tempered
radicals rely on allies who represent both sides of their ambivalence—
people who help them stay connected to their different "selves." This
is critical to guard against silence and co-optation *and* to temper the
possible impulse to explode in anger or push too hard. In the heat of a
conflict, it is far too easy to head in one direction or the other, to either
compromise your principles and values or to make hotheaded comments that undermine your goals. Tempered radicals rely on allies who
help them stay focused on their "non-negotiables" and allies who keep
them tempered so they stay credible. Often, striking this balance takes
the advice of more than one person; it means seeking out people who
may be more radical than you and those who are more tempered and
prone to compromise. It is hard to maintain a balance between competing pulls without help. This observation applies in general, but it
appears to be particularly important to people in the heat of a conflict.

Some tempered radicals shun relationships such as the ones Joanie
developed with her founder or Cathy had with her boss. These allies
are completely and unapologetically insiders, so how could they possibly be trusted? That's why it was crucial for Cathy and Joanie to have
allies who keep them connected to their "outsider" selves as well. In a
given tension, being able to look to these different allies can be
tremendously important.

Different Roles of Third Parties: A Summary

Third parties can play a number of important roles to help tempered radicals "negotiate" effectively and broaden their impact:

1. Preparing for a negotiation
   - Helping tempered radicals step back
   - Pushing tempered radicals to look inward
   - Helping uncover other parties' real concerns/issues

2. Lending legitimacy, clout, and connections

3. Providing emotional, social, and task support

4. Mediating when things get tough

5. Lowering adversaries' anxiety and resistance

6. Helping sustain multiple "selves"

7. Framing issues
   - Helping interpret actions and make sense of immediate conflict
   - Helping interpret the local issue in terms of its broader significance

---

Help frame issues. Finally, third parties can help frame the meaning of issues. How a specific encounter is handled and the broader learning that results is often influenced by someone's explicit characterization of the event. In his letter to the police, Al framed the issue as one with broad significance. He took it away from the problem of one biased officer and one wronged woman and interpreted it as an example of institutional racism within the force—as a community problem that he cared about.

Al's letter certainly paved the way for a productive response. But he or others could have done even more. After the initial meetings between Cathy and the police, Al or other third parties could have explicitly interpreted their joint attempts to address the larger issue as a constructive intervention into a systemic problem. They could have said: "Yes, this is a big problem, but it is not an intractable one. If we work together to chip away at it we can make an appreciable difference in people's lives." In doing this interpretive work, a third party helps create learning about the broader problem and lets others know that people are making a difference through their efforts to address it. If there is one type of action that can broaden the learning that comes from a specific incident, it is this kind of "framing" work, and because of its importance we will take a deeper look at the tactics of framing meaning in the next chapter.

Tempered radicals need other people. I often advise people to think of constructing a "Personal Board of Directors" with people who bring very different perspectives, skills, and networks to the table. These Personal Boards of Directors—or as Dr. Frances Conley calls them, "Kitchen Cabinets"[21]—can help tempered radicals stay focused on their ideals and make the most of their opportunities to inspire learning and positive change in their organizations.

Conclusion

Far too often people take things at face value—Cathy is being harassed by racist police officers; John is being pressured to violate family obligations; Joanie's program is being written off as "do-good" idealism. If nothing else, we have seen how problems themselves have multiple faces. One of the most important ways tempered radicals make a difference is by transforming problems that seem personal and local into issues with broader and more complex implications. This not only changes how we see the problem, it also can open avenues for acting and effecting change. Transforming the issues begins with a deliberate process that includes many of the strategies used in successful negotiations.

To approach a difficult situation or conflict as a negotiation is to take the stance of agent rather than victim. Cathy is perhaps the best example of this. She turned a painful and personal encounter into an opportunity to grow personally and make a positive and broad impact in her community.

By staying anchored to her underlying goal of alleviating racism in the community, she placed herself squarely in the driver's seat. This has had a lasting impact on Cathy, and many others who have been inspired by her actions, that goes far beyond her work with the police. Her words best summarize this chapter:

> My experience with the police shapes now how I think about people in the boardroom of corporations. I go into a room and see people

who have very different attitudes than I do. Particularly when I work with older men in older industries. I'm sure they make assumptions about me. They have been allowed to discount people like me throughout their lives.

But now I see myself as part of a movement that helps move people along slowly. I try to make them aware of how people treat me because of my race and gender. I continually watch and take opportunities to influence them gently when the opportunities come up. I try to keep a close eye on the system and I don't take things as personally as I used to. I now know that I'm representational and it isn't about me per se. I see things changing slowly and I want to be part of the solution.

The next chapter builds on many of the themes from this chapter. Whereas here we focused on strategies to respond effectively to difficult situations, in the next chapter we move on to a more proactive method of looking for opportunities to make an impact. We focus on the strategy of "small wins" as a method of initiating small doable changes and creating learning from proactively framing the meaning of these initiatives.

6

Leveraging Small Wins

Do not be fettered by too many rules at first. Try different things and see what answers best. Look for the ideal, but put it into the actual. Everything which succeeds is not the production of a scheme, of rules and regulations, made beforehand, but of a mind observing and adapting itself to wants and events.

— Florence Nightingale

FROM THE TIME he was hired in the mid-1960s, Peter Grant felt that Western should hire more people from ethnic and racial minority groups. He believed not only that more diversity would make it easier for existing employees from minority groups to excel, but also that the broader perspectives that diversity would bring to the organization would strengthen the company. Further, he knew that some of the embedded practices, particularly related to recruiting, were making it hard to find and attract the candidates he believed they should recruit. It wasn't that other people were opposed to his ideas, it's just that they didn't see the need as clearly as he did and certainly didn't see the impediments.

Peter could have made a big public issue about his concerns, but he believed generally that if he made any outright attempts to change recruiting policy or challenge some of the underlying assumptions, he might be threatening to his colleagues and might arouse a great deal of resistance. So he chose to start quietly.

I am particularly indebted to Professor Karl Weick for the insights and inspiration that provide the foundation for this chapter.

As he went about his normal recruiting activities, Peter worked hard to identify solid minority candidates. When he did, and then success-fully recruited them, he asked them to make a commitment—that they too would hire other minority candidates: "I'd say, 'one of your jobs is to hire other people from minority groups. If you can't do that, if you're not committed to that, then you shouldn't take this job.'" He also asked them to actively maintain relationships with their new hires at Western. Peter believes strongly that the only way change will occur is "if we all bring others along." With each hire, he communicated this.

For many years, Peter kept to this process. As all this minority hir-ing was taking place in the context of a substantially larger and broader recruiting activity, it didn't draw attention. Over time, how-ever, these scattered initiatives added up. In his first two years with the company, Peter estimates that he directly or indirectly helped recruit forty minority candidates. Over ten years, he guesses that number grew to 1,500. After 20 years, Peter had made his way into the exec-utive ranks and was actively involved in many aspects of Western's management activities. After 30 years with Western, he was addressing issues of diversity much more actively and openly. But by this time, he estimated that the process he had started with tiny steps decades ago had been responsible for the hiring of more than 3,500 minority employees and the creation of a support network that makes it more possible for them to succeed.*

Peter's quiet recruitment policy is an example of what Karl Weick calls a "small win." A small win is a "limited doable project that results in something concrete and visible."[1] Peter knew what he wanted to achieve—dramatically increase the representation of minorities at Western and create a context in which they could succeed. He started where he could, with initiatives that were *doable*. In starting small, he made immediate tangible progress and over time created a cascading process that not only made a meaningful difference by itself but helped set a context for more change later on.

Compared to strategies outlined in previous chapters, the small wins approach presumes an agenda for change and a proactive approach to seeking opportunities to put this agenda into motion. It is a conscious

---

*Three of his colleagues corroborated these figures with their own independent esti-mates, which were slightly higher than Peter's "conservative" estimate.

Examples of Small Wins

These examples were provided by a tempered radical who sought to promote social responsibility and environmental consciousness in her company:

- Place a green bin under everyone's desk so they don't even have to get up and walk to the nearest recycling receptacle. The cleaning staff is paid to collect all the recyclable waste.
- Put a bottle bank in the parking lot so people don't have to make an extra trip to recycle glass.
- Configure computers to shut down automatically after short periods of inactivity so people don't have to remember to turn monitors off.
- Purchase low-energy light bulbs in bulk so employees can buy them cheaply and use them at home.
- Set up a carpool for lunchtime supermarket shopping.
- Switch tea and coffee sourcing to fair-trade suppliers.

---

strategy for living in line with values and effecting change without directly confronting the system in an open and aggressive manner.

Let's look at how Joanie Mason used small wins to pursue her agenda at Shop.co. Initially she reported directly to Alice, the founder and CEO of the company. Joanie needed the cooperation of the product development group to launch her products, but their cooperation—like that of other groups in the company—was sometimes less than forthcoming. Though many of the individuals in the group wanted to support the fair-trade projects in principle, they usually included the products in the product line only as socially responsible "add-ons."

When the company was reorganizing many of its divisions, Joanie saw an opportunity to make some changes. She thought she might get less resistance from the product development group if she herself became part of the group. So she requested that her group be moved into the product development division and that she report directly to the director of that division. No one resisted this request; in fact, many people saw it as a voluntary demotion since Joanie would no longer report to the CEO.[2]

Her project gained momentum. As an "insider" in the group, she had more success getting colleagues in product development to appreciate the merits of her fair-trade products and how these products could enhance the overall product line. Soon her colleagues asked her to attend product development brainstorming sessions to generate ideas for the next season's wares. Her group became part of this process, and quickly her colleagues in the "regular" product groups began to think of the fair-trade products as integral to some of their lines. She also looked for opportunities to talk about her new reporting structure and how it was more appropriate for her to be integrated into the product development process rather than in a separate program disconnected from the core activities. When possible, she used her move as an occasion to create conversation about the role of fair trade within the company.

Like Peter, Joanie had an agenda for change. She had previously tried more direct routes to pursue it. She had worked for months trying to change directly what was valued in the organization, trying to get people to support in practice the kind of programs that were consistent with Shop.co's articulated values. Some of these efforts had made clear progress in some groups, but they had required a great deal of time and energy. Joanie's move into product development was less threatening than her other efforts and more doable. Her requested change in reporting structure created little resistance. Yet with this one small act, and her framing of it as a deliberate effort to integrate her programs into the product development process, Joanie completely shifted how a critical department thought about, valued, and treated the fair-trade products. Not bad for one small act!

Why Start Small?

As an approach to change, the small-wins approach contains several advantages, some of which are comparable to the benefits of quiet resistance discussed in chapter 3. First and foremost, small wins are powerful because they are doable. This approach encourages people to *act* by doing what they can do *now*, rather than being overwhelmed by the challenge or searching endlessly for the "perfect" approach to their problem. When he was a new hire, Peter probably could not have imagined challenging Western's formal recruiting policy. But his job responsibilities included hiring, so it was natural for him to recruit minority candidates himself.

Because of their perceived "doability," small wins also precipitate a sense of hope, self-efficacy, and confidence. Greater self-efficacy and confidence lead to heightened ambition and more effort, which in turn are more likely to lead to desired results.[3] The capacity of small wins to generate hope and to attract involvement of other people makes them a cornerstone of community organizing efforts. Saul Alinsky, the "grandfather" of community organizing, believed the reverse was also true: that when people believe they do not have power to change their situations, they stop looking for opportunities to make a difference and—guess what?—they don't find any.[4] These initiatives are therefore as much about creating positive momentum as they are about accomplishing a task. Small actions toward desired ends get the ball rolling, both for individuals and for groups.

One attractive element of a small-wins strategy is that it minimizes anxiety and personal risk. Because it reduces the scope of an initiative and raises people's perceived capability to accomplish desired ends, it lowers the anxiety associated with change efforts.[5] In addition, small wins are usually small enough that they do not engage the organizational immune system, at least until they accumulate enough to take on larger significance. This dynamic was clearly at play for Peter as he chose his strategy for creating what turned out to be significant change.

Another benefit of small initiatives, whether they result in wins or failures, is that they can bring about significant learning. As Kurt Lewin once observed, there is no better way to learn about systems than to try to change them, even in small ways.[6] Small actions can uncover unknown allies and information, sources of resistance, and additional opportunities for change. Small wins provoke questions and stimulate conversations.

In addition, one of the most important advantages of small wins is that they express and sustain tempered radicals' "different" values and identities. They are concrete reminders that individuals will not suppress these parts of their selves. Small wins may be the best antidote against co-optation because they demonstrate who we are and what we care about.

Critics of this approach are quick to point out the strategy's shortcomings. They argue that small wins can "lull people into a false sense of complacency." And, they argue, "Big problems deserve big solutions, not minor tweaks." But small wins demonstrate that things need not be as they are. A departmental recycling program doesn't solve the problem of global warming, but it does demonstrate that waste *can* be reduced. A change in meeting times to accommodate an employee's schedule does not change the culture of a workplace, but it does show that work practices need not be inhumane and all-consuming. Small wins are *small proofs*. Even when the changes are minor—and remain minor—small wins are qualitative, if not quantitative, demonstrations that things can be different.[7]

Critics complain that small wins remain small. Who says so? If one person is committed to ensuring that they don't stay small, then they don't have to. With some effort, small wins can be bundled together and their significance made explicit to promote broader learning—and learning leads to further adaptation.

Positioning to Create Small Wins

In prior chapters we focused on how people react to threatening situations, and we looked at suggested strategies for preparing to respond more effectively. There also appear to be a number of conditions that prepare people to locate and create small wins.

Cultivating a "Blurry Vision"

Tempered radicals who want to advance change cannot operate without a general vision of the changes they are seeking, and yet visions that are too clear and specific can be overly constraining. Blurry visions of the future allow people to be flexible and take advantage of opportunities when they present themselves. This does not imply that tempered radicals abandon all sense of direction. It simply means that they hold visions that are sufficiently ambiguous to allow for strategic flexibility.[8] I doubt, for example, that Peter had a vision that was more concrete than wanting to promote social justice and diversity in the workplace. Joanie wanted fair-trade programs to be integral to Shop.co's business. The vagueness of their visions enabled them to be flexible in choosing strategies and responding to opportunities.

Scouring Daily Details for Opportunities

As I have emphasized throughout the book, opportunities for learning and change often lie in the details of organizational life—in everyday practices, mundane interactions, and "normal" ways of understanding. Tempered radicals also find opportunities for small wins in the details.[9]

A great example of this came when an employee at Western noticed one day that the organization was offering a parenting workshop for its employees. She took this offering as an invitation to push for a similar workshop for "alternative parents": gay parents, single parents, and custodial grandparents. This seemed like a reasonable request to the human resources manager in charge of these workshops, so the employee organized and publicized the workshop. Several months after the workshop was held, one participant, who was also on the organization's diversity task force and was now more attuned to the number of "alternative families" at Western, noticed the seemingly small detail that the employee handbook defined "family" strictly in terms of the "traditional family." After several months, she and other gay employees convinced officials to change this formal definition to be more inclusive of different kinds of families. This nontrivial and very symbolic win generated immediate learning and paved the way for some material changes in benefits offered to "families."

Making change in response to these kinds of details means looking for practices as well as language that can be redirected or redefined in minor ways to produce qualitatively different outcomes. Above all, this approach requires a capacity to improvise—to be sensitive to the details of surrounding conditions and willing to act on opportunities as they arise.[10]

Challenging the Organization's Tolerance

Because of the diversity of views in an organization, it will often not be clear how small a small win must be to avoid arousing resistance. But people often imagine tolerance levels to be more constraining than they actually are. Recall Tom Novak from Western, who brought his male partner to a high-profile social function. He had imagined that this behavior would result in all kinds of negative repercussions, but his imagination proved to be far worse than reality.

Similarly, in a former job at Ford Motor Company, Roger Saillant was sent to Mexico to build and run a new factory. Roger was expected to comply with Ford's well-established norms for designing and building a plant, including which architects to work with, what materials to use, and, most important, what the building should look like. Roger believes that the right way to operate in a foreign culture is to be a gracious guest and to build a plant that appeals to local tastes and fits into the local environment. So despite the prevailing norms, he contracted with the local college of architecture to design his plant. Several of his colleagues warned him against this move, advising him that taking this step would lead only to a much tighter "leash" from headquarters, if not to his undoing. Though this action did provoke skepticism, his boss and other senior executives at corporate headquarters gave him more room to do his "thing" than his colleagues, and even Roger himself had anticipated. Later, after the plant was built within budget and on schedule and he had succeeded in creating unprecedented goodwill within the local Mexican community, many colleagues praised Roger for being willing to push back on established norms to do what he believed was right and effective.

Small wins may not always result in such happy endings, but the danger of imposing imagined constraints on what we can and cannot do is that we inadvertently collude in maintaining the limits we desperately want to challenge. When we find ourselves backing away from action that we fear is too risky, it may be wise to challenge the assumptions that lead us there. Have we actually witnessed negative outcomes that would justify our concerns? By gently pushing the limitations of what the organization will tolerate by initiating small wins, we keep the organization in flux and push its constraints outward without bearing undue risks.

Scoping and Timing Battles Wisely

With a limited stock of energy, time, and credibility, tempered radicals have to pick their battles carefully. Decisions about which changes to pursue are based more on locating a ripe opportunity than finding the perfect solution or ideal moment. Picking the right opportunity entails a sensitivity to timing, to relative "risk and reward," to the stake one has in the potential outcome, and to the match between one's interests and skills and the opportunity. Being sensitive to the receptivity of others in a given moment can also be important: Will the other party in this circumstance be receptive to the changes? The beauty of blurry vision is that it affords the flexibility of waiting for an appropriate time and opportunity to act. It also provides the flexibility to spot particularly good but unexpected opportunities.

Joanie Mason's idea to move into the product development organization at Shop.co didn't come to her in a vacuum. It came to her in the context of a larger reorganization that was going on around her. The timing couldn't have been better to suggest a change in reporting structure without provoking resistance or suspicion.

Sheila Johnson at Western explained that her judgment about which battle to fight hinges partly on timing and partly on what is at stake:

> I always stop and think, "Is it a large enough issue that I'm willing to stand up and say this?" . . . I probably fight longer and harder for a woman of color than I do for a white woman. I think my fight would matter more and I try to make a difference where it counts.

Designing Small Wins for Feedback and Learning

Small wins have been treated as vehicles of system learning. They provoke questions about why things are the way they are and can be thought of as "experiments." Experiments are intended to disrupt "normal" ways of doing things, yet because they appear to be mere "trials," they do not provoke as much anxiety or resistance as would a more permanent change. But much can be learned from what exactly gets disrupted and what doesn't.

Like medicine, in which the reaction to a treatment confirms or disproves a diagnosis, the validity of a small-wins experiment lies in whether and to what extent the small win produces the anticipated outcomes.[11] Joanie certainly had no guarantee that her move into the product group would bring fair-trade products into the mainstream, but if nothing else she would have gained invaluable information to help her design her next "experiment."

John Ziwak tried to initiate a policy in his business development department at Atlas to prevent dinnertime calls at home. His boss agreed to this as an informal norm and goal, but he would not adopt it

---

Positioning to Create Small Wins: A Summary

1. Maintain a "blurry vision." Develop a vision of change that allows for multiple specific outcomes and alternative paths, to create flexibility and allow for opportunism.

2. Create opportunities in the details. Look for opportunities and be ready to act on them.

3. Challenge your sense of organizational tolerance. Use small wins as a way to push existing conventions and constraints outward.

4. Scope and time your challenges wisely. With limited resources, time, credibility, and energy, pick your battles based on timing, scope of impact, probability of success, and so on.

5. Design small wins to generate learning. Think of small wins as experiments that probe conditions and help you and others learn.

---

as a written rule because the time-sensitive nature of their acquisitions work sometimes demands crisis-like availability. John realized that it was probably not reasonable to create "absolutes" in policies related to time. He would have to be more flexible or else his boss would reject outright any attempts to initiate family-friendly practices. This important lesson helped John shape how he framed later initiatives.

To learn from small-wins attempts, as John did, requires close attention to what happens as a result of them: What changes and what doesn't? Who gets excited and who resists, and why? Karl Weick suggests that one of the most powerful outcomes of small wins is that they help cultivate organizational wisdom by distinguishing between the things that we can change and the things we can't.

Framing the Meaning of Small Wins

Once someone has successfully initiated one or more small wins, he or she may want to extend their potential impact. Doing so requires others in the organization to understand the significance of the interventions. To promote this kind of learning requires an active process of framing the meaning of the small wins.

As I touched on briefly in the previous chapter, people's understanding of what an action means can be every bit as important as the action itself. The most effective way tempered radicals extend the impact of small wins is by making explicit their significance or bundling several of them together and retrospectively framing them as a coherent package or "program" that serves the same ends. This gives individual small wins greater punch.

Recall Martha Wiley's responses to an employee's request for more flexible work arrangements. Martha admitted that she had no intention of directly trying to change Western's formal policy on work schedule and flexibility. She simply looked for opportunities to try flexible arrangements with those who wanted to work this way, and over the years she initiated several "experiments." Eventually, because word of her experiments traveled, she realized that all her ad hoc accommodations had added up to a successful program for employees in her department.

Clearly the accommodations Martha made for her employees' schedules were important to each of them personally. But greater significance came from the bundling of the initiatives as a "program" and Martha's subsequent efforts to frame them explicitly as a solution to the bigger problem—that long, rigid work schedules posed a hardship for certain workers.

The Importance of "Framing" Meaning

Let's step back and look at additional reasons why framing the meaning is such an important part of the change process. First, helping others see what the small win means allows people beyond the initiator to *learn* from the change. In Martha's case, her colleagues learned that flexibility can actually increase people's productivity because inflexible hours are so constraining for some workers. Martha explicitly challenged assumptions otherwise. The framing of Roger's Saillant's initiative in Mexico as a step toward working *with* local communities served to question existing norms and provided broader organizational learning about more responsible and effective ways to enter a host culture.

Second, bundling and framing also create coherence out of what might otherwise be perceived as a disconnected set of ad hoc initiatives. Framing a series of small wins as a successful "program," a workable "alternative," or a viable "practice" gives the set of activities significance. Martha's scheduling accommodations would come to be seen not just as successful management on her part, but as an indication that these arrangements may be more attractive alternatives to the status quo throughout the company.

Third, framing small initiatives in the context of big ideals can help ward off frustration and burnout. This can be extremely important. Tempered radicals are not typically given the mandate for large-scale transformation and usually operate in a contained arena with limited scope of influence. But many have big ideals. It is easy to become frustrated when what you want to do is, say, eliminate environmental waste and all you see are the limited results of a departmental recycling program. For this reason, the capacity to frame your own and others' circumscribed efforts in terms of the broad ideals they are meant to advance can be crucial to keep yourself going and to generate others' involvement.

Fourth, when we name the broader significance of a small win, it naturally begs two questions: What other small wins will contribute to the same agenda, and what else can I do along the same lines? This broader view helps prevent complacency. Following the workshop for alternative parents at Western, participants began to look for other programs that were overly restrictive. When Martha explained to a colleague in another department that her flexible schedules were designed to accommodate the lives of working parents, the colleague decided to address her department's needs by discouraging mandatory late-afternoon meetings. Change more readily begets change when the bigger purpose is made clear.

Finally, explicitly linking small wins to their larger purpose by deliberately framing their meaning effectively names the concerns and ensures that the problem does not go unrecognized or get trivialized by others who may not see the connection. If Martha never publicly named the bigger problem with which she was concerned (the systemic issues that impede workplace humanity and equity), people may have continued to think that she was simply addressing the idiosyncratic needs of a few employees. Her framing of the bigger issues led to broader organizational learning about cultural norms that impede anyone with set outside responsibilities. This learning, in turn, paved the way for additional adaptations in informal norms and policies about flexible work.

Vehicles for Framing Meaning

How do people frame and communicate the meaning of small wins? Although a wide variety of mechanisms and mediums were used by the tempered radicals I observed, in this chapter we'll focus on the use of stories and language to frame meaning, and oral, written, and symbolic expressions to communicate it.

Revealing and revising stories. The stories people tell about themselves, others, and their activities consciously and subconsciously create meaning and define the way people understand their "realities."[12] Small wins create opportunities to question and revise people's implicit "stories" about reality and thereby create openings for people to change their understandings of the world around them.

Stories that have been told and retold within a culture become so much a part of consciousness that we don't see them as stories at all. They define what we see as "plain truths"—the way things "are." For example, stories about what is "good," who is deserving, and what is "normal" are so ingrained and taken for granted that the stories themselves are transparent. All cultures have these "dominant narratives."[13]

Other stories make dominant narratives more apparent, so that they no longer function as unassailable truths. These stories expose the transparency and limitations of dominant narratives by posing alternative truths and views of reality. These "subversive narratives" create openings for learning and change by questioning prevailing understandings.[14]

The story of meritocracy in U.S. culture is a dominant narrative that provides ready explanations for who gets ahead in organizations, who doesn't, and why. The accepted story is "people who try hard and have the capability will get ahead." The converse is, of course, implicit: "Those who don't get ahead must not be as able or hard working as those who do." The story of meritocracy justifies a wide range of existing organizational arrangements, including organizational hiring, evaluation, and promotion systems, but it is so institutionalized within U.S. culture that its truthfulness is rarely acknowledged or challenged.[15]

Western has its share of practices that reinforce this dominant story of meritocracy, and most employees there probably assume that merit is the driver of success. These dominant narratives can be disrupted, however, even if only temporarily, and such disruptions provide alternative explanations and create openings for new kinds of work practices. For instance, Martha's flexible work scheduling raises questions about the "truth" of meritocracy. If people with outside constraints can perform more effectively with flexible scheduling, then maybe some "poor performers" who didn't get that option were not incapable of being successful. This question raises the possibility that systemic biases might be a factor in job performance. In this way, small wins can implicitly or explicitly call into question the dominant narratives that explain and hold in place existing practices. They also create openings for alternative truths of why things are as they are, which can teach powerful lessons and pave the way for subsequent changes in practices.

Let's look at another example. An investment firm wanted to increase the number of women and minorities it was hiring from business schools. Since they believed their past failure to hire women and minorities had to do with "pipeline" issues, they reasoned that the more candidates they saw, the greater the chance of identifying good candidates. So the firm increased the number of thirty-minute interviews it held on campus. The change had no impact.[16]

The dominant narrative at this firm was that the organization was gender- and race-blind and that its recruiting practices were *neutral* (meaning they affected men and women of different races equivalently) and *impartial*. This narrative made the recruiting practices virtually incontestable and implied that the candidates themselves were somehow unworthy or insufficiently qualified for the job. That was the widely held meaning of their "failure."

One member of the firm saw the flaws in this story. He saw that the standard thirty-minute on-campus interview was not long enough for the middle-aged, white male senior managers conducting most of the interviews to connect sufficiently with minority and women candidates to see beyond first impressions. In recognizing this, the firm implemented several small changes: they changed the length of the first interviews (to forty-five minutes), changed the questions they asked during the interviews (to emphasize potential contributions versus "deal experience"), and increased the number of candidates they admitted into the next round of interviews, which allowed for longer, more comfortable conversations.

These small changes worked to produce a very different pool of qualified candidates and resulted in several successful hires. But the bigger impact came from the learning that both preceded and followed these small wins. Members of the firm recognized how their standard recruiting practices screened out desirable candidates and learned that these practices thought to be neutral were not. Once they recognized and revised their dominant narrative about the neutrality of work practices, they went on to look for other practices that may have been inadvertently creating obstacles for women and minorities, and ultimately they made additional adaptations to chip away at some of those practices.

By taking on the quality of uncontestable "truth," dominant narratives keep existing arrangements in place. Alternative stories can be an important vehicle to jar widely held understandings and open the way for learning and subsequent adaptation, as was the case in the investment firm. Small wins can be both the result of the new stories and the occasion to create them.

Using language to create meaning. In telling stories about small wins (and in everyday conversation for that matter), tempered radicals make choices about what language to use to frame the meaning of small wins.[17]

On the one hand, it is important to frame small wins in a language that is already familiar and legitimate to insiders. Small wins can be justified by showing how they contribute to outcomes the organization already deems important. Martha Wiley can talk about her flexible work arrangements as a way to improve retention and save recruitment costs. Peter Grant can describe minority outreach and networking programs as a cost-effective recruiting and professional development program. Roger Saillant can describe his collaboration with the local college of architecture as primarily a way to expedite the construction process. Framing small wins in the language of an organization's instrumental/economic interests increases the likelihood that the dominant group will adopt them.

If our intent is to effect change, however, relying solely on language and criteria that are already legitimate will do little to unfreeze people from their current way of thinking.[18] Talking only in terms of the prevailing vocabulary and related meaning systems can lead people to think in those restricted terms. If we talk about a corporate environmental program strictly as a plan to reduce costs, we may come to think of cost savings as the principal criterion, and we may lose sight of the motive of sustainability.[19] If Peter discusses his recruiting practices only as a cost-effective measure, the benefits of a diverse workforce may go unnoticed. Thus language can be one of the most powerful mechanisms for unwittingly shifting people's priorities as well as supporting the ones in place.

It is important to use language that duly reflects commitments and values. This requires staying *within* the experience of the people we are trying to influence *and* moving outside this experience at the same time. Staying inside means relying on accepted rationales to show the benefits of small wins. Moving outside requires introducing alternative rationales and words to communicate the subtle and broader implications of the initiatives. This boils down to the importance of speaking in multiple languages, rather than watering down one—using insider language to temper the message and outsider language to push the edge, but just enough.[20] If you do one and not the other, you risk losing legitimacy or diluting your change agenda.

Joanie at Shop.co accomplished this. She talked about her new place in the organization as a smart organizational move, one that put her activities more efficiently within the logical department. She also talked about her desire to integrate fair-trade programs into the company's core activity to improve the conditions and economic viability of impoverished communities around the globe.

As the success of his efforts grew, Peter began to talk more and more about the impact he was having on increasing the diversity of Western's workforce, and creating a network for minorities that helped address the disadvantages of not being part of the "old boys' network." Peter added his version of the story to the more widely accepted talk about efficient recruiting and effective development and retention.

I must acknowledge that speaking in multiple languages to the same constituency is often easier said than done. Jennifer Jackson, a leader of the gay employees' group at Atlas, claimed that her struggle to find a way to be heard without losing her own voice was one of the most difficult things she confronted early in her career. The dual pulls she faced as a tempered radical played out as a linguistic juggling act:

> We had goals and desires for our group, yet we also had the best interest of the company at heart. We gave them good reason to trust

us and they did. But we never watered down our own desires. . . . Our group asked for a nondiscrimination policy to protect gay employees. We discussed how Atlas could make a difference by setting an example for society. We also pointed out that doing this *would help Atlas* effectively access ten percent of the best employees available, since at least ten percent of the best employees are gay and lesbian. We also argued that it would increase gay and lesbian employees' commitment to Atlas. We pressed the personal, the political, and the corporate issues. It all helped.

Another linguistic strategy involves using the vocabulary that is familiar to insiders to your own advantage. This is the linguistic equivalent of the martial art jujitsu, where the defender uses the energy and strength of the adversary to build power. Tempered radicals can effect change by holding the organization or a part of it to its espoused rhetoric. If she had needed to, Joanie could have held members of the product development group to the group's own rhetoric—"coming up with innovative and socially responsible products"—to influence them to consider products outside their normal line. Peter could have used management's espoused commitment to diversity to justify his hires. "Linguistic jujitsu" can thus justify small wins in language that is *supposed* to reflect an organization's practices and values.

Language is not only a vehicle for creating the meaning of small wins; language can also be the target. Small changes in language—either revising the meaning of an established word (e.g., "family") or changing the word itself (e.g., "chairman" to "chairperson")—can alter how people think and act. Feminists working toward making the world more inclusive, for example, have long seen language as a crucial lever for change. As words become more inclusive and less universally male, so too do roles, expectations, and actions.

Using Multiple Mediums to Communicate

Whether in narrative or any other form, meanings must be communicated through some medium in order for learning to occur. Oral communication may be the most common in organizations, occurring informally and spontaneously in the course of in-the-moment conversations at meetings, around the coffee pot, or in the restroom, as

---

Framing and Diffusing the Meaning of Small Wins: A Summary

Vehicles for Framing Meaning

1. **Stories:** Dominant cultural narratives promote the "truths" of the status quo; subversive narratives create opportunities for change by identifying the flaws in the dominant narrative and offering alternative views. Small wins can create occasions to develop subversive narratives and new stories.

2. **Language:** Balancing insiders' language (and rationale) with language of the change agenda; small wins can also be created from small alterations in language.

Mediums for Communicating Meaning

1. **Informal interactions and conversations.**

2. **Formal/structured conversations:** Debates, interviews, performance reviews, speeches.

3. **Written communications:** Newsletters, articles, memos, letters, reports, conference proceedings, mission statements, and so on.

4. **Symbolic communication:** T-shirts, bumper stickers, buttons.

---

well as in more structured settings such as job interviews, structured discussions, or performance reviews. We've seen repeatedly how interactions provide opportunities for resistance; when people interact, they actively negotiate and communicate meanings.

We communicate meanings through formal and scripted mediums as well. Speeches and informal conversations can create and disseminate meanings. Researchers who have studied protest movements have recognized the importance of conferences, workshops, and celebrations as forums for challenging traditional understandings and creating new ones. Professor Mary Fainsod Katzenstein, for example, looked at how feminist movements within the Catholic Church have relied primarily on these discursive processes as their means of protest.[21] Through workshops, conferences, and other forums that allowed for formal talks and informal conversations about the meaning of faith, the implications of inclusion, and the history of women and the Church, feminists challenged prevailing doctrine and generated new understandings and possibilities. Their aim was to use all these discursive mechanisms to disrupt and revise existing narratives for those who felt alienated from the Church but still committed to being part of it.

Written mediums—conference papers, published articles, newsletters, editorials, mission statements, memos, and the like—are also vehicles for communicating meaning. People rely on these mediums to challenge dominant narratives and introduce alternative "truths."

Finally, visual expressions in the popular culture, such as T-shirts and bumper stickers, serve as significant symbols and mediums of communication.[22] The multicultural department at Atlas distributed T-shirts at their annual diversity conference. The messages on the shirts created openings for fresh conversations. People said that when they wore their T-shirts to work, others asked them questions about diversity, which provided occasions for serious discussions, discussions that in other situations would have felt forced.

Conclusion

Small wins are doable initiatives. They are not logical first steps in a linear change sequence. Rather, ideas for small wins emerge from opportunities, and opportunities often lie in the details of everyday life. Anyone who wants to initiate small wins must be alert. The approach calls for skillful improvisation rather than brilliant strategy. Even though the small-wins strategy is a humble, incremental approach to change, the impact of small wins does not necessarily remain small.

One important way people encourage the spread of a small win is to frame it in terms of its larger significance. A small win will more likely lead to significant change when it is used as an occasion to question existing understandings and beliefs and to foster system learning and adaptation. This is accomplished through the active framing and dissemination of their meanings.

Small wins are driven by people's beliefs, values, and identities. They are actions of self, more proactive than many of the expressions we've seen in previous chapters. But small wins also shape people's values, beliefs, and identities. By acting on them, people affirm, extend, and revise their "selves."

Small wins are clearly not the only proactive strategy with which to advance progressive change from within an organization. Big wins, of course, are also important. But big wins usually are more risky and are difficult to successfully accomplish alone, without the support, resources, and clout of a collective body. In the next chapter we turn to strategies for organizing collectives for bigger wins. As we will see, small wins can be critical to laying the groundwork and generating the involvement of others for these larger institutional changes.

Organizing Collective Action

I'm one person, and I can't do it alone. I can yell and scream and push and all that, but I really am just one voice out there. There has to be a large number of people doing the same things I'm doing, and I haven't seen that happen yet.

— *Atlas employee*

DAVID WELTON, a self-proclaimed tempered radical who worked in a large bank in Switzerland, had just returned from a two-week seminar on social responsibility, part of a two-year master's degree program on the same topic.[1] David was hired as part of a cohort of "Future Leaders" who had been recruited for a special two-year internal training program with rotations throughout the bank. Members of this program had unusual access to key executives and were perceived as the next generation of leaders.

David felt that part of his role would be to advance and implement programs that support socially responsible and environmentally sustainable business practices at the bank. He believed that the first step was for the bank to implement a social audit of its practices to determine where it stood in various areas of social responsibility and environmentalism, how it was judged by different stakeholders (including employees), and what relevant areas most needed work. This institutional agenda was ambitious, and he knew he could not push it through on his own.

David spent much of his first year in the Future Leaders program educating and developing enthusiasm for this agenda among other members of his cohort. Although this cohort was an existing group—members were in frequent contact and shared similar professional goals—they had no real collective identity or sense of purpose. He wanted to change that.

David described to his peers the bank's role in the global economy and how employment and lending practices throughout the world had a variety of economic and social impacts in local communities. He explained how the bank, with minor adjustments to its policies, could make positive contributions to these communities. He also pointed to the credibility of this cohort within the bank and how they, working as a collective, had a unique opportunity to influence the bank's leaders to alter the practices and set an example for other institutions.

By the end of the first year, David had convinced his cohort to take this on as their shared agenda, which created the basis for a much stronger collective identity. No longer were they just a collection of fast-track individuals. They now felt a common sense of purpose and responsibility.

At the annual meeting with the bank's top executives, the Future Leaders cohort was asked to present their agenda for the future and a plan for implementing their top priorities. Speaking for his cohort, David presented a compelling case for placing social responsibility on the bank's agenda and a plan for implementing a social audit of its current practices. The social audit would serve to raise awareness while putting in place a set of clear metrics with which to measure progress on key targets for change.

The executives approved this initiative and authorized a task force co-led by David and another Future Leader to begin the implementation. In looking back on this accomplishment, David knew that it was the unanimous support of his cohort and the legitimacy they held as a group that enabled him to move this progressive agenda through the system. He never could have done it on his own.

I have emphasized throughout this book how individuals can effect significant change by working persistently and opportunistically toward incremental adaptations. And the efforts of multiple individuals working independently toward comparable ends, what Joanne Martin and I call "disorganized co-action," will have an even greater impact.[2] But there are limits to what individuals—and even large numbers of individuals acting independently—can achieve on their own.

In chapter 5 we talked about the benefits of relying on third parties—among other things, they can extend your networks, provide social support, help frame meaning, and keep you tied to your values and identities. Allies remind you that your struggles are not yours alone. Having people with whom you can compare your experiences helps you identify larger patterns outside yourself that need to change.

But when the target of change is something as large, or immediate as a new organizational practice or policy, a redistribution of resources, or a clear and discrete institutional shift in direction, it may require the force of a collective body to generate movement. It stands to reason that people can drive large-scale immediate change more effectively by working in concert with others toward a common goal, particularly when they do not have formal authority to mandate the desired changes.

The biggest advantage of working in concert with others is that collectives have greater legitimacy, power, and resources than individuals. David probably would not have received the senior executives' attention or support for launching his progressive social audit initiative. He may have changed a few minds, garnered some support along the way, and possibly made the social audit happen months or years down the road. But to catalyze such an immediate and institutional-level response, he required the muscle of a collective. In his case, the muscle was particularly forceful because the Future Leaders group held a great deal of credibility with important stakeholders.

Consider any recent social movement and its accomplishments. Could a collection of mothers working as disconnected individuals—even as highly motivated and persistent individuals—have accomplished a fraction of what "Mothers Against Drunk Driving" has achieved as a collective movement? One motivated person realized that she could do much, much more with the force of a coalition of mothers behind her. From the civil rights movement to more localized neighborhood movements to collectives within organizations, the same principle holds true.[3]

Clearly, it does not always make sense to join forces with others. Sometimes it makes sense to work alone; sometimes tempered radicals simply need the help of allies and friends; and sometimes, to make the desired kind of difference, it is best to join forces with others and work as a collective body for commonly valued changes. These choices are not mutually exclusive. Most tempered radicals do all of the above.

The question is therefore not, "Am I lone agent or community organizer?" The important question to ask is, "Under what conditions, for what issues, and in what circumstance does it make sense to join forces with others toward a collectively valued end?" And, when it does make sense, how do you mobilize independent individuals to act as a group with a collective purpose and identity?

Different Routes to Organizing Collectives

My observations of the tempered radicals who have successfully organized collectives are consistent with the findings from the large body of research on social movements. This research has converged on the importance of three conditions for fostering collective action: (1) the presence of immediate political opportunities or threats; (2) available structures for members to organize themselves into a collective; and (3) the framing of collective identity, opportunities, and threats.[4] I'll explain each of these briefly.

First, sociologists have observed that collectives tend to form and ignite into action when something happens to pose an immediate threat to the interests of a set of individuals, or to create a sudden opening of political opportunity for a set of individuals to exploit. The existence of a threat or opportunity can topple the basis of a system's stability and has the potential to galvanize a set of individuals into a collective movement.

Second, the availability of resources and credible structures at the time of an opportunity or threat helps determine whether a collective entity actually forms to respond to the situation.[5] Employee groups, union committees, or, in David's case, the Future Leaders cohort provide readily available and legitimate structures for collective action.

Third, the framing of a problem or set of interests serves as the link between impending threats or opportunities and action. With framing, a threat or opportunity is actively interpreted in terms relevant to the interests of a group of people. At a minimum, it makes the group feel that by acting together they can address the problem or exploit the opportunity. Some researchers refer to these frames as "collective action frames."[6] Effective collective action frames define, at a minimum, a shared identity and purpose, a sense of indignation (or opportunity), and a hope that collective action will make a difference. Without effectively framing a situation, people will not likely identify as members of the collective or be galvanized to act as one.

David Welton came into a situation ripe for collective action. Even though few people in the Future Leaders cohort identified with the group or felt it served any purpose beyond a professional program, the existence of the group provided a ready *structure* for coordinated action. David made it clear to his peers that as a group they had a unique political *opportunity* to make a difference because of their positioning as "future leaders." His success in mobilizing this group was partly a result of his capacity to provide a compelling collective action frame—a shared purpose, a shared sense of opportunity, and common feeling that as the next generation of leaders they were in this together and had a responsibility to make a difference together.

Although the three conditions that foster collective action are common, the exact paths people take to form collectives, and their reason for doing so, vary. My research pointed to three distinct paths: organizing a group to respond to a shared threat or opportunity; igniting a group with the spark of a lone individual's action; and forming a group to combat social isolation. The first of these paths is the course David followed. It reflects a conscious effort to mobilize a group to address a threat or opportunity. The second path reflects instances when a lone individual's action catalyzes the interests of others and intentionally or otherwise frames a group identity and purpose. The third path begins with the purpose of generating social and professional support; once formed, the group takes on a shared change agenda. These three paths are different routes for creating involvement and mobilizing a group toward a common end.

Organizing to Respond to a Shared Threat or Opportunity

At Atlas, Jennifer Jackson recruited a group of gay, lesbian, and bisexual (GLB) employees to combat a legislative initiative that threatened their well being.[7] She reported to me,

> It was for Prop. 64, the initiative to restrict public health policies regarding AIDS that I decided I needed help. Out in the world, people were organizing to fight, but not here at Atlas. At a political

meeting I went to, I wanted to stand up and say, 'I'm going to do fund-raising among all the rich apathetic gay people I know here at Atlas.' But then I realized I only knew three people. So I thought, "I'm going to start a group."

Given the direct threat Proposition 64 posed to the GLB community, Jennifer found it easy to frame the issue in a way that gave people a sense of collective purpose and identity. It was harder, however, to find an appropriate structure for the group. Since at that point Atlas had no precedent for identity-based employee groups, Jennifer needed to create one. She wanted Atlas to formally sponsor the group because she believed more people would join an official group. She also thought that the Atlas name would give the group legitimacy in the community. To get the group sanctioned, she sent a letter to the vice president of human resources to explain its purpose. Written in cooperative, tempered language, the letter said, "We are not mad at you. We think Atlas is a good place for gay employees. We just have some issues we want to discuss with you that will make it an even *better* place."

Jennifer's strategy worked. Atlas management agreed to the formation of a formal group for gay, lesbian, and bisexual employees. When she announced its formation and its intent to fight Proposition 64, only a dozen individuals showed up at the first meeting. These people then talked about the group to others, and by the third meeting fifty employees, many of whom had previously been silent about their sexual orientation, signed up to participate and to work on Proposition 64. While clearly they were part of a much bigger movement to defeat the initiative, the Atlas GLB group played a visible and potentially significant role in helping focus corporate attention on the issue.

Jennifer's actions had further benefits as well. First, Atlas agreed to sanction other employee groups. As of this writing, eleven such groups are active. Second, operating on the momentum from the legislative initiative, the group found other issues of common concern to address and worked on getting sexual orientation written explicitly into the company's nondiscrimination clause. After a year and a half of ups and downs, the group had not only successfully broadened the nondiscrimination policy but also secured domestic partner benefits. Jennifer had little doubt that the group's collective influence and collaborative relationship with management set them up for these successes.

Here a loosely connected set of individuals were mobilized as a collective force by the presence of a meaningful shared threat, paired with a framing that pointed to the importance of acting together to redress the threat. Once they had a structure, they were poised to act on other issues as more opportunities and threats arose.

Individual Action to Ignite Collective Action

When one or more tempered radicals take a small action, it creates an occasion for uncovering and framing an issue with broader appeal. This is equivalent to the strategy of using small wins to generate involvement.

The case of Biology Professor Nancy Hopkins at MIT illustrates this path to collective action.[8] Out of frustration, anger, and despair, Hopkins decided that she had to do *something* about the persistent gender discrimination she witnessed at the School of Science. She decided to write a letter to the president of MIT about a problem that she believed she alone saw. She was reluctant to send the letter because she feared that it might affect her reputation with her senior colleagues. So before sending it, she decided to show it to a respected female colleague, which was not easy for her to do:

> Looking back, I can see how difficult it was to show this woman my letter. I had to steel myself emotionally. I think the reason it was so hard is that we grew up believing that if you are really good enough, you can make it on your own. Even in the face of discrimination.[9]

To Hopkins's surprise, the colleague she showed it to asked to cosign the letter and to go with her to see the president. It turned out that she too had experienced and witnessed the kinds of biases Hopkins described, but like Hopkins, feared she was alone and chose not to talk about it. Hopkins's letter changed that; she now felt motivated to do something about it. At this point it occurred to the two women that other female faculty might feel the same way, so they visited with all seventeen tenured women in the School of Science to talk about their experiences. They discovered that *all but one* agreed with their description of the way gender discrimination played out at MIT. All had previously refrained from saying anything, even to each other, but now all asked to sign the letter, which they decided to address to the

Dean of Science. Whereas all of them once saw the discrimination as an individual problem, they now framed it as a shared problem that riddled the whole system.

The group of women faculty asked the dean to address the problem by setting up a committee to collect data and thoroughly investigate the matter. The dean and president agreed with the analysis in the letter and agreed to follow the recommendations. After they secured this support, the women scientists and several administration officials worked collaboratively on the issue, never proceeding without the consensus of all involved.[10] The women were relieved that they could establish this working relationship with the administration and avoid resorting to formal complaints, litigation, or other adversarial means of redress. The results of these efforts have not yet fully unfolded, but every school at MIT has now adopted a process to examine itself for subtle forms of gender bias. And because of its willingness to address these issues so deeply and publicly, MIT has been held up as a model for other institutions to follow. In January 2001, MIT hosted a "summit" meeting with a handful of officials from five other top universities to address the issue of "women academics in science and engineering." Hopkins now spends a good deal of her time talking with officials in other institutions who want to take on similar change initiatives.

Hopkins's initial act of drafting a letter to the university president uncovered allies and created an occasion for conversation. Women debated its content and asked to sign it. This concrete act invited the collective framing of the issue. The framing helped mobilize the women to act together because it delineated their shared interest. Ultimately the women continued to push for change partly because the president's and dean's initial responses showed them they had a real opportunity to effect change. After this ad hoc group's initial push, the administration created a formal structure to work for further change.

It would seem that the logical way to effect large-scale change would be to identify a common threat, organize a collective, and then mobilize the collective to act on the problem. Professor Hopkins and the lessons of community organizers throughout the past century suggest the potential efficacy of this alternative path: act first, organize second.[11]

Organizing for Personal and Professional Support

Action can be the impetus or reason for forming a group, or it can be a by-product of a collective formed for other purposes. Tom Novak's involvement with other gays and lesbians at Western was purely social at first and then evolved as necessary into a collective force for change. It began when Tom and a few others who had marched together at an AIDS walk decided to circulate an informal invitation. In Tom's words:

> The flyer said, "If you're interested in socializing with gay and lesbian employees at Western, call or e-mail one of us, and we're going to put something together." We planned a picnic on a Sunday in a park about six weeks later. We expected about fifteen people to show up but almost a hundred people came, right out of the blue.
>
> That picnic was one of the most emotional experiences I've ever had because these people who literally worked on the same floor with each other for years were for the first time seeing one another. For people who had only spoken on the phone through the course of their business day, suddenly there was a face, and it was a gay or lesbian face, it was a friendly face. I think it changed people's lives, which may sound like gross overstatement, but I don't think it is.

According to Tom, the picnic enabled gay and lesbian employees to understand that there are more gays and lesbians in corporate America than they ever realized: "I always knew that I wasn't alone, but watching those connections get made was just unbelievable. I felt incredibly proud."

Women at both Atlas and Western have formed groups to network and develop relationships with other women so they could combat some of the isolation they feel. Some come together to share experiences and to get and give moral and social support. At Western, many senior white women meet regularly for social meals, at which they compare experiences, help each other, and provide emotional support. According to one member, "It's not the Old Girls' Network per se, but in a way I guess it is."

A group of black executive women from Western also meet regularly to compare their experiences as black women. Occasionally this group takes on causes in the community, but members vary in their activist inclinations and mostly they get together to socialize and to "feed each others' souls."

All these groups have formed as networks for social and professional support. They serve the express purpose of bringing people together to share professional tips, insights, and contacts with one another. But this does not mean that such groups have no political consequence. Membership in identity or interest-based groups gives people the psychological strength they need to resist conformity pressures or to turn impending threats into opportunities for greater learning.

In addition, given the appropriate catalytic conditions—either a perceived threat to the collective or a political opportunity—and a compelling framing of these situations, members of these social groups are ready to move into collective action.[12] For example, when the Boy Scouts banned gay men as leaders, the informal gay and lesbian group at Western came together to protest. Gay and lesbian employees who thought their involvement in the group was only social immediately became a focused collective body. They helped mobilize interested straight employees and then joined with them to apply pressure on senior management to stop funding the Boy Scouts. Even though this group remained an informal entity, the right catalyst inspired the members to work effectively as a collective body for change. The group eventually worked for and secured domestic partner benefits for gay employees.

Dilemmas of Organizing Collectives

Organizing people to act collectively brings no shortage of challenges. Collective action is usually more threatening than individual action to those in charge, so this step can entail additional risk and require a further level of commitment. Recall from chapter 4 four black men heading out to lunch together. They were not even trying to organize anything; they were just going to lunch. But their mere gathering triggered suspicion. Because collective efforts are more visible than independent actions, they tend to trigger more resistance.

Another reason tempered radicals often choose to act independently is that it is simply less complicated to do so. They are free to pursue their agenda at their own pace, at their own level of radicalism, with their own strategies, and toward the specific ends that are most important to them. They don't have to negotiate agreement among people, worry about tradeoffs, or coordinate different approaches. Individuals have limited time and energy to pursue change agendas—on top of the demands of succeeding in their official jobs—and they sometimes simply choose not to spend them on organizing others.

As we've seen earlier, however, there are many advantages in moving from an individual actor to a member of a larger collective force, and tempered radicals lead or join these efforts all the time. My research identified two sets of additional issues affecting their strategies. The first concerns the challenges of effectively framing collective agendas to encompass the interests and identities of diverse constituencies. The second concerns the pros and cons of working as a collective within the structure of formally sanctioned employee groups versus informal, organic groups. These issues map onto two of the three critical conditions for organizing collectives described earlier; we'll look at each in turn.

Developing a Collective Framing among Diverse Constituencies

Jennifer Jackson's first challenge in organizing the group of gay, lesbian, and bisexual employees to respond to impending legislation was to develop an effective framing that could galvanize a previously unorganized group of people into a collective. Fortunately for her, she had a pretty easy job identifying a common "we" that was being threatened and creating a clear, shared sense of purpose for acting together. Some issues, however, do not so readily lend themselves to clear targets of change or to well-defined groups with clear identities. In some cases, people disagree about what a threat means, who is affected by it, and what the group's shared agenda should be. It is the classic problem of building coalitions across disparate groups that share some, but not all, identities, priorities, and agendas.

The traditional solution to this dilemma is to locate and highlight that which is shared across diverse people and to downplay the differences. This solution is akin to what social movement researchers refer to as "the lowest common denominator approach" to politics, where the identity of a group and target of change is that which is common across groups.[13] This approach is appealing in its emphasis on a common target of change, but it is problematic in *what and who* it ignores in the name of consensus. Often, the sense of identity or targets for change become so diluted that many people lose their excitement or even willingness to remain a part of the collective. This dynamic helps explain why some coalitions fail to organize successfully around issues of real and common importance. White women and women of color, black women and Latina women, straight women and lesbians share real concerns about inequities that face women in organizations. Yet when a collective effort reduces women's issues to "lowest common denominator" concerns, it too often ignores issues of racism or heterosexism in favor of only the most basic forms of gender discrimination that all women share. This boiled-down version of "gender issues" more often than not tends to be based on straight white (professional) women's experiences, as if these experiences are universally shared by all women.[14] In these situations, women of color and lesbians become understandably frustrated and alienated when their white heterosexual colleagues ignore their specific concerns in their attempts to advance change for "all" women. Accordingly, women's groups tend to be segregated, and many women of color, particularly black women, tend to join race-based groups rather than women's groups. As a result, sometimes they have to subordinate their gender identity and silence their gender-related concerns in favor of promoting racial solidarity.[15]

Because any one person has multiple identities, subordinating a part of oneself to fit into a collective can feel demeaning. These are the same forces at play that silence tempered radicals' different "selves" within the dominant culture. One woman almost dropped out of the gay and lesbian organization at Atlas because she felt the group ignored lesbian employees' experiences, which were different from those of gay men. Even though Jennifer, a lesbian, founded the group, men soon joined her in leading it and some women felt that the group did not adequately represent their interests. These women felt the group simply reproduced some of the gender biases they experienced within the broader organizational culture.

Effectively managing the reality of multiple interests within collectives requires that the group emphasize not only what is shared—the identities, values, or concerns that bring the group together—but also the differential experiences of that which is shared. For example, you can focus on a general problem such as gender injustice to galvanize the support and enthusiasm of a broad group of women, and at the same time you can foster an active dialogue regarding each person's *distinct experiences* based on differences such as those based on race, sexual orientation, or class.

In many ways, leaders of collectives who want to embrace constituents with significant differences face the same challenges that tempered radicals pose for their organizations as a whole. How can they inspire a commitment to a common purpose while also making room for different experiences and personal agendas? The accompanying box shows that it is important to consciously manage certain matters, such as the overall purpose, the internal culture of the collective itself, the organizational structure and leadership, and the choice of allies and third-party resources for outside support.

Mobilizing a group of people with diverse interests and perspectives toward a common end should involve efforts to generate dialogue and debate. Mobilizing isn't necessarily more effective when it is smooth and easy. Dialogue enables people to identify the shared issue as well as areas of contention. Early conversations among the female faculty

---

Considering Differences within a Collective

Research by Sharon Kuntz suggests that the following considerations help deal effectively with differences among members of a collective while also enabling commitment to a common purpose.[16]

Clarifying the issue and the movement: To galvanize support and inspire action, clarify your purpose by framing the issue broadly, but clearly. Be sure, however, to actively encourage subgoals that reflect the distinct experiences of different participants; doing so helps ensure inclusion and avoid alienation.

Internal culture: Focus on the culture of the collective itself, as indicated by norms of behavior, clothing, music, food, language, jokes, and so on. Be sure to encompass different identity groups within the collective. Diversity of cultural expression increases the commitment of members whose differences might otherwise preclude alignment.

Organizational structure and leadership: Ensure that the collective's leadership and structure do not reflect only a dominant group but a multiplicity of identities and interests.

Outside support: Solicit support from people or groups who identify with possible subgoals as well as the core issues, to create a sensitivity to all constituents relevant to the collective and thus to create a sense of inclusion.

---

about the problems at MIT enabled the participants to find common territory, to discuss differences in their experiences, and simply to get to know one another. These conversations set the stage for forming and acting as a collective.

Sanctioned versus Unsanctioned Employee Groups

Is an employee group formally sanctioned by the organization or not? Pros and cons are associated with both formal and informal groups. As it happens, Western and Atlas, my two primary research sites, differed in their approach to employee coalitions, which makes for an interesting contrast.

Sanctioned groups. Atlas formally sponsored and sanctioned employee groups: not only the GLB employee group but also groups for professional women, administrative women, blacks, Latinos, Asian Americans, Pacific Islanders, and a few interest-based groups, including one formed to address the needs of single parents. The formal sanctioning meant that each group had "Atlas" in its name (e.g., the Atlas Gay, Lesbian, and Bisexual Employee Group), received modest financial support, could meet in Atlas facilities and on Atlas working time, and could use Atlas's channels of communication, such as phones and e-mail. Atlas also developed a well-staffed department of multiculturalism to support these groups and a multicultural task force comprising representatives from the different employee groups. In exchange for its support, Atlas management could ask these groups for feedback on company activities, products, and marketing materials, and could rely on them to expand networks for labor, customers, and suppliers. The company viewed the groups as legitimate and, in many cases, constructive resources.

Official sanctioning provides other important advantages to members of these employee groups. Most notably, management's support provides a legitimate structure and protection for those who want to engage in collective action.[17] This legitimacy may be particularly significant for workers who feel that their efforts to promote learning and change involve a certain degree of professional risk.

Sanctioning may also foster a more cooperative working relationship between the employee collective and its supposed adversary. A cooperative relationship developed quickly at MIT; and some, including Nancy Hopkins herself, see that relationship as central to the women's success. While the women faculty may have had to temper their agenda a bit to keep the administration on board, their incremental, reasoned agenda may also explain why so many women have been eager to sign on to the cause, why, over time, they have been able to address some of the deepest and stickiest issues, and why so many people at other institutions are eager to emulate their model.[18]

The most fundamental advantage of organizing in the context of sanctioned groups is that such groups are less likely to disintegrate when there is no immediate cause for action or when some members do not think a collectively held issue is legitimate. The formal structure keeps a "minimal group" alive that can easily mobilize should a need arise.[19]

Officially sanctioned employee groups have disadvantages as well. For example, Atlas management attempted to define the collective purpose for some groups. When they did, they defined the purpose of the groups to be for social and professional support, and not for political advocacy. In addition, because the groups were meant to encompass everyone who shared a broadly defined identity or interest (e.g., all Asian Americans), they found it difficult at times to mobilize around causes. In order to define the issue broadly enough to fit the group, they typically resorted to finding the lowest common denominator, which diluted the issue and failed to engender much support.

Unsanctioned groups. Unlike Atlas, at the time of my research Western did not sponsor or sanction identity- or interest-based employee groups and forbade employees from using company resources, such as copy machines and e-mail, to organize group gatherings.[20] Western officials told me that such groups were "too close to unions," and Western has always opposed unionization. Despite this opposition, some tempered radicals regularly initiated informal identity-based coalitions and many groups of employees met regularly, usually away from work and after formal work hours. Tom Novak's picnic at the park for gay and lesbian employees is an example.

Even with the inconveniences, the lack of official sanctioning gives employees more freedom to define their collective identities and agendas. One of the black employee groups at Western is composed of an informal network of senior black employees, most of whom Peter Grant initially hired. They look to Peter for leadership and mentoring, and they look to each other for information, expanded networks, and alternative job prospects. When necessary, they work behind the scenes to provide resources, information, and help for each other, and they regularly support each other's efforts to effect change. Western's informal collectives vary their levels of political activity, based primarily on whether an immediate issue impels them to action—such as the Boy Scouts' exclusion of gay leaders or the issue of securing domestic partner benefits—rather than a purpose defined by senior management.

A major drawback of groups in organizations that remain unsanctioned is that they lack legitimacy and resources; as a result, they often have narrower reach within the organization. They evolve organically, through personal invitations and informal networks, growing by word of mouth. Accordingly, informal groups tend to be more exclusive, either by design of the members (as was the case among the group of senior white women) or unintentionally as a result of how they evolve. Clearly some groups can start informally and later seek sanctioning. Conversely, in some organizations, sanctioned groups form opportunistically *because* of the availability of resources and support, and then evolve into more informal factions and subgroups.[21]

Whether the group is formally sanctioned or not, what appears to be most crucial to involve any particular individual in a collective effort is the pre-existence of social ties to the collective or to other individuals in the collective.[22] Formal groups may be more enduring and therefore attract individuals with greater certainty, but informal groups also serve to maintain social ties. That the Future Leader group already existed, even as a loose cohort of people, made David Welton's task of mobilizing a group infinitely easier. Because people felt connected to David, a modest amount of interest in his agenda was sufficient to motivate people in the cohort to join the collective enterprise.

Conclusion

There appear to be several paths along which tempered radicals travel from individual to collective actor. In all cases they depend on the three basic conditions of collective action: existence of threat or opportunity, a viable existing or potential structure for organizing, and an effective framing that links a threat or opportunity to a collective purpose and identity. These conditions can be activated at different points in the organizing process and with different motives.

The path you choose to take to mobilize others depends on any number of factors: Is there already an existing collective poised to be galvanized into action? If so, what sort of framing would solidify the collective identity and purpose to move the group into action? Is there an impending threat that would naturally stir the concerns and energy of others and lead to a clear and shared agenda? Or is there enough uncertainty about who a collective would include, and what the shared agenda would be, that you need first to stir conversation through a catalytic action?

Probably the most direct path involves the emergence of an impending threat or opportunity in the face of an obvious group whose interest would be affected by these. This is the hand David Welton was dealt. If you have no existing group but are faced with a threat, you need to identify loosely linked people and frame the threat in such a way that a collection of people *form* a collective with a common purpose and identity. Jennifer Jackson worked with this set of conditions well. In the absence of an existing group or sense of shared threat or opportunity, it may require the spark of an individual's action to start conversation, identify allies, and ignite collective action. Nancy Hopkins's initial small action generated a series of conversations that led to broad and influential collective involvement.

In their efforts to form and mobilize collective bodies, Nancy Hopkins, Tom Novak, David Welton, and Jennifer Jackson were performing an essential task of leadership. Whether or not they held official leadership roles within their organizations, the work of creating a collective agenda and mobilizing a group of people to pursue it is the work of leadership.[23] Each of these individuals played a part not only in organizing a collective body, but in enabling it to work through internal conflicts, mobilize support, and deal with resistance. Jennifer and David both spoke about these situations as invaluable leadership experiences. Gay and straight employees alike point to Tom as the unofficial leader of the gay and lesbian employees at Western. Women academics throughout the country look to Nancy Hopkins as a leader of a diffuse, though strongly held, collective agenda.

While tempered radicals certainly lead important change through quiet and individual actions, joining forces and leading collective action clearly broaden the impact and often deepen the benefits of those changes. In the final chapter of the book we consider the different ways tempered radicals exhibit leadership in organizations and society. First, however, we look at the variety of challenges tempered radicals face in organizations and the kinds of contexts that are more and less conducive to their efforts.

challenges for Tempered radicals

It is not the critic who counts; not the man who points out how the strong man stumbles, or where the doer of deeds could have done them better. The credit belongs to the man who is actually in the arena, whose face is marred by dust and sweat and blood; who strives valiantly; who errs, and comes short again and again, because there is no effort without error and shortcoming; but who does actually strive to do the deeds; who knows the great enthusiasms, the great devotions; who spends himself in a worthy cause; who at the best knows in the end the triumph of high achievement, and who at the worst, if he fails, at least fails while daring greatly, so that his place shall never be with those cold and timid souls who know neither victory nor defeat.

— *Theodore Roosevelt,* History as Literature

Facing the Difficulties

"The day came" he reflected, "when I wished to break my silence and found that I could not speak: the actor could not longer be distinguished from his role." . . . [Who] knew better than anyone else how a mask could deform the face beneath.

— Henry Gates, in "The Welfare Table," recalling a
reflection of his mentor, James Baldwin

MORGAN DAVIS is an environmentalist who worked in the non-profit sector before returning to business school at the age of 35. For twelve years he devoted his life to improving the quality of water in the Pacific Northwest and battling corporate giants that continued to dump waste in Puget Sound. He then decided that he may be more effective working within the corporate world. Not only did he want the material benefits he knew were available, but he also believed that he could have an even bigger impact on environmental issues if he worked inside the system that created many of the problems.

Business school provided Morgan with a great transitional opportunity. With a top-notch business education and access to a network of business school colleagues, he planned to find a job in environmental management after business school. He was confident that his experience in the field, his business education, and a summer internship in manufacturing would land him a job in which he could have a direct impact on the future of corporate environmentalism. He knew that some companies were beginning to take a proactive stance and he wanted to be part of this wave.

During his first year of business school, Morgan took the usual required courses and a few electives. Like so many of his classmates, he became attracted to the lures of the high-tech world and decided to spend his electives learning more about marketing in high-tech companies. He didn't think of these choices as a big deal; when else would he learn about marketing in the high-tech industry? He was confident that he could take manufacturing and environmental courses the following year. Based on his strong performance in the marketing classes, he was offered a summer job in a high-technology start-up. Though his gut told him that he was straying from his commitments, he told himself that the job was not permanent and was too good of an opportunity to pass up. The following year in school, Morgan found himself making a series of small decisions that took him farther from his original agenda, including a decision midway through his second year to return to his summer employer for a once-in-a-lifetime opportunity in a start-up.

Five years out of school, after switching jobs two more times within the high-tech industry, he found himself in a high-power all-consuming job as vice president of marketing at another fast-growth high-tech company. Morgan was successful by any traditional measure. Yet he continued to be nagged by this dull sense of confusion and regret. How, he wondered, had he gotten so far from the commitments that directed him to business school and the corporate sector in the first place? Each step along the way seemed reasonable enough, yet with each step, he feared, he had lost a small part of himself—a part he valued and did not want to lose.

Morgan started his journey into the business world as a tempered radical. He held progressive values and a clear agenda around corporate environmentalism and he had every intent to take a job in which he could significantly influence corporate practices toward this end. But ever so slowly, his progressive ideals and commitments seemed to fade away, and before he knew it, they were all but gone.

People like Morgan are everywhere—individuals who put aside their "different" values, identities, and ideals in the course of living up to a career that consumes them. For some people who may start out feeling at odds with a majority culture, this happens as part of a conscious choice to live by the rules of the game. And for many, the compromises they make along the way are well worth the spoils of the game. Some people never look back.

But there are those like Morgan who look back and are not so content with who they have become and the "selves" they have given up. Others who retain and act on their "different" values, identities, and commitments in the context of institutions that make it difficult for them to do so endure considerable psychological and professional turmoil along the way. It's not easy to be a tempered radical.

Throughout the book, we have focused on strategies that tempered radicals use to hold onto their different selves and advance progressive change agendas, and I have emphasized efforts that have been more or less successful in these regards. But my focus on successes does not mean that these efforts are free of risk or difficulty.

Plenty of tempered radicals express their different selves, resist expectations, and challenge prevailing practices only to find themselves without a job or last in line for promotion. Even some of the people I've cited in this book—Sheila Johnson and Martha Wiley, for example—believe that their resistance has probably slowed their careers. They claim that they do not regret their choices, but they believe that they have paid a price for rocking the boat. If they were not also excellent at their jobs, these individuals and other tempered radicals would have little hope of surviving, let alone succeeding. As one tempered radical explained, "They trust me to deliver results, and that is the only reason I'm still here."

We explore two related questions in this chapter: What makes it so difficult for tempered radicals to hold onto their different selves and act on their progressive values and agendas? And what particular factors in their work environments exaggerate and diminish the difficulties of these struggles? In other words, under what conditions is it more or less difficult to be a tempered radical?

Challenges Faced by Tempered Radicals

When tempered radicals navigate between the competing pulls toward conformity and rebellion, they cope with at least four kinds of strains: (1) the difficulties of ambivalence, (2) the incremental lures of co-optation,

(3) potential damage to their reputation, and (4) frustration and burnout. The first two are psychological strains associated with sustaining a dual stance; the second two result when tempered radicals act on their differences.[1]

The Tolls of Ambivalence

To be ambivalent means simultaneously holding opposing feelings toward the same object, say, love and hate or attraction and repulsion. We tend to think of ambivalence as an unstable state, yet tempered radicals and others manage to sustain their ambivalence over long periods. But doing so takes certain psychological tolls.

Anxiety. Psychologists have shown that ambivalence produces anxiety.[2] To eliminate anxiety, people sometimes defend against ambivalence by repressing or "splitting off" one of the contradictory feelings and exaggerating the impulse for the other.[3] In organizational settings, people tend to repress the part of themselves that differs from the majority and emphasize the part of themselves that is impelled to fit in. In this way, a basic psychological drive to alleviate the anxiety from ambivalence can lead people toward conformity.

Guilt. Ambivalence can also produce feelings of guilt—that you've have fallen short of commitments, say, or have let others down. This guilt is a natural psychological by-product of not being able to realize aspirations of success fully or live up to promises for organizational change completely.[4] For instance, a university administrator who worked tirelessly to promote gender equity in her institution but felt that her efforts fell short: "I flagellate myself in the most extraordinary and creative ways even though the problems are institutional and it didn't matter what I did. I don't sleep well."[5]

You may know rationally that there is only so much you can do, but you still may feel that you could have done more for a constituency or cause you care about. This guilt can fuel the drive to eliminate one set of commitments.

Loneliness. Tempered radicals' dual stance positions them as both insiders and outsiders in their organizations, but they are not fully in either camp. As a result, they are neither completely accepted by organizational insiders nor completely accepted by outsiders who share their "different" identities or values. Feeling somewhat alien in both worlds leads to loneliness.

As tempered radicals advance up the organizational ladder, their sense of isolation often intensifies. This happens particularly for some groups, like white women and people of color, because the higher they rise, the fewer peers they have who are like themselves or who face similar circumstances.[6] Some report that they have no one in their peer group with whom they can enjoy a casual conversation over lunch. In addition, the higher people rise, the more distance they put between themselves and other "outsiders" like themselves.

Accusations of hypocrisy. Tempered radicals face another difficulty associated with their ambivalence, specifically their effort to play both sides and being able to play neither completely. They are vulnerable to being viewed as hypocrites insofar as coworkers and friends from outside the organization may accuse them of not "walking their talk."[7] This perceived inconsistency damages their reputations and alienates them from people who could be natural allies. While many of his colleagues at Western recognized Peter Grant's persistent efforts, some people outside the company tended to consider him a hypocrite. Some community members appreciated his efforts, but others saw him as someone who talks about his commitment to the community but has "made it out of the community" by playing by the very rules that exclude people from the community. Peter's explanation that his commitment to success was partly *for* the black community did little to appease his old friends who complained that he had grown too important for them. This kind of situation can be very painful for tempered radicals who are in fact trying hard to do well by others.

These struggles come with the territory of ambivalence. It is neither psychologically nor behaviorally easy to navigate between competing pulls and sustain selves at odds with one another. These strains can lead people to give up one side of their selves or the other. In the face of all of the organizational lures toward conformity, the side most often repressed is that part at odds with the prevailing majority.

To resist these lures and sustain their ambivalence, tempered radicals make ongoing, deliberate efforts to maintain affiliations, to take satisfaction in their efforts, and to make explicit the connection between their local efforts and the broader significance of them. Unfortunately, there is no magic pill to fight successfully against some of these natural psychological strains associated with ambivalence. Rather, it is important to look for small ways to lessen these strains and, most important, recognize that ambivalence is a necessary and natural state.

Incremental Lures toward Co-optation

Despite rhetoric touting the importance of organizational adaptation, most organizations implicitly reward people for maintaining, not disrupting, the status quo. In exchange for people's conformity, organizations promise inclusion, legitimacy, status, opportunities, recognition, and material compensation. I am not suggesting that conformity comes with a guarantee of these rewards or that they are impossible to obtain if you don't conform completely (as many tempered radicals have proved). But the chances of obtaining these rewards are often perceived to be far greater for those who play by the rules.

It may seem that by a certain point in your career, the risks associated with deviating would be cushioned by your tenure, position, and reputation. In fact, however, as people move up the ranks, they often become increasingly averse to the risks of standing out and challenging cultural expectations. They simply have too much at stake. A gay senior executive at Atlas who was only selectively "out" at work explained,

> I can see from my experience so far how much *more* closeted I've become as I've moved up. I'm sure that if I ever made it to director level, I would not talk about being gay to anyone, ever. It just gets harder because there is now too much at stake.

Beyond the real material incentives to conform to dominant cultural expectations (and silence the part of the self that is different), a number of psychological mechanisms induce conformity.[8] The psychological impulse to conform to a group majority is so powerful that it has been the focus of an entire tradition of research in social psychology, much of it inspired by the observations of the horrors of conformity demonstrated during the Nazi regime.[9] This research shows how the fear of exclusion and social ostracism by a group majority can drive people to act, speak, and even think in a way that is opposite to what they believe to be true and right.

In one classic study, experimenters asked individuals to estimate the length of lines that were projected as light onto a wall.[10] To test people's propensity to conform to views they disagreed with, they put lone individuals in a room with a group of experimental "confederates" who deliberately gave the same wrong response. Subject to this social influence, where *all other group members agreed* on the same answer, individuals tended to go along with the wrong response and change their beliefs about the length of the line. Instead of sticking with their own perception and risk being socially ostracized for deviating from the rest of the group, they chose to silence their judgments.

A related body of work looked at the effects of perceived authority on people's propensity to comply. Stanley Milgram demonstrated that people are even willing to inflict pain on others to comply with perceived authority.[11] His experiments brought together two individuals: one was assigned the role of "student" (but was actually a confederate of the experiment) and the other, the role of "teacher" (the experimental subject).

A university official (the authority) informed the "teachers" that the study was about learning and reinforcement. The "student" was supposedly wired to a chair in a separate room and would answer the teacher's questions by pressing levers that would illuminate a display light for the teacher. Each time the student gave a wrong answer, the teacher was instructed to administer what he or she believed to be an electric shock. The "authority" told the teacher that the intensity would increase with each wrong answer.

Approximately two-thirds of the teachers did just what they were told, even though they perceived that they were sometimes inflicting severe pain on the student. Afterward, the teachers explained their actions with comments such as "He [the university official] told me to." A terrifying number of experimental subjects silenced their own beliefs about what was "right" to comply with the perceived authority.

People are subjected to the same sort of social influences in groups in the workplace, and resisting these influences can be psychologically just as difficult. Such acts of deviation—the heroic acts of organizational "whistle-blowers" addressing violations of environmental or health and safety standards as well as the less dramatic everyday acts of tempered radicals—require self-knowledge and conviction to overcome enormous pressure to conform and to suppress beliefs that challenge the majority.

Overcoming these pressures, particularly the subtle pressures faced by tempered radicals, can require mindfulness of the sort we've seen throughout the book. Although whistle-blowers face obvious dilemmas, tempered radicals must be especially vigilant because their subtler choices may seem inconsequential. The compromises they must make sometimes appear to be reasonable and insignificant, part of the price of membership. And membership is typically attractive.

The problem for tempered radicals comes when these compromises add up. As Morgan from the opening learned, all too frequently and sometimes before we know it, we have left behind a small part of our self by making a series of seemingly inconsequential decisions. To avoid this trap, I describe some of the "reasonable compromises" that are particularly likely to add up and unwittingly lead people down a slippery slope of co-optation, a process that entails incrementally increasing people's investment in groups into which they are being assimilated.

Waiting for a "better time." Faced with a choice about whether to embrace a risky agenda, some people may decide that the present moment is not a good time. Deferring can entail simply waiting a few minutes or a few days until you find an appropriate response, locate a better moment, or simply let a situation cool off. Or waiting can be indefinite, a decision that you are not in a position to stick your neck out right now, and that you would be better positioned to take a stand and make a difference once you have gained more credibility, power, and legitimacy in the system. Then you will have the security to act more boldly.

This strategy is known as banking "idiosyncrasy credits."[12] The concept is based on the notion that people collect credits by conforming. Later, they can cash in some of their credits to deviate from the majority and advance change.

This logic seems reasonable enough. And it is, except that all too often the wait never ends, for several reasons. First, people never really know when they have amassed "enough" credits. Since what constitutes "enough" security or power is ambiguous, there is always the temptation to defer just a bit longer, so the deferral keeps going.

Second, by the time people decide that it is a good time to speak up, they may find that the opportunities to do so have passed. Third, after expending so much energy to gain inclusion as an insider, people have more at stake reputationally and materially, which causes them to become more risk averse over time, not less. And if a person's direction or career has proved successful, it becomes far too costly to change directions, as Morgan learned the hard way. If he returned to his plan five years out, he would forfeit the network and reputation he had established in the high-tech world and would have to build them again from scratch in the world of corporate environmentalism.

Using "insider" language. We have already seen how language can be a vehicle for influencing how people think and understand their realities. It is also a mechanism of co-optation. When people talk exclusively in the language of the dominant culture, they come to think this way as well.[13]

Sociologist Carol Cohn observed the co-opting potential of language during her research on the world of defense intellectuals, the people who strategize about the contingencies of war. When she first arrived to do research at a military "think tank," she entered as a critic and did not understand how the professionals in these organizations could talk about weapons of destruction so casually. Their vocabulary included euphemisms like "limited nuclear war," "clean bombs," "counter-force exchanges," and "collateral damage." An "exchange" sounded more like a friendly conversation than a bloody battle. "Collateral damage" did not have the same sting as widespread civilian deaths.[14]

To gain credibility and to converse within the organization, Cohn learned to speak the language of insiders. It was difficult at first, but over time she became more fluent and less anxious about using their language. "Part of the appeal was the power of entering the secret kingdom, being someone in the know," she wrote. "Few know, and those who do are powerful."[15]

As her comfort with the language increased, however, her capacity to speak and think critically about the system disappeared:

I found that the better I got at engaging in this discourse, the more impossible it became for me to express my own ideas, my own values. While the language gave me access to things I had been unable to speak about before, it radically excluded others. I could not use the language to express my [real] concerns because it was physically impossible. This language does not allow certain questions to be asked or certain values to be expressed.[16]

Language literally changed her consciousness.

A seasoned group of executive women at an investment bank had this experience as well. The group started as a forum to initiate significant changes to eradicate obstacles that got in the way of women's advancement. When approaching senior management, members of the group believed that using "deal-making" language to present their ideas would help their cause. They framed the benefits of their solutions in economic terms, such as lower turnover costs for the bank.

Their strategy had an unintended consequence, however. By framing the group's agenda in terms of quantifiable economic benefits, the outcomes became more central to the group. The instrumental, deal-making language did not include a vocabulary to describe sources of discrimination, the core purpose of their effort. The women were so good at using insider language to avoid threatening those in power that they soft-pedaled and disguised the message. They unquestionably appeared more legitimate, but as a result they lost their radical edge. As we discussed, people who advance diversity or other agendas that challenge the status quo see this happen all the time; in an effort to use a language that is soft enough to be heard, they silence their challenges and change agendas.

Using insider language is like wielding a double-edged sword. On the one hand, it is imperative to use terms that allow us to gain credibility and communicate effectively inside the culture we are trying to influence from within.[17] On the other hand, adopting insider language carries the danger of changing how we think and silencing our own perspectives. This is why, in chapter 6, we talked about the importance of learning to speak in the language of insiders *and* outsiders.

Developing a professional image. In any profession, people learn soon enough that to get ahead they have to assume an appropriate image, one that conveys what their organization is trying to portray about itself. In some companies, the process of learning the appropriate self-presentation may be every bit as important as grasping the technical aspects of the job.[18] As Ellen Thomas experienced when she was advised to unbraid her hair, pressure to adopt the "right image" is often about conforming to prevailing definitions of "professionalism." Sometimes conforming to the right images comes with a high cost and can be an all-consuming and highly scrutinized enterprise. As another tempered radical explained, "I cannot remember a time when the way I dressed, my makeup, or my hair was not an issue. A woman's image was frequently raised as an issue and often thought to reflect on her level of maturity and judgment."

The process of adopting an acceptable professional persona does not only mean learning to emulate insiders' behavior. In some cases, it can also entail remaking a significant aspect of one's self. A recent study of the career transitions of male and female management consultants and investment bankers found that those who successfully made the most senior-level transitions were professionals who internalized their finely honed personae as part of their own identities. During the early stages of their career, the young professionals learned to emulate a persona that conveys confidence and expertise in their fields. For most people, this persona is at first only an "act." But it doesn't stay that way. To continue leaping over higher hurdles in these demanding careers, professionals would incorporate these personae into their sense of self. What begins as managing the impression one makes ends up resulting in a transformation of self.[19] Some people make this transition more seamlessly than others. And others never do make it.

When you play a professional "part" over long periods, it can become increasingly difficult to separate your "self" from the part you are playing. To avoid this slippery slope, it is important also to find ways inside and outside your work environment to express the part of your self that is different from the "part" you are playing.

Proving loyalty. We have seen how people who stand out as different face ongoing pressures to prove their loyalty to the majority. One way people do so is to distance themselves from others who are similarly "different." For example, women who are in a small minority come under heightened pressure to prove that they are "one of the boys." They distance themselves from other women—by refusing to take up women's causes, by avoiding women's programs and groups, and by rejecting overtures to mentor other women. Laughing at or telling sexist jokes, becoming fluent with sports metaphors, and putting down other women sends a message that they are not at all like the other women.

Rosabeth Moss Kanter identified this dynamic in her classic book *Men and Women of the Corporation*.[20] She found that this heightened pressure to distance oneself from members of one's own identity group becomes especially strong when members of the minority group make up less than 15 percent of the relevant population. When the ratio is this low, the contrast between the groups becomes more obvious, which makes members of each group more aware of the differences between them. In the presence of a "token" woman, men become more conscious of being men, and women become more conscious of being women. Most important, everyone becomes aware that the token woman *is not* a man, which generates pressure for her to prove that, for the purpose of work, she is one of the guys.

Other minority–majority relationships fall prey to this dynamic. People of color in predominantly white settings are implicitly pressured to distance themselves from their own identity and from members of their own racial and ethnic communities to demonstrate their allegiance to the majority.[21] Early in her career, Sheila Johnson felt pressured to distance herself from other blacks, and she avoided at all cost any association with issues concerned with diversity or race. It took several years for her to reclaim this part of her identity—a part that she later realized was core to her sense of self.

Besides losing a part of your self, the danger of this dynamic is that you also distance yourself from the very ties that keep your threatened identity alive. This may seem worth the price of inclusion, but in the long run alienating others who share your "different" identity can be costly to yourself and to others.

Complying with gender roles. By virtue of their unique historical, cultural, and social relationship to the dominant group in most social institutions, white women face particular pressures to submit to conformity pressures that members of other groups do not face in the same way. When white women look at the majority group, they see people who look like their husbands, brothers, and fathers.[22] They see familiar people who re-create familiar expectations for roles and relations. Thus when women challenge conventions or resist stereotyped expectations for gender roles, they not only threaten men's notion of what it means to be a "good man," but they may also throw into question their own socialized notions of what it means to be a "good woman." One senior executive at Western understood this well. She saw her success tied to her willingness to embrace a traditional "feminine" support role, even as she carried out her responsibilities as an executive:

> Part of being a woman here is playing the traditional role of women. I know that there are a lot of executives who will tell me things that they won't tell men simply because they know I'm not after their job.

She accepts that her access to power is partly due to her cultural proximity to those in power and her willing conformity to traditional gender roles and relations.[23] Aida Hurtado has referred to this process as a kind of "seduction" that leads to women's (particularly white women's) willing collusion in their own silence and subordination.[24]

In situations like these, women have a choice. Resisting these seductive forces may limit access to some degree, but it reinforces their commitment to changing a system that keeps in place these traditional gender roles and relations. Whatever the choice, however, it is helpful for women—or anyone—to build bridges with others who face similar circumstances and actively promote a dialogue that sheds light on these patterns so that they can make choices with a greater understanding of the consequences.

ALL THE PROCESSES mentioned so far represent mechanisms that take people down a path of compromise and ultimately co-optation. Often these processes are so subtle that people aren't aware that they have made choices or that their incremental decisions have long-term cumulative consequences. The slipperiness of these mechanisms and the subtlety with which they operate is why tempered radicals must be on the alert to resist them and keep alive their "different" selves.

Damage to Reputation

Tempered radicals who avoid the pulls of co-optation and who express their differences or take on an agenda for change jeopardize the material and professional rewards of conformity. Those who take on an agenda for change that challenges the status quo also risk becoming associated with a heated issue or gaining a reputation for being a troublemaker. Fear of damaging their reputations in these ways can be sufficient to keep some tempered radicals silent.[25]

Consistent association with a single issue brings the additional danger of being perceived as a one-issue person. The vice president of marketing at Link.com (a pseudonym), one of the most successful high-technology companies in Silicon Valley, experienced this fate. After many years on a core team of executives who built the business, the retiring CEO gave her a plaque at his retirement party. It read, "Natalie Kramer: Building Gender Awareness at Link.com." While she had in fact worked hard to promote equity in the company, she did not want this to be her primary legacy. Somehow, her work on gender equity overshadowed her contributions to the company's growth and her phenomenally successful marketing career at least in the eyes of some of her colleagues. That she was being seen as a "one-issue" person felt degrading; she feared that this reputation had damaged her credibility with some of her colleagues.[26]

Frustration and Burnout

Beyond the psychological tolls of ambivalence and the vigilance required to resist conformity pressures, the road of tempered radicalism can be paved with potholes of setback and frustration. This is partly because of the slow, incremental, and diffuse nature of the kinds of changes tempered radicals advance. They become frustrated when they can't see how or if their efforts add up, and they can become cynical about the futility of trying.

But tempered radicals persist despite receiving little recognition for their efforts and no guarantee that their efforts will result in desired outcomes. Joanne Martin summarized her own frustrations as a tempered radical:

> It is a struggle to swim against the tide, and those of us who do it often feel unjustly devalued and marginalized. Is this because our values are not those of the mainstream? . . . You never know. I say this not to discourage others, but to say that getting tired, or feeling

discouraged, is inevitable when the tide is running. Moments of ease—when the tide turns in your favor, or even just when it pauses between rise and ebb—are all too rare.[27]

Like other tempered radicals, the diffuse nature of Martin's accomplishments and the end products of her tireless efforts are difficult to track. For her, like others, it has been a road of integrity and satisfaction but also of frustration, setback, and bouts of burnout.

Sometimes feelings go beyond frustration and burnout. Some contexts are unbearably toxic. When our values or identities are so deeply misaligned with those dominant in a culture that there is no way to live a life that feels authentic, it may simply be a bad situation in which to remain. Giving up too quickly is a danger, but tempered radicals also must recognize when it is time to acknowledge that the right choice is to move on.

Factors That Shape the Climate for Tempered Radicalism

All the foregoing challenges (except moving on) may be an inevitable part of the tempered radical's swim against the tide. But the swim is easier and more gratifying in some contexts than in others. What conditions differentiate a friendly context—where you can fruitfully act on your values, identity, and beliefs—from a toxic one—where you're constantly trying to stay afloat?

Cultural and Subcultural Support

I had originally thought that Western and Atlas would differ in their tolerance for tempered radicalism. In fact, this was an important factor in my choice of these research sites. I reasoned that Western's traditional culture would be far less tolerant of differences and less open to acts that challenged existing practices than would be Atlas's informal, youthful, and innovative culture. Further, I thought that Shop.co's fragmented, chaotic, and progressive culture would welcome differences and support experimentation.

On the one hand, I was correct. Some norms were more flexible at Atlas. People could dress however they wanted and in some departments show up to work at noon. And consistent with Shop.co's progressive culture, people dressed informally and interacted more casually across hierarchical lines. In addition, people at Shop.co discussed important issues, such as the company's position on human rights in the world, that would not even have hit the screens in other companies.

On the other hand, I was wrong about the differences. It became very clear in my research that a culture's apparent informality or progressiveness does not determine the amount of day-to-day freedom people have to express and take action on their differences. What does appear to matter is how discrepant the dominant values are from someone's personal values, the extent to which dominant practices and assumptions construct a person as an outsider, and, most important, what the implicit consequences are of not conforming and fitting in.[28]

Like Western, Atlas and Shop.co enforced a set of dominant rules. Although the specific rules varied across companies, people in each company felt pressure to play by them and to fit in. Atlas workers reported that they felt pressure to behave in the confident, outspoken, and always available "Atlas way" to get ahead within the company. There was a good deal of consensus about what "the Atlas way" meant and who could and could not pull it off. It was particularly difficult, for example, for women of color to be successful in this cultural context. Even if they wanted to fit in, cultural expectations made it difficult for them to do so. In addition, even though there was relative flexibility around when professionals showed up for work, people were expected to put work first and to be available at all times. These expectations carry important implications for employees who have outside responsibilities; this was the tide against which John Ziwak had to swim. Similarly, even though Shop.co had relatively progressive values, specific practices, such as their incentive system, favored economic priorities, rewarded those who lived by them, and penalized those who wouldn't.

One additional measure of the pervasiveness of the prevailing culture is the prevalence of "subcultures" that reflect and support different values or identities.[29] While Joanie Mason's struggles at Shop.co were very real, the founder and a subculture of employees did in fact support her efforts. The mere existence of her job and the presence of allies and a supportive subculture no doubt eased her struggles, or at least gave her a degree of respect and legitimacy.

Subcultural support, whether in the context of a formal group in an organization or an informal collection of individuals, can sometimes make a person feel part of a group. As a member of a group, tempered radicals are less likely to feel alone, more likely to feel part of something larger than themselves, less likely to stand out as the lone "deviant" or troublemaker, and more likely to get something done. Ironically, individuals can become anonymous in the context of a larger group and at the same time feel personally affirmed through membership in the group. Thus the existence of identity-based or interest-based groups or identifiable subcultures provides comfort, affirmation, and safety, as well as legitimacy, for tempered radicals.

In addition to the forcefulness of the dominant culture and existence of subcultures, a few other structural and cultural factors appear to influence the climate for tempered radicals. These conditions vary from organization to organization and even from department to department. Let's look specifically at three that surfaced as relevant in my own and others' research.

Demographic Composition

The composition of the organization, specifically the proportion of traditional "insiders" to "outsiders," particularly within top management, shapes how receptive the culture is for tempered radicals. When tempered radicals can look around and see others who share their identities, values, and beliefs, or simply others who deviate from the majority in comparable ways, they are more likely to feel that they can claim and act on these identities. Robin Ely's research has shown, for example, that in organizations whose leadership is comprised of at least 15 percent women, junior-level professional women are more prone to self-identify as women, more apt to develop healthy relations with other women, and more likely to identify with the senior women in the organization.[30] In other words, the composition of the leadership group, not just the demographics of the immediate work group, shape women's experiences, identities, and relationships.

The relative proportion of majority to minority members also appears to influence how willing people are to act or speak up on behalf of their marginalized groups. Research by Susan Ashford and colleagues has shown, for example, that the relative proportion of women in senior positions influences women's willingness to speak up on behalf of gender issues. Women tend to think, "If I see more women at the top, it must be OK to identify as a woman, and thus my reputation should not suffer if I speak up as a woman or on behalf of women." On the other hand, when an organization has relatively few women at the top, it sends a signal that being a woman is incompatible with success; thus women are less likely to self-identify, speak as, or act on behalf of women.[31]

Other underrepresented groups in my sample highlighted the symbolic significance of demographics. A gay woman at Western argued that the recent promotion of an openly gay man to senior vice president did more good for gays than any benefit package they could have won. She believed that his achievement signaled official acceptance, which would in turn make it more acceptable for other gay people to be open and to express this part of themselves:

> Every time a gay person reaches a senior position, it is a statement that management is entrusting the company into the hands of "one of us." Being awarded with top positions is the ultimate sign, particularly if the person who was promoted lives by his own rules rather than conforms to traditions. They start to change what others perceive as possible.

The inclusion of traditionally excluded people into circles of power can send strong signals to others inside and outside the organization, particularly if the inclusion is not seen as a superficial gesture, but a genuine sign of acceptance and respect.[32]

Cultural Legitimacy of an Issue or Identity Group

Relative representation is not the only way an organization signals its openness to people who are "different" from the majority. Most Atlas employees thought that the company's formal support of identity-based employee groups demonstrates acceptance of all people, regardless of their identity. Some Latino employees said the existence of a Latino group makes them feel that it is legitimate to express this part of their identity and still be a valued Atlas employee. A few of the more cynical tempered radicals thought that management supported these groups to contain when and how employees can express their identities, rather than to express genuine acceptance of different groups of people. For most people, however, the existence of these groups seemed to have a positive impact on their feelings of acceptance.[33]

Similarly, the perceived legitimacy of an issue influences how "heated" and risky the issue seems.[34] When top management demonstrates interest in or support for an issue, the issue seems more legitimate and people get a sense that their reputations won't be damaged if they become associated with it.[35] I suspect that once the president and dean at MIT formally acknowledged and became collaborators on the gender equity problems at their university, people were much more willing to speak up. The administration's support generated resources, created a structure to deal with the issue, and focused attention on it. But more than that, the public acknowledgment gave the issue legitimacy within the school, making it safer and more credible for women throughout the university, and even previously silent people from other marginalized groups, to speak up about their own experiences or their observations of others'. Management provides this protection by making an issue a priority, framing it as an opportunity for learning, and creating a clear process or structure to deal with it.[36]

Although Western did not sanction identity-based employee groups, the CEO had made several public statements about the importance of diversity. For some people, his support of this issue made it legitimate to raise topics related to diversity. Whether this kind of senior-level support for an issue actually creates a more nurturing environment for tempered radicals who care about that issue depends in large part on how consistently the rhetoric matches day-to-day reality. When diversity programs espouse values and expectations that contradict existing work practices and cultural norms, people become frustrated. For example, Peter Grant felt supported by the CEO's endorsement of diversity, but the support was somewhat undermined by the lack of sensitivity Peter experienced in his day-to-day work life. Joanie Mason experienced a comparable mismatch between rhetoric and reality at Shop.co. Thus, although macro-level support from the top of an organization is important, it goes only so far if it just pays lip service to an issue and isn't carried through into people's daily interactions and experiences.

These three conditions—cultural and subcultural support, demographic composition, and cultural legitimacy—as well as some others

---

Macro Conditions That Shape the Environment for Tempered Radicals

The following questions should help decipher how supportive a climate is in general for a tempered radical.

1. Cultural and subcultural support
   - How different are your values and beliefs from those at play and enforced in the dominant culture?
   - Are there subcultures that support your deviant values and beliefs?
   - What are the costs of not conforming to the dominant culture?

2. Demographic composition
   - What is the relative proportion of people like you throughout the organization?
   - What is the relative proportion of people like you in your immediate work group?
   - What is the relative proportion of people like you in leadership roles?

3. Cultural legitimacy of relevant issues and concerns
   - How legitimate are the issues and concerns you care about?
   - Does rhetorical support of the issue match day-to-day practice?
   - How safe is it to talk about and take up this issue within the organization?

---

play an important part in shaping how welcoming an environment is for tempered radicals.[37] Unfortunately, any one individual has very little impact on influencing these conditions. But they can be seen as criteria for screening a work environment or for evaluating the source of frustration. All my research clearly indicated, however, that the climate of tempered radicals' *local* work groups and their particular relationships within them overwhelms the importance of these general conditions.

Local Relationships

Just as everyday interactions can be the source of power plays and identity threats, so too can they be the wellspring of validation and affirmation. The tempered radicals I interviewed at both Western and Atlas consistently reported that more than any other factor, their relationship with their immediate supervisors either made it safe for them to speak their minds and be themselves or not.[38]

Recall the encounter in which Tom Novak's long-term mentor advised him to bring a female date to a high-profile social function. As painful and devaluing as this advice was, it was more than counterbalanced by the encouragement Tom received from his immediate boss to bring his partner to the function. Her support not only helped him decide to bring his partner but reaffirmed his ability to be himself at work. Tom told me,

> It's the simple stuff that really makes a difference. Her invitation [to come with my partner] was different from all the other invitations I've ever received. It was a 'come into my life' kind of invitation. It meant to me that I was OK, that as a gay man I was good enough to sit at the company table and that meant I could be myself and still be a real part of this organization. I think that when there is such visible acceptance, minds get changed somehow.

Several months after the event, Tom's eyes still filled with tears as he recalled how much this gesture meant. It is this kind of affirmation— or the lack of it—that shapes how valued people feel, how much of themselves they can bring to work, and how safe they feel to deviate from cultural patterns. It turns out that many of the actions, like that of Tom's boss, that make for supportive relationships simply reflect someone's effort to value people—all people.

One of Martha Wiley's employees spoke of the compassion Martha brings to her work group and the small ways she acknowledges people's value in the company: "In many ways she is just a great manager of people. Probably because she herself has always done things differently, she tries to bring out the uniqueness and best in each person. She doesn't push for one right way." Another said of his boss: "She doesn't get on a soapbox. She just talks to you as one real human being to another." He too felt validated by the simple signs of respect from his supervisor. The practice of bringing out the best in each person and treating people with respect is no more than good management. It also happens to make people more comfortable being who they are and saying what they think is true—a particularly healthy environment for tempered radicals.

In my research, tempered radicals also felt that their struggles were less difficult when their managers demonstrated a high tolerance for experimentation and deviation, or when they felt the differences they brought to a group were treated as an asset to a group's effectiveness.[39] A senior manager in human resources at Western was charged with the job of starting an employee referral reward program. She proposed using radical language and ideas to go "beyond people's comfort zones because otherwise we would just get the same results we had always been getting." She knew that some people would object to her radical ideas and that her initial proposal would be edited and diluted. But she felt safe pushing the limits because her supervisor believed in experimentation and had always encouraged her to do things differently when she wanted to, even if it led to some mistakes or disagreements.

Similarly, some people explained that what made the biggest difference in their ability to be themselves and speak their mind freely was how deeply they trusted their supervisor to give them the benefit of the doubt. A tempered radical at Atlas claimed that this made all the difference in the world to who she could be at work:

> I feel safe with Chris [her boss] because I've always felt I could say anything to her and she wouldn't misconstrue it. It makes a huge difference for me to know that she will give me the benefit of the doubt. She genuinely wants me to succeed and believes completely that I will. I believe she will always be honest with me, so I'm honest with her and take risks with her as my boss. With someone else I would have to be much more careful about what I say.

Another factor that surfaced as relevant, particularly in Martha Wiley's work group, was people's sense of independence. Just as independence gives her the confidence to speak up and stand firm on her beliefs, Martha encourages her employees to develop a sense of independence for themselves. As a result, they develop their own sense of power and confidence to express their values and challenge both Martha and the organization.

Other tempered radicals emphasized the importance of having a champion—someone who cares about their professional development and will interpret their actions for others in a positive light. This champion might be an immediate boss or a close peer. A Latino manager who reports directly to Tom Novak explained,

> When I have frank discussions with Tom about a plan for my own development, I feel that there is a conscious plan to keep me and groom me. When he is honest about my weaknesses and helps me come up with a plan to develop in these areas, it says "we value and care about you.

An outspoken assistant counsel at Atlas derived safety from knowing that her boss would go out on a limb to defend her, even when he disagrees with her. She felt that their disagreements—and there were many—had generated learning and growth for both of them and she trusted her boss to defend her, despite these differences.

Sheila Johnson experienced the opposite—a relationship plagued with suspicion—which made life extraordinarily difficult for her. She felt that her previous boss scrutinized her every move and that he seemed eager to prove that she was not up to the job. Sheila recalled a time when she circulated a memo that she had spent hours writing. Rather than engage her in a discussion of the memo's substance, her boss focused on the one typo in the three-page document. Sheila viewed this encounter as a blatant reminder that she was not safe, that her competence would always be suspect, and that she would not be given the benefit of the doubt no matter what her performance might demonstrate: "My glass was always seen as half empty, no matter what."

In this relationship, Sheila felt anything but an invitation to deviate from the rules or voice her own views. She frequently spoke up anyway because she had reached a point in her life where her commitment to do so was more powerful than her fear. But rarely did she feel safe, and she knew that her boss would not appreciate or commend her for raising a difficult issue, challenging an offensive comment, or simply expressing views that differed from the majority. This relationship made her life as a tempered radical extremely difficult.

In a similar way, a gay woman at Western was undermined, not by her boss but by her coworkers. After going out on a limb by speaking up to senior management on behalf of gay employees, she felt betrayed when the other gay employees distanced themselves from her and refused to support her actions. Clearly, such a reaction would make her think twice before going out on a limb again. Her experience attests to the importance of having strong and supportive relations not just with immediate supervisors but also with dependable allies who can provide support along the way.

Conclusion

Life is not always easy for tempered radicals. By virtue of who they are and what they care about, their path involves what Joanne Martin refers to as a "swim against the tide."[40] The effort to battle the tide simply to avoid being swept away with it can be enormous, and making progress in opposition to it is that much more difficult. But as we've seen, the level of difficulty depends partly on the strength of the prevailing culture and whether we have any help moving against it.

While there can be little doubt that organizations and units within organizations differ in how culturally nurturing or hostile they are to tempered radicals, it is also important to pay attention to the more mundane features of organizational life that may matter the most. Individual managers, like individual tempered radicals, can make a huge difference in whether the context feels safe or risky, accepting or hostile, and adaptable or entrenched. Supportive, nurturing relationships with supervisors and peers can be the organizational equivalent of life vests for tempered radicals battling a strong tide.

It should not be surprising that the people who provide these vests to others—the best managers of tempered radicals—are often themselves tempered radicals. Indeed, the work of consciously fostering the efforts of other tempered radicals may be one of the most essential accomplishments of a tempered radical. And, if you believe that the kinds of change initiated by tempered radicals is critical to organizational learning and adaptation, then you can view such support as an essential component of leadership. It is to this topic of tempered radicals as "everyday leaders" that we now turn.

Tempered Radicals as Everyday Leaders

Tempered Radicals have not been killed off. They are irritants to their organizations in the way that pearls are irritants to oysters. There is something about these individuals that their organizations want to keep and nurture—even if the relationship is mutually painful.

— *Keith Hammonds,* Fast Company

WHEN I ASKED people at Western who they thought had made a real difference for the company, people of color uniformly pointed to Peter Grant. They described him as an inspiration, a giving coach and mentor (to themselves or others they knew), and a catalyst of a quiet and slow cultural transformation. It was not only people of color who perceived Peter this way, however. Many of his white colleagues marveled at all he had accomplished and everyone he had inspired over the course of his career. One middle manager described how Peter had kept him going when he was ready to throw in the towel, showing him how his struggle to get ahead was not just his own. "He was tough on me. He made me realize how this was not just about me and not just for me. He didn't let up on me, but it was the most caring exchange I can ever remember having at work." Another executive told how Peter had helped her land a plum job in another area of the bank, which turned out to be a platform for a brilliant career. Over the years, she tried to follow his lead, actively recruiting and mentoring other minorities. People who had never even met Peter could tell stories of his will and persistence and his never-ending efforts to create a more inclusive and humane workplace. They were inspired by Peter's story, if not directly by the man himself.

Despite this legacy, I doubt that Peter Grant will be written into Western's history books as one of the company's more influential "leaders." He never formally led the company or held one of the few top positions. He never visibly took the helm of a dramatic transformation or organization-threatening crisis. Yet people throughout the organization viewed him as one of the most important people in their professional lives. They were mentored by him, inspired by him, and nurtured by him. This, I would argue, is a critical and drastically underacknowledged sort of leadership in organizations and society.

Like Peter, other tempered radicals I've described act as "everyday leaders" who make a difference in the course of their daily actions and interactions. They often do not flash brightly on the organizational radar, because by design their actions are rarely dramatic. Some never rise higher than middle management, and some stay firmly in the rank and file. They lead not as white knights steering grand revolutions but as improvisers with big ideals who seize the moment.

Everyday leaders do not quench the thirst for quick fixes, "killer apps," or grand transformations so prevalent in this day of overnight heroes and demons. Everyday leaders are quiet catalysts who push back against prevailing norms, create learning, and lay the groundwork for slow but ongoing organizational and social change.

If we look, we can find traces of this humble form of leadership in our neighborhoods and local schools. We can see everyday leaders in the trenches of communities working to transform whole nations— look to South Africa, Northern Ireland, or Bosnia for people who act everyday in big and small ways to create more just and humane societies. As I mentioned earlier in the context of the civil rights movement, quiet, persistent individuals worked tirelessly behind the scenes to advance their agenda and to lay the foundation for the more dramatic acts that mark the history of the movement.

Look closely at the modern history of Poland, which was transformed into a democratic state largely through the efforts of everyday leaders. The democratic opposition originated in the Worker's Defense Committee (the KOR), which began as a few people meeting in coffee shops to talk about their visions of a democratic state.[1] When they met, these individuals acted *as if* they were free and could speak freely. They were "positive deviants" who created constructive alternatives by *acting* differently.[2] Their small actions proved that things could be different and pushed the boundaries of liberty just slightly outward. Over years these actions gained momentum, spread, and laid a platform for a profound societal transformation.

The point is that hundreds of leaders played important if not crucial roles in this movement. Sometimes history takes notice and we learn the names of a few of the more visible leaders, like Adam Michnik or Lech Walesa. We learn the names of Rosa Parks, Martin Luther King, and a handful of other brave individuals who have been written into history for their roles in the civil rights movement. But left out of these accounts are the names of countless people who modeled alternative ways of doing things, chipped away at existing institutions, inspired others to act, and played crucial roles in generating the momentum of social change.

The same is true of the tempered radicals I have profiled. They don't create legacies as heroic leaders. More often than not it is difficult to attribute significant changes to a particular individual's actions. Yet the footprints of tempered radicals are all around us and their leadership takes many different forms.

Perhaps the most important way tempered radicals "lead" is by creating supportive local contexts and nurturing relationships with their peers and employees. We saw in the previous chapter how tempered radicals were themselves some of the best managers of other tempered radicals. Isabel Nuñez was seen as a manager who valued, trusted, and cared deeply about her employees. She sought to understand her employees and to learn from their disagreements. In return, her employees felt they could express their differences and be honest and open with her and with each other. Martha Wiley's employees looked to her as one of the best managers of people because she pushed them to be their best, created opportunities for them to shine, and championed their successes. She also encouraged them to develop a sense of independence, to think independently, and to challenge prevailing practices. Beyond this, Martha created a local context that was adaptable, capable of learning from her employees' initiatives. People in her group experimented with different work arrangements, and these experiments influenced how others in the group thought about their own work and lives, which encouraged more experimentation. The capacity to build a local context supportive of tempered radicals' actions and capable of adapting and learning from them is itself an important aspect of leadership.[3]

By creating supportive local context and nurturing relationships, tempered radicals also lead by exercising influence toward achieving desired ends. Not only did Peter directly or indirectly affect the hiring of more than 3,500 minority candidates at Western (according to his own "conservative" estimate), but he sustained many of these individuals and their own efforts to make a difference by his unending support, the network he helped maintain, and his quiet efforts to champion their successes and push back on obstacles that were in their way. Thus a network of hundreds, if not thousands, of minority employees worked in their own ways to make their local environments more inclusive and open.

While influencing other tempered radicals and creating supportive contexts for learning from them may be the most obvious way in which tempered radicals inspire change, they also exercise leadership and effect change in other important ways. Sometimes they inspire change simply by behaving differently, and their small deviant actions challenge norms and set an example that others emulate.[4] Recall Alan Levy, who took days off for the Jewish holidays. His deviation from the norm encouraged more people to observe their own traditions and attend to their own priorities. Workers in his department stopped challenging coworkers who observed their cultural and religious traditions. Some of these coworkers moved into other departments and enacted these same norms. While it may be impossible to trace the company's adoption of its policy of providing a number of "personal days" off to Alan Levy's initial deviant behavior, his coworkers had little doubt that Alan's action, and others like it, spread and played a part in influencing policy. Under certain conditions, small positive deviations amplify and change the context such that these once deviant behaviors become the new norm. As sources of deviation, tempered radicals can be crucial catalysts of constructive adaptation in a system.[5]

Other tempered radicals lead change more deliberately by initiating small wins that result in new relationships, understandings, and patterns of behavior. When Joanie Mason changed her reporting structure, the relationship between fair-trade products and "regular" products shifted, which resulted in a different way to work together and integrate the two product lines. Martha Wiley experimented with flexible work arrangements and strategically framed these accommodations as a significant deviation from normal practice. She used these small wins as an occasion to create learning in the system.

Scholars of leadership have argued that the capacity to push people to confront the conflicts and adaptive challenges facing a system is one of the most crucial and difficult aspects of real leadership.[6] If so, then tempered radicals represent an important population of leaders. When John Ziwak sat his team down to talk about institutional assumptions and practices regarding personal time, he pointed to how these assumptions did not meet the current needs of a growing proportion of the workforce. In his own small ways, John pushed the system to adapt to these needs.

When tempered radicals push people to question their understandings and deeply ingrained work practices in this way, they force them to confront difficult adaptive challenges. These confrontations can occur through explicit conversations or through small but meaningful prods to the system—prods that reveal assumptions and biases, contradictions between rhetoric and reality, and unintended consequences of existing practices. When Joanie worked with Shop.co purchasers to help them deal with the cost premiums of buying materials from developing communities, she opened the possibility of revising other purchasing and accounting practices. When they did so, Shop.co discovered that it inadvertently discouraged socially desirable practices that were more costly in the short run but more desirable over the long term. At another European manufacturing company, a tempered radical intervened in a similar way and raised questions about how raw material costs were reported. It prompted company accountants to spread costs over a longer and more appropriate time horizon and align economic incentives with the organization's environmental sustainability programs. This action triggered a more aggressive sustainability program in the manufacturing department as well as in other areas of the company.

We have seen examples of these kinds of meaningful prods throughout the book in mundane self-expressions, opportunistic and strategic responses to everyday encounters, and small wins. These acts that challenge a system to adapt may not be dramatic or even visible, but they may be the most consequential things tempered radicals do.

We have also seen tempered radicals lead and effect change more publicly and aggressively. Through different paths, David Welton, Jennifer Jackson, Tom Novak, and Professor Nancy Hopkins created sufficient energy, hope, and common purpose to bring together independent individuals and mobilize them as a collective force. Community organizers and activists have long defined leadership as the capacity to mobilize collective action: in Saul Alinsky's words, "to build confidence and hope . . . to win limited victories, each of which will build confidence and the feeling that 'if we can do so much with what we have now, just think what we will be able to do when we get big and strong.'"[7]

Last, but certainly not least, tempered radicals lead through inspiration. They inspire change and they inspire other people, not through daring acts of courage, but through their ability to keep going, to tough it out, and to rise above their own frustration, humiliation, and anger to act on behalf of their larger ideals. This is courage of a different sort, and it is truly inspirational.

Peter Grant and Sheila Johnson, for example, persisted through endless frustrations and setbacks. What kept them both going through the countless insults and frustrations was their understanding of what they were up against, their appreciation for the length of time it takes to make real change in a system, and, most important, their courage and commitment to hang in for their larger ideals. Both of them believed that their best strategy was to keep succeeding and, in whatever way they could, to keep chipping away slowly and steadily to transform the very system in which they work to succeed. As we've seen in particular with Peter, the legacy of his persistence, courage, and conviction has inspired dozens if not hundreds of others to keep going and to follow in his lead.

In a similar way, Cathy Jones, stopped by police for being the "wrong" color and driving a sports car, chose to contain her emotions and direct her energy toward working for her bigger ideal of alleviating racism. If Cathy had succumbed to her impulse to seek revenge, she would have been acting as victim—either as an object of police racism or as an object of her own fury and sense of powerlessness. In either case, she would have been driven by some other force besides her own ideals and choices. Cathy's *refusal* to give in to her own anger required enormous courage and discipline, and a *deliberate* choice to stay anchored to her ideals and work as part of the solution, however incomplete it may be. Other people, including the police, took inspiration from Cathy's ability to turn this humiliating situation into an opportunity to become an agent of positive change. She surprised even herself; she did not realize she had within her this courage and commitment.

Tempered radicals lead change and they lead people. They lead by creating relationships and local environments that support other tempered radicals, by acting as agents of "positive deviation," by instigating small wins and creating learning, by pushing people and systems to confront their latent conflicts and adaptive challenges, by organizing other people to act together toward shared goals, and by inspiring change and people.

TEMPERED RADICALS reflect important aspects of leadership that are absent in the more traditional portraits. It is leadership that tends to be less visible, less coordinated, and less vested with formal authority; it is also more local, more diffuse, more opportunistic, and more humble than the activity attributed to the modern-day hero. This version of leadership depends *not* on charismatic flair, instant success, or inspirational visions, but on qualities such as *patience, self-knowledge, humility, flexibility, idealism, vigilance,* and *commitment.* And, although tempered radicals often act as individual agents of change, they are not lone heroes. Whether their objective is simply to stay true to their values and identities or to affect broad institutional change, everyday leaders are quick to acknowledge that they *cannot do it alone.*

Conclusion: How and Why Tempered Radicals Keep Going

Throughout this book, we've explored the many faces of tempered radicals. We've seen the tensions they experience and the range of strategies they use to fulfill their commitments and achieve their goals. We've also looked at the challenges they face and the sometimes paradoxical ways they address them.

Possibly the most fundamental thing to remember about successful tempered radicals is that they know *who they are and what is important* to their sense of self. They realize that they have multiple selves, some aspects more enduring and "core" than others, and they are clear about the ways these core values or identities are at odds with the dominant culture. Though tempered radicals stay anchored to their core commitments, they must also remain flexible about how and when to fulfill them.

Tempered radicals *favor action*. Some people act with modest and self-directed objectives; others act with more bold and outwardly focused ambitions; and most move back and forth along a spectrum between these extremes, choosing their actions based on circumstance, interests, risks, and even energy level. Regardless of how quiet or bold their actions, tempered radicals sustain their "selves" and avoid conforming completely by acting.[8] Even as they favor action, however, tempered radicals must also be notably patient, willing to wait for opportunities and outcomes.

Along with a proclivity toward doing something comes a *perspective of choice* and an awareness of circumstances that present choices: choices, for example, about when to speak up, when to go along, when to bring up an issue, when to let it slide, how to understand ourselves, and how to interpret others and the world around us. Above all, tempered radicals reserve the choice to be an agent rather than a victim of their circumstances, and with this stance comes a tremendous sense of freedom and power. I go back to Cathy, who chose not to remain victimized by the racial injustice that surrounded her or be paralyzed by her own justifiable rage; instead, she chose to work toward a solution of the much larger problem of racism. Acting as an agent with the power to make choices can be critical to preventing cynicism, burnout, and co-optation.

Tempered radicals see *choices in everyday actions and interactions*, in the mundane details of organizational life. They recognize how dominant interests surface in large institutional policies, and they also appreciate how these larger forces manifest and create choice points within local interactions and the mundane minutiae of organizational life. A former student recalled how she chipped away in all sorts of opportunistic ways at a culture that inadvertently kept women from leadership positions at her professional services firm. For example, as part of her role in human resources, she had to write case studies for leadership training. She decided to populate the case studies with women in leadership roles. That prod may seem trivial, but it forced people to talk and think differently, and these gradual changes reflected and catalyzed a cultural shift. Details are the raw materials of culture, and we have seen repeatedly how small prods and adaptations can slowly but steadily add up to shifts in cultural norms.[9]

To make a difference by working the details, tempered radicals have to be on their toes—poised to *recognize and act on opportunities* as they present themselves. This opportunistic stance requires the skills of improvisation—paying attention to, building on, and creating small deviations in what is happening around you.[10] When Joanie Mason switched her reporting structure, she took advantage of the reorganization that was already occurring to justify her own move. My former student had to write case studies about leadership for training sessions; why not sprinkle them with *she's*? Attending to these sorts of everyday details enables us to spot opportunities, but it also alerts us to risks and constraints. Being attentive to the details and their consequences can also be a powerful antidote to co-optation.

Tempered radicals don't remain stuck in the details, though. Tempered radicals create connections between the personal and political and between the local and global. When they create connections between small events and their systemic implications by using language and stories to *frame their larger meaning*, they *push others to learn* from their efforts. Just as important, they affirm to themselves that their efforts do make a difference. By naming the broader significance, they remind themselves and others that small acts count toward big ideals.

Finally, tempered radicals are individual actors, yet they *depend on connections to others*, both people who share their identities and change agendas and those who don't. For reasons we've discussed throughout, these relationships are essential to keep tempered radicals going, to help them affirm their sense of self, to aid them in their efforts to broaden their impact, and to forge collectives when necessary to drive larger institutional change. Perhaps most important, relationships prevent isolation and loneliness—a fate that all too often saps the energy and effectiveness of many tempered radicals.

This is what effective tempered radicals do. They know "themselves," favor action, recognize that they have choices (including the choice not to act), pay attention to details, look for opportunities, create learning by framing local events in terms of their broader significance, and forge connections with other people.

In addition, successful tempered radicals *choose their workplaces wisely* and pick battles within contexts in which there is some chance of accomplishing something. Sometimes, no matter how clever or careful one may be, the opposing forces are too strong to battle. It is important to know when to stop fighting and instead look elsewhere for a less toxic and more welcoming setting. And I can't emphasize enough how important it is to build strong relationships at work, particularly with immediate supervisors and peers. Almost every tempered radical in my research spoke to the importance of a supportive boss and a broader network of peers and colleagues from whom they gain (and to whom they give) support.

Even with favorable conditions, I am not suggesting that it is easy to be a tempered radical—but neither is it impossible. The people portrayed here are ordinary people. All have advanced steadily in their careers while straddling the competing pulls that can often be difficult to sustain. It is a road that requires a good deal of commitment, patience, and persistence to avoid wandering away from ideals when lured by something easier. There is no question that this kind of vigilance can be exhausting.

Why then is it worth it? What keeps people on this road, pushing for change, despite the constant tension and inevitable setbacks?

As I said at the beginning of the book, for many, being a tempered radical simply beats the alternatives. Some people are different and they just can't bring themselves to conform, don't want to be ardent radicals, and won't surrender to victimization.

But that is an oversimplification. Tempered radicals persist because they feel it is the only choice that allows them to be true to themselves. It's about being able to get out of bed in the morning and feel good about who they are. For these people, integrity and doing "the right thing" cannot be pushed aside. That's how Sheila Johnson feels. After a period of trying to conform, she no longer can turn her back on the blatant injustices that she witnesses. She will not sell out. It is that simple.

For some, the choice isn't that clear. Some people know they would have an easier time and enjoy an accelerated career if they assimilated more completely. But they gain satisfaction from the knowledge that they are living by their ideals and are working to make a difference for others. To live by your ideals—your values, identities, beliefs, principles—is to gain a deep satisfaction that you have lived a life of integrity. While this may sound grandiose, we have seen how staying grounded in this notion can be the daily motivation necessary to avoid selling out.

People who are inclined toward a more radical voice and may have more naturally worked as activists outside traditional institutions sometimes choose a tempered course because they value the platform that comes with operating within a mainstream organization. Sharon Sutton is an African American professor of architecture who holds radical beliefs about the practice and purpose of architecture (e.g., physical space should be designed with the primary purpose of liberating people), and she wants to advance social justice within her profession. She has chosen to work at a major university and has made many compromises to keep her job. She has done so consciously because she believes the university gives her a stage from which she has far more power and reach to advance her social change agenda.

Others keep going because they believe that unless someone throws a pebble into the river most people won't even be aware of how powerful the current is. They don't believe their efforts will change the course of the river; they simply hope to raise questions that make others more aware of what they are doing and more conscious of the implications of their own actions. In the words of one:

> [My efforts] mattered to those who argued against me, because by providing a clearly articulated alternative I (and other tempered radicals like me, of all persuasions) force others to be clearer about what they are doing and why they are doing it. In the end, maybe they will become a bit more open and inclusive.[11]

I have observed tempered radicals for fifteen years. Few of them would readily embrace the titles of "radical" or even "leader," and few would lay claim to grand achievements. Some look back over their years of efforts with disappointment at how little they seem to have moved their organizations. Yet they keep trying.

Against the prevailing imagery of the lone leader who steers dramatic change, the impact of tempered radicals' efforts will undoubtedly appear insignificant. I hope that I have shown that the problem is the yardstick of heroism against which they are measured (and measure themselves), not the significance of their efforts.

Throughout the book, I have demonstrated that the efforts of these everyday leaders *do* make a difference, no matter how far or how little they have moved their agendas, and no matter how long it takes for their efforts to accumulate into meaningful change. In all sorts of ways, their efforts matter to themselves, to other people, and to the organizations in which they work.

Tempered radicals inspire change. Yet their leadership resides equally in their capacity to inspire people. They inspire by having courage to tell the truth even when it's difficult to do so, and by having the conviction to stay engaged in tough conversations. They inspire by demonstrating the commitment to stay focused on their larger ideals even when they suffer consequences or get little recognition for doing so. Their leadership does not rely on inspiring through periodic heroism and headlines. Their leadership inspires—and matters—in big and small ways every day.

Appendix A:
Research Design and Methods

For a description of my general research design, including the logic behind my choices for primary research sites and a description of the cultures of these three organizations, see the preface.

Research Sample

My research samples differed at my three primary sites—Western Financial, Atlas Tech, and Shop.co—depending in part on the way I gained access into each organization. At Western, my primary contact was the Executive Vice President of Human Resources. Through her, I arranged to interview senior-level employees who had "identities of difference" as well as those who were self-described change agents and "progressives" in this conservative organization. These criteria were intentionally vague to keep the net broad. She arranged for the first wave of interviews with officers (vice presidents, senior vice presidents, and executive vice presidents) who met these criteria. Some of these officers held positions as regional directors or branch managers as well. I expanded the original sample by asking each individual to recommend others at Western, using the same criteria. This expanded sample included managers and assistant vice presidents as well. Overall, the sample included all but one of the most senior-level white women and women of color (except a few of the Asian American women vice presidents), most of the senior black and Latino men, five Asian and Asian American men, and all the openly gay men and lesbians. I interviewed six white straight male employees who identified themselves as internal change agents or "progressives." The sample also included some peers and direct reports of these individuals. All told, the sample included fifty-eight people at Western. I interviewed some of these people several times. (See table A-1.)

At Atlas, I developed access through the Director of Multiculturalism. Here, I asked to interview identifiable change agents at all levels of management. He gave me an initial list of twenty-two change agents at different levels. After each interview, I asked informants for a referral based on the same criteria, which led to an additional twenty-two informants. In total, these forty-four individuals included men and women mostly in middle management, with a few at upper levels and a few at entry levels of management. Some of these people had come up through technical ranks; others had risen through marketing, business development, and human resources. The people I interviewed at Atlas were identified by my initial contact or by their peers as people who had made a difference in the organization, particularly with respect to the organization's inclusiveness and diversity. When possible, I tried to interview colleagues and subordinates of individuals in my original sample. The forty-four individuals also included the heads of most of the employee groups, including the gay and lesbian employee group, the founder of the women's executive forum, and the heads of the black, Latino, and Asian American employee groups. I interviewed other members of these groups and several white men who had been advocates in the organization for more inclusive norms and recruiting practices.

At Shop.co I gained access through an entirely different process. My research there took place after the initial wave of my interviews at Western and Atlas, but I had initially designed it for an entirely different research project sponsored by the Ford Foundation. The results from these interviews turned out to be highly relevant to my concerns in this project as well. Located in rural England, Shop.co is known for its progressive business practices, but it is nonetheless a publicly traded corporation. As a result, the organization suffers several "disconnects" between its espoused values and its day-to-day practices. Many powerful people in this company, including the founder/CEO, are committed to aligning practices with ideals, including aligning day-to-day practices and policies with the ideal of gender equity. The CEO/founder brought me in to identify the cultural factors and work practices that create systemic obstacles and to develop methods of change to eradicate them. Several colleagues joined the research team for this action research project.[1] Action research entails a process of iterating between inquiry and intervention. In this case, we actively intervened in processes that appeared to have a differential impact on men and women, and we analyzed which interventions took hold.

Over the three years, we worked in multiple departments at every level of this global corporation, from the board of directors to the shop floor. We focused primarily on middle management, however. We interviewed eighty people, many of them multiple times. All but a few were white, and most were European. The criterion we used to choose our research subjects was simply whether they were directly or indirectly implicated in a cultural dynamic we were trying to understand or involved in a change we were trying to implement. Over the course of the study, other members of my research team and I conducted extensive observation to supplement people's verbal accounts.

In addition to the informants in these three organizations, I also interviewed eight people who had identified themselves as organizational change agents. These individuals held very specific change agendas related to social responsibility in for-profit companies. They believe that business—as perhaps the preeminent social institution of our time—should take more responsibility for its role in society. For these individuals, this belief fueled change agendas related to human rights, environmental sustainability, "fair trade"/supply practice, and social auditing. Some of these individuals were interested in bringing out the "human spirit and creativity" of the workforce, believing that organizations have been needlessly oppressive to the human spirit. Six of these people were students or former students in a master's of social responsibility program at the University of Bath. This is a part-time degree program for working adults committed to these ideals.

Over the past ten years, I have also built the concepts and strategies of tempered radicalism into my teaching, exposing these ideas in MBA classes at the University of Michigan and Stanford University, academic seminars, and senior executive programs. I have worked with these ideas in workshops with male and female professionals from all over the world. When appropriate, I have archived records of these discussions, student papers, and the hundreds of e-mails I have received from people who read the original article.

I also continued to interview people when opportunities presented themselves. People referred me to friends and colleagues, who in turn referred me to others. This "snowball" portion of my sample included people from a wide range of occupations as described in the preface. The informants from the "opportunistic" portion of my sample, including the eight change agents who advance agendas related to social responsibility, totaled an additional fifty-six women and men from four countries, a variety of ethnic groups and races, ages, sexual orientations, ideologies, religions, and levels of seniority in their fields.

Methods and Analysis

All interviews at Western and Atlas and some at Shop.co were tape recorded and professionally transcribed. For most interviews at Shop.co, one researcher conducted the interview and another took notes during the interview. Interviews with other informants that could not be taped were recorded by hand as close to verbatim as possible. After each interview and following each day of observation, I wrote up extensive interview debriefs and field notes. In these records I tried to capture nonverbal cues, recorded observations about the surroundings, noted inconsistencies in what the informants said or between what they said and how they behaved, and so on. These notes proved to be among the most useful sources of data.

At Western and Atlas, I followed a semistructured interview protocol that varied somewhat depending on the particular informant. For example, for direct reports of "tempered radicals," I emphasized their impressions of their bosses and peers and asked questions about their own experiences and willingness to speak out, and how their supervisors entered into these experiences. For many of the interviews at Shop.co, I was interested in uncovering practices that created the gap between rhetoric and reality, particularly (but not strictly) as it applied to gender equity. Among the self-identified tempered radicals and the opportunistic portion of my sample, I emphasized their experiences as change agents and their perception of where their efforts fell short and where and how they felt they made a difference. These interviews were less structured to leave room for stories about the informants' differences and the challenges they faced as they tried to advance changes. Appendix B shows some sample interview protocols.

To analyze the interview data, I used a method of coding familiar to most ethnographers. This method involved a first pass through the data to develop macro-level categories. I then repeated the analysis with a more fine-grained coding scheme, which resulted in additional categories. These data were then coded into a software program called "Ethnograph." My inferences were based on these analyses and the analyses of data from additional field notes.

Once I had a conceptual framework based on these analyses (and an outline for the book), I went through the data once more to determine which individuals would most effectively illustrate core concepts. I chose protagonists based on a wish to locate "best illustrations" as well as a desire to balance the sample in terms of demographic diversity and the kinds of changes the informants seek to advance. I needed to rely on other informants as further illustrations because the primary protagonists could not alone illustrate all core concepts. These secondary characters are interspersed throughout.

Representation	Numbers	Executive VPs	Senior VPs	VPs	Assistant VPs	Managers
Table A-1: Sample Population at Western						
White straight women*	14	4	5	3		2
White lesbians	6		1	3		2
White men	6	1	1	2		2
Asian American women	5		1	3		1
Black men	5	2	2	1		
Asian American men	5		2	2		1
Latina women	4			4		
Black women	4		1	1	2	
Latino men	4		1	1		2
White gay men	3			1		2
Pacific Islander woman	1		1			
Asian American gay man	1					1

*All others present themselves as heterosexual unless noted.

Table A-2: Sample Population at Atlas

Representation	Numbers	Senior VPs	VPs	Directors	Managers	Individual Contributors
White straight women*	11	1		3	3	4
Asian American women	5			1	1	3
White lesbians	4			1	2	1
White gay men	4			2		2
White men	4		1	2	1	
Latina women	3			1	1	1
Black women	3			1	1	1
Asian American men	3		1		1	1
Asian American gay men	3		1		1	1
Black men	2				2	
Latino men	2			1	1	

*All others present themselves as heterosexual unless noted.

Table A-3: Individuals in Opportunistic Sample*

Occupation	Number	Representation
Businesspeople	11	5 white women, 3 white men, 2 Latino men, 1 Asian woman
Professors	9	4 white women, 2 black women, 2 white men, 1 Latina woman
Lawyers	4	2 white women, 2 white men
Social workers	4	3 white women, 1 Latina woman
University administrators	4	2 white women, 2 Latina women
Nurses	3	2 white women, 1 white man
Physicians	2	2 white women
Journalists	2	1 white woman, 1 white man
Public officials	2	1 black man, 1 white woman
Resident (M.D.)	1	1 white man
Architect	1	1 black woman
Engineer	1	1 white man
Schoolteacher	1	1 white woman
Public health administrator	1	1 white woman
Publisher	1	1 white woman
Admiral, U.S. Navy	1	1 white woman

*This does not include the six students from the master's program in social responsibility and two additional self-appointed change agents.

Appendix B:
Sample Interview Protocol

Protocol Used at Western and Atlas

A. Background information

1. Name
3. Age
4. Title
5. Years in organization
6. Years in job
7. Professional and educational background
8. Professional, community, civic memberships/affiliations

B. Identity

1. I'm interested in how individuals who are somehow different from those in the majority move ahead and keep their sense of self. Let me ask you to think about yourself in this organization. What cultural identities come to mind? That is, list five ways you would describe yourself in terms of identities.
   - How important is each to you?
   - Can you give me an example of a time at work when being X was highly salient to you?
2. I'd like you to think about your professional identity. How important is your success here to you?
   - Has this changed at all over your career?
   - What must happen for you to keep succeeding here?
   - How do you react to praise and criticism of this organization?
3. Please tell me the last time you were aware of being a(n) _____ [identity descriptor].
4. Have you ever felt advantaged by being a(n) _____ ?
5. Have you ever felt disadvantaged by being a(n) _____ ?

6. Can you tell me about a time when you felt pressured to wear a "mask" or be "one of the boys"?
   - What was the incident?
   - What did you feel like?
   - What did you do?
   - Was there any time you felt that you should have kept the mask on, but didn't? What happened? How did it feel? What would you do differently?
7. Are there any situations in which you express yourself as a _____ here?
   - Do you mentor people?
   - Hire?
   - Work outside the organization?

C. Change

1. Can you think of a time when you felt that it was okay, from the organization's standpoint, to express yourself as a(n) _____ . Or to work explicitly with other _____ , or on behalf of _____ . Do you ever advocate on behalf of _____ ?
   - What do you take away from this?
   - Would you do it again?
   - What would you advise others about working on behalf of _____ ?
   - Has this changed at all over the course of your career?
2. Can you think of an instance in which you felt it was not okay to be a _____ or to speak up or advocate on behalf of _____ ?
   - Do you ever speak up when you hear a joke or slur? Example?
   - Advice?
   - Has this changed since you joined the organization?
3. Can you think of a specific instance where you wanted to do something but didn't?
   - What happened?
   - How did you feel?
   - Would you do the same thing? What would you do differently?
4. What would pushing too hard or taking too much risk look like?
5. Have you ever felt like you were being put on the spot for the _____ perspective?
   - What did you do?

6. Think about the small stuff you do everyday, the way you dress, the words you use. Are you deliberate about any of these things in terms of expressing yourself? Do others notice?

7. Has your awareness or desire to change things been heated up or cooled off during your career? Can you tell me about a time when you felt a strong desire?

8. Can you think of any examples of situations involving issues of being a(n) _____ where you behaved differently at one point than you do now?

9. How would you like the organization to change to be more _____?
   - Do you see yourself as someone who wants to make these changes?
   - Can you give an example of a time you did this?

D. Connections/community

1. How do you relate to other _____ here? Any connection or sense of community?
   - What would you like to advise those ahead of you? Those behind you?

2. Do you belong to any organization or community that reaffirms your _____ identity?

3. Can you tell me about a time when a group of _____ got together?
   - How did this evolve?
   - For what purpose?
   - What happened?
   - What was the organization's reaction?

4. Do you have any particularly close allies or friends in the organization?
   - When do you go to them?
   - Can you describe a time when they helped you?

5. How would your colleagues describe you?

E. Managers and perceptions of others

1. Can you think of others in this organization who have succeeded in making change or advancing _____?
   - How have they done it?
   - Have others made a difference here?

2. What about others who have tried to make change but failed or left?
   - Are there others who have pushed too hard?

3. Who in this organization represents the position of _____ ?
4. Who has made your life safe here?
5. Who has made the most difference in terms of influencing the climate here? What about making it difficult for you?
6. What is your relationship with your manager? With your peers?

F. Others

1. Are there others I should talk to? Why?

Notes

Preface

1. Debra Meyerson and Maureen Scully, "Tempered Radicalism and the Politics of Ambivalence and Change," *Organizational Science* 6, no. 5 (1995): 585–601; Keith Hammonds, "Practical Radicals," *Fast Company*, September 2000, 163–174.

2. Linda Smirich, a well-respected scholar, presented a similar dilemma at a conference that fueled our concerns: "Can a Radical Humanist Find Happiness Working in a Business School?" (paper presented for symposium entitled "Alignment in the Development of Social Science—Toward a New Role for Organizational Development," presented at the Annual Meetings of the Academy of Management, Chicago, August 1986). A number of subsequent conversations with Linda about her experiences helped us refine our ideas.

3. Joanne Martin, "Swimming Against the Tide: Aligning Values and Work," in *Renewing Research Practice*, ed. Ralph Stablein and Peter Frost (Thousand Oaks, CA: Sage, forthcoming).

4. Though I eventually left a traditional tenure-track job, I have continued to act in a way that builds my legitimacy within my profession and follows an academic path, even as I work from the margin of the academic institutions that employ me.

5. These were part-time students with full-time jobs who enrolled in this degree program jointly sponsored by The New Academy of Business and the University of Bath, both in England.

6. In each case, the representation of women within the top three levels of the organization (under the CEO) was relatively high (23 percent at Western, 21 percent at Atlas, and nearly 40 percent at Shop.co). However, in each case, these numbers thinned dramatically within the top *two* layers. At Shop.co, for example, only two women, including the founder/CEO, occupied officer level positions. The composition of ethnic minorities varied more. At Western, people of color comprised 9.7 percent of the spots at the top three levels, and at Atlas, the number was 12 percent. The majority of these people at Atlas were Asian Americans, whereas at Western the numbers were spread more evenly across ethnic groups. Numbers were not available for Shop.co, though my estimate is that the proportion of ethnic minorities in senior management was no more than 5 percent.

7. I use *protest* to mean active engaged forms of activism designed to challenge and disrupt the working of power, not just resist them. On protest and activism, see Frances Fox Piven and Richard A. Cloward, *Poor People's Movements: Why They Succeed, How they Fail* (New York: Pantheon Books, 1979) or Ruth Fainsod Katzenstein, *Faithful and Fearless: Moving Feminist Protest Inside the Church and Military* (Princeton, NJ: Princeton University Press, 1998).

Chapter 1

1. *Merriam-Webster's Collegiate Dictionary*, 10th ed. (Springfield, MA: Merriam-Webster, 1998).

2. Debra Meyerson and Maureen Scully, "Tempered Radicalism and the Politics of Ambivalence and Change," *Organizational Science* 6, no. 5 (1995): 585–601.

3. In her autobiographical account, *Trespassing: My Sojourn in the Halls of Privilege* (New York: Houghton Mifflin, 1997), Gwendolyn Parker describes the feeling of being an outsider even as she climbed up the ladder of success at American Express Company.

4. Sharon Sutton, *Finding Our Voice in a Dominant Key* (unpublished manuscript, University of Michigan, 1991).

5. See Sigmund Freud, *Civilization and Its Discontents* (New York: Norton, 1961).

6. On ambivalence see Gideon Kunda's *Engineering Culture* (Philadelphia: Temple University Press, 1991). Kunda describes the way people construct their selves in relation to a culture that attempts to be all-consuming. See also Ken Smith and David Berg, *Paradoxes of Group Life* (San Francisco: Jossey-Bass, 1987) and Blake Ashforth and Fred Mael, "The Power of Resistance: Sustaining Valued Identities," in *Power and Influence in Organizations*, ed. Roderick Kramer and Margaret Neale (Thousand Oaks, CA: Sage, 1998), 89–102. Both these works speak to the opposing inclinations of self in relation to conformity-inducing social institutions. See also Neil Smelsner's 1998 Presidential Address to the American Sociological Association: Neil J. Smelsner, "The Rational and the Ambivalent in the Social Sciences," *American Sociological Review* 63 (1998): 1–15 for a discussion of the ubiquity of ambivalence in social life and the conditions that foster it.

7. These two strategies are comparable to the strategies of "exit" and "loyalty" described by Albert Hirschman, *Exit, Voice and Loyalty* (Cambridge, MA: Harvard University Press, 1970), in this classic treatment of people's ambivalence toward the state and constraining social institutions.

8. Meyerson and Scully, "Tempered Radicalism."

9. *Merriam-Webster's New Collegiate Dictionary,* 10th ed. (Springfield, MA: Merriam-Webster, 1998).

10. Karl E. Weick, "Small Wins," *American Psychologist* 39, no. 1 (1984): 40–49.

11. Karl E. Weick and Robert E. Quinn, "Organizational Change and Development," *Annual Review of Psychology* 50 (1999): 361–386 and Karl E. Weick, "Emergent Change as a Universal in Organizations," in *Breaking the Code of Change*, ed. Michael Beer and Nitin Noria (Boston: Harvard Business School Press, 2000), 223–241.

12. Michael Tushman and Elaine Romanelli, "Organizational Determinants of Technological Change: Toward a Sociology of Technological Evolution," in *Research in Organizational Behavior* 14, ed. Barry Staw and Larry Cummings (Greenwich, CT: JAI, 1992), 311–347.

13. Weick and Quinn, "Organizational Change and Development."

14. One's identity—and therefore one's deviance based on identity—is defined in part by one's cultural and historical situation. What being an Indian woman means is different in the United States than it is in India. After an Indian woman spends time in the United States, it means something different to be a woman when she returns her home country. The point is, it is hard to answer the question "who am I?" in a vacuum. People's identities change over time and place, and they change as their place in a web of relations changes. This notion is relatively alien to Western notions of the "self" as autonomous and stable, but it is familiar within Eastern conceptions of self as defined relationally. See Dorinne Kondo, *Crafting Selves: Power, Gender, and Discourses of Identity in a Japanese Workplace* (Chicago: University of Chicago Press, 1990) and Hazel Marcus and Shinobu Kitayama, "Culture and the Self: Implications for Cognition, Emotion, and Motivation," *Psychological Review* 98, no. 2 (1991): 224–253. What this means for tempered radicals is that the tensions they experience and their feelings of deviance are specific to time and context. And, although I view ambivalence as a starting point, how people experience ambivalence, the extent to which their selves are at odds, and what they do with these felt tensions can vary enormously over time and situation.

15. It has also been found that people's conception of the "self" is culturally specific, e.g., Marcus and Kitayama, "Culture and the Self."

16. William B. Swann, Jr., "Identity Negotiation: Where Two Roads Meet," *Journal of Personality and Social Psychology* 53, no. 6 (1987): 1038–1051; Viktor Gecas, "The Self-concept," *Annual Review of Sociology* 8 (1982): 1–33. See also Erving Goffman, *The Presentation of Self in Everyday Life* (New York: Doubleday, 1959).

17. Karl E. Weick, "Small Wins."

18. Jane E. Dutton, "The Making of Organizational Opportunities: An Interpretive Pathway to Organizational Change," in *Research in Organizational Behavior* 15, ed. Barry Staw and Larry Cummings (Greenwich, CT: JAI, 1992), 195–226.

Dutton describes the psychological mechanisms by which "opportunity framing" motivates action. The first of these is the suppression of perceived threat, which lowers anxiety and allows for greater search for response options. The second is a "positive gloss" effect, which heightens one's sense of mastery and efficacy, which in turn provides motivation for action.

19. Ibid.

20. Ronald Heifetz, *Leadership Without Easy Answers* (Cambridge, MA: Harvard University Press, 1994). Heifetz, who teaches a popular leadership course at Harvard's Kennedy School of Government, argues that enabling a system to meet its adaptive challenges is the most crucial component of leadership.

21. Patricia Hill Collins, "Learning from the Outsider Within," *Journal of Social Problems* 33, no. 6 (1986): 53. Sociologists have made similar observations about the creativity and insight black women bring to the field of sociology as a result in part of their "outsider within" status in the field. Outsiders within occupy a special place—they become different people, and their difference sensitizes them to patterns that may be more difficult for established sociological insiders to see.

Chapter 2

1. How a person experiences his or her identity depends on a number of social and individual conditions. For example, a person is more likely to be aware of an identity when he or she is one of relatively few people who share it. As Rosabeth Moss Kanter has shown, social identities are more likely to be salient in situations of relative scarcity. See Kanter's *Men and Women of the Corporation* (New York: Basic Books, 1977).

2. Roderick M. Kramer, "Intergroup Relations and Organizational Dilemmas: The Role of Categorization Processes," in *Research in Organizational Behavior*, ed. Barry M. Staw and Robert Sutton (Greenwich, CT: JAI, 2000), 1–37, and Marilyn Brewer, "The Social Self: On Being the Same and Being Different at the Same Time," *Personality and Social Psychology Bulletin* 17, no. 5 (1991): 475–482.

3. In chapter 1 I discussed how someone's sense of self is partly malleable. So too are experiences of difference. A stream of research sees the self as socially constructed. The work of Kenneth Gergen, *The Saturated Self* (New York: Basic Books, 1991), is illustrative of this approach.

4. Erving Goffman, *Stigma: Notes on the Management of Spoiled Identity* (New York: Simon and Schuster, 1963). In his study of social stigma and deviance, Goffman argued that deviance is defined only in relation to conventional definitions of normality. He also pointed out the subjective and socially fabricated notion of this standard. Standards of normality gain their power when people

take these standards so much for granted that they see them as objectively defined and "true." The subjectivity of such standards comes into focus when people from other cultures with different standards call them into question.

5. This example was developed in Debra E. Meyerson and Joyce K. Fletcher, "A Modest Manifesto for Shattering the Glass Ceiling," *Harvard Business Review* January/February 2000, 129–130.

6. Goffman, *Stigma*.

7. William E. B. DuBois, *The Souls of Black Folk* (1903; reprint, New York: New American Library, 1961). In DuBois's now famous words:

> It is a peculiar sensation, this double-consciousness, this sense of always looking at one's self through the eyes of others, of measuring one's soul by the tape of a world that looks on in amused contempt and pity. One ever feels his twoness, an American, a Negro; two souls, two thoughts, two un-reconciled strivings; two warring ideals in one dark body, whose dogged strength alone keeps it from being torn asunder (45).

8. This dual posture has also been referred to as a bicultural stance. See Ella Bell, "The Bicultural Life Experience of Career-oriented Black Women," *Journal of Organizational Behavior* 11 (1990): 459–477. Sociologists, psychologists, and educators have studied the impact of bi-culturalism as it relates to a number of outcome variables. For instance, the impact of biculturalism as it relates to a number of outcome variables, such as the "self-concept," achievement motivation, and learning. Educators concerned with the impact of traditional and nontraditional schooling on biculturals have paid particular attention to how various teaching methods and socialization practices of schools affect bicultural students.

9. Maureen Scully, "Meritocracy," in *Dictionary of Business Ethics*, ed. R. E. Freeman and P. H. Werhane (London: Blackwell, 1997), 511–514 and "Manage Your Own Employability: Meritocracy and the Legitimation of Inequality in Internal Labor Markets and Beyond," in *Relational Wealth: A New Model of Competitive Advantage*, ed. Carrie Leana and Denise Rousseau (New York: Oxford University Press, 2000), 199–214. Scully's work shows how people's ambivalence about their life chances prevents them from acting and protesting the system, which helps keep in place the status quo. John Jost's work on system justification is also relevant. He and his colleagues find that members of low-status groups (based on any number of status indicators, including the status of one's organization) show a consistent tendency to feel ambivalent toward higher-status groups. See John Jost and Diana Burgess, "Attitudinal Ambivalence and the Conflict between Group and System Justification Motives in Low Status Groups," *Personality and Social Psychology Bulletin* 26 (2000): 293–305.

10. Among the Asian and Asian American executives I interviewed at Western and Atlas, with one exception, none suggested that they experience their "selves" as different in this way. On the other hand, the Pacific Islanders and Hispanic professionals I interviewed were quite mixed.

11. Deborah B. Gould, "Sex, Death, and the Politics of Anger: Emotions and Reason in ACT UP's Fight Against AIDS," (Ph.D. diss., University of Chicago, 2000). Ambivalence directed inward is based in feelings of shame, which is an unfortunate product of growing up as a homosexual in a heterosexist society.

12. Kathleen Hall Jamieson, *Beyond the Double Bind: Women and Leadership* (New York: Oxford University Press, 1995). Jamieson explores a number of double binds that achievement-oriented women face in contemporary society.

13. While stereotyping affects all marginalized groups, particularly when they are in a drastic minority, stereotypes tend to bite women especially hard when they ascend to relatively senior positions in organizations. Preconceived ideas about appropriate behavior for women, combined with what is expected of leaders, give women leaders (or potential leaders) only a narrow range of acceptable behaviors. Typical images of leadership and success have developed in the image of stereotypical masculine behaviors. When women behave in ways consistent with these traditionally defined leadership behaviors—when they are tough, aggressive, and competitive—others tend to claim that they are too masculine, or "unfeminine." For further discussion of how this plays out in the course of normal interactions, see Cecilia L. Ridgeway, "Social Difference Code and Social Connections," *Sociological Perspectives* 43, no. 1 (2000): 1–11.

14. See Kathleen Jamieson, *Beyond the Double Bind*, and Meyerson and Fletcher, "Modest Manifesto."

15. Robin Ely and Debra Meyerson, "Theories of Gender in Organizations: A New Approach to Organizational Analysis and Change," in *Research in Organizational Behavior*, ed. Barry Staw and Robert Sutton (Greenwich, CT: JAI, 2000), 103–152.

16. Immigrants should vary in their experience. If they immigrate by choice, they should feel less political pull and less antagonism toward the mainstream; this society represented a desirable alternative to what they left behind. If immigration was not by choice, or not by their ancestor's choice, as is the case with many African Americans, they may be more aware of political dynamics and of their group's political exclusion; members should feel more disempowered by their difference from the dominant group. This possibility was pointed out at a talk I delivered to the faculty seminar at the Institute for Comparative Studies on Race and Ethnicity, Stanford University, December 1999.

17. *New York Times Magazine*, 16 November 1997, 82.

18. Ibid.

Chapter 3

1. See Paul Rogat Loeb, *Soul of a Citizen* (New York: St. Martin's Griffin, 1999), particularly chapter 2.

2. Ibid., p. 35.

3. Elizabeth Janeway, *Powers of the Weak* (New York: Knopf, 1980). See also Carolyn G. Heilbrun, *Writing a Woman's Life* (New York: Ballantine, 1988), 18.

4. Janeway argues that "the refusal to accept the definition of oneself that is put forward by the powerful" is one of the most important sources of power and resistance held by the "weak" in society. Janeway calls this "the ordered use of power to disbelieve." She writes, "By disbelieving, one will be led toward doubting prescribed codes of behavior, and as one begins to act in ways that can deviate from the norm in any degree, it becomes clear that in fact there is not just one right way to handle or understand events." *Powers of the Weak*, 167, quoted in bell hooks, *Feminist Theory from Margin to Center* (Boston: South End Press, 1984), 90.

5. Claude Steele and Joshua Aronson, "Stereotype Threat and the Intellectual Test Performance of African Americans," *Journal of Personality and Social Psychology* 69, no. 5 (1995): 797–811, or Claude Steele, "Race and the Schooling of Black Americans," *Atlantic Monthly*, April 1992, 68–78.

6. See also Jennifer Crocker, Brenda Major, and Claude Steele, "Social Stigma," in *Handbook of Social Psychology*, ed. Daniel T. Gilbert, Susan Fiske, and Gardner Lindsay (New York: McGraw-Hill, 1998). This research points to the debilitating effects of social stigma and low status on people's self-esteem and sense of self.

7. In his talk at the 1999 Center for Gender in Organizations Annual Conference in Boston, Ron David used the human body as a metaphor to describe the importance of healing communities to build people's capacity for resistance. The human body heals at the same time it builds resistance. Human communities need to find ways to let people heal as a stage in resistance. bell hooks, *Yearning: Race, Gender, and Cultural Politics* (Boston: South End Press, 1990), also describes the importance of safe "places" for marginalized people to "come home to" and heal. She focuses on black women's role in creating a "homeplace" for black people:

> This task of making homeplace was not simply a matter of black women providing service; it was about the construction of a safe place where black people could affirm one another and by so doing heal many of the wounds inflicted by racist domination. We could not learn to love or respect ourselves in the culture of white supremacy, on the outside; it was there on the inside, in the "homeplace," most often created and kept by black women, that we had

the opportunity to grow and develop, to nurture our spirits. This task of making a homeplace, of making home a community of resistance, has been shared by black women globally, especially black women in white supremacist societies (42).

8. This notion has also been challenged, however. Some argue that social identity categories, based on fixed identities, are a basis of group oppression. I am suggesting they are also a basis of political power and psychological strength.

9. Ella Bell and Stella Nkomo, "Armoring: Learning to Withstand Racial Oppression," *Journal of Comparative Family Studies* (1996): 3. See also Bell and Nkomo, *Our Separate Ways* (Boston: Harvard Business School Press, 2001).

10. Erving Goffman, *The Presentation of Self in Everyday Life* (New York: Doubleday, 1959). In this volume, Goffman details the ways in which the presentation of self involves an elaborate and staged performance, complete with settings and props. Maintaining an onstage persona typically requires a physical and psychological delineation of a front stage, where one must carefully manage impressions for an audience that presumably matters, and a backstage, where one is less subject to normative and performative expectations. In this backstage physical and psychological region, people express their feelings and act more honestly. Regions may be physical places—like a physical backstage—or demarcated symbolic locations that suggest safety.

11. James Scott, *Domination and the Arts of Resistance: Hidden Transcripts* (New Haven: Yale University Press, 1990). Scott describes the hidden transcript that takes place in reaction to power and subordination.

> Here, offstage, where subordinates may gather outside the intimidating gaze of power, a sharply dissonant political culture is possible. Slaves in the relative safety of their quarters can speak the words of anger, revenge, self-assertion, that they must normally choke back when in the presence of masters and mistresses (18).

Scott argues that these private acts and the social sites in which they take place represent significant resistance in their own right. They also nurture and give meaning to the more public displays of resistance. See also Robert Bies and Tom Tripp, "Two Faces of the Powerless: Coping with Tyranny in Organizations," in *Power and Influence in Organizations*, ed. Roderick Kramer and Margaret Neale (Thousand Oaks, CA: Sage, 1998), 203–220. Bies and Tripp explore the more subversive forms of resistance, such as sabotage, withholding information and support, and rumor spreading as expressions of power in the context of powerlessness.

12. For discussions of organizational culture and the relationship between dominant culture and deviant subcultures and individuals, see Joanne Martin, *Cultures in Organizations* (New York: Oxford University Press, 1992). Also see

Edgar Schein's classic text, *Organizational Culture and Leadership* (San Francisco: Jossey-Bass, 1985), for a discussion of the different aspects and layers of dominant culture.

13. Drawing on Frances Fox Piven and Richard Cloward's classic work on organized protest movements, *Poor People's Movements: Why They Succeed, How They Fail* (New York: Pantheon Books, 1977), 24–27, Mary F. Katzenstein writes,

> Piven and Cloward are right to focus on disruption as the defining feature of protest actions. Disruption, they argue, occurs when people "cease to conform to accustomed institutional roles, withhold their accustomed cooperation, and by doing so, cause institutional disruption." . . . . I will argue there are a wider pool of actions and words that convey exactly this refusal to "conform to institutional roles."

Disruptive, role-shattering behavior, she argues, is a form of protest. See *Faithful and Fearless: Moving Feminist Protest Inside the Church and Military* (Princeton, NJ: Princeton University Press, 1998), 7–8.

14. Karl E. Weick, *The Social Psychology of Organizing*, 2nd ed. (New York: Random House, 1979).

15. The term *enactment* refers to the process by which actions alter the context that in turn shapes future actions. Mary Parker Follett, an early scholar of management, was among the first to call attention to the way individuals shape their environments: "We are neither the master nor the slave of our environment. We cannot command and the environment obey, but also we cannot, if we speak with the greatest accuracy, say that the organism adjust itself to the environment, because it is only part of a larger truth. . . . [This]is a *creating process*." *Creative Experience* (New York: Longmans, Green, 1924), 118–119, quoted in Karl E. Weick, *Sensemaking in Organizations* (Thousand Oaks, CA: Sage, 1995), 32.

16. Goffman, *The Presentation of Self*.

17. Anat Rafaeli, Jane Dutton, Celia V. Harquail, and Stephanie Mackie-Lewis, "Navigating by Attire: The Use of Dress by Female Administrative Employees," *Academy of Management Journal* 40, no. 1 (1997): 9–45.

18. Maureen Scully and I met and interviewed Conley during the earliest stage of our research on tempered radicals.

19. On the subject of office decor as cultural manifestation, see Mary Jo Hatch, "The Organization as a Physical Environment of Work: Physical Structure Determinants of Task Attention and Interaction" (Ph.D. diss., Stanford University, 1985).

20. Magali Larson, *The Rise of Professionalism* (Berkeley: University of California Press, 1977). For a feminist critique of the profession, see Debra Meyerson,

"Feeling Stressed and Burned Out: A Feminist Reading and Re-visioning of Stress-based Emotions within Medicine and Organization Science," *Organization Science* 9 (1998): 103–118.

21. Victor Turner, *The Ritual Process* (Ithaca, NY: Cornell University Press, 1969).

22. Ruth Behar, *The Vulnerable Observer* (Boston: Beacon Press, 1996). In this volume, Behar explores the relationship between the researcher's human experience and the researched.

23. I first heard the term "shadow job" at a conference on women in management at Stanford's Graduate School of Business in the mid-1990s. Female executives talked about all the unseen work they were expected to do on top of their regular jobs. Similar notions have been developed in Joyce K. Fletcher, *Disappearing Acts: Gender, Power, and Relational Practice at Work* (Cambridge, MA: MIT Press, 1999).

24. On the importance of networks and how they work informally, see Herminia Ibarra, "Homophily and Differential Returns: Sex Differences in Network Structures and Access in an Advertising Firm," *Administrative Science Quarterly* 37 (1992): 422–447; or Joel Podolny and James Baron, "Resources and Relationships: Social Networks, Mobility, and Satisfaction in the Workplace" (research paper no. 1340, Graduate School of Business, Stanford University, Stanford, CA,1995).

25. White men are often evaluated based on "potential"; when they lack particular qualifications, they are often viewed as a glass "half full." Women and people of color are evaluated on what they have actually achieved. Thus their "glass" of qualification is more likely to be interpreted as half empty. This is why it can be crucial for people of color and women to have champions who actively interpret their unrealized potential in a positive light.

Chapter 4

1. Erving Goffman, *Encounters: Two Studies in the Sociology of Interaction* (Indianapolis, IN: Bobbs-Merrill, 1961). Encounters, according to Goffman, are a particular kind of face-to-face, focused interaction that have clear beginnings and ends. Doug Creed and Maureen Scully, "Songs of Ourselves: Employees' Deployment of Social Identity in Workplace Encounters," *Journal of Management Inquiry* 9, no. 4 (2000), also build on the notion of "encounters."

2. Erving Goffman, "The Nature of Deference and Demeanor," *American Anthropologist* 58 (1956): 473–502.

3. These types of encounters can be viewed as events in which larger cultural and political arrangements manifest themselves and thus as potential sites of

"micro-mobilization." See William Gamson, Bruce Fireman, and Steven Rytina, *Encounters with Unjust Authorities* (Homewood, IL: Dorsey, 1982).

4. Barry Staw, Lloyd Sandelands, and Jane Dutton, "Threat-Rigidity Effects in Organizations: A Multi-level Analysis," *Administrative Science Quarterly* 26 (1981): 501–524.

5. Goffman, *Encounters*.

6. Jane E. Dutton, "The Making of Organizational Opportunities: An Interpretive Pathway to Organizational Change," in *Research in Organizational Behavior* 15, ed. Barry Staw and Lloyd Cummings (Greenwich, CT: JAI Press, 1992), 195–226. For the effect of positive illusions, see Shelley Taylor, *Positive Illusions: Creative Self-deception and the Health Mind* (New York: Basic Books, 1989). Positive illusions create a sense of mastery, which heightens effort, which in turn increases the likelihood of achieving positive outcomes. Taylor's research documents the effects of this psychological dynamic on cancer patients' recovery rates.

7. In Eastern and some Native American cultures, silence is not viewed as a void and is more likely to be viewed as a deliberate choice.

8. Deborah Kolb and Judith Williams, *The Shadow Negotiation* (New York: Simon and Schuster, 2000). "Responsive" turns are responses to what Goffman describes as "moves" in Erving Goffman, *Interaction Ritual: Essays in Face-to-Face Behavior* (Chicago: Aldine, 1967).

9. In *Shadow Negotiation*, Kolb and Williams also prescribe humor as a tactic, but they fold it into the other types of turns.

10. This scenario was extended from part of a teaching case, Ellen Waxman and George Maxe, *Telemachus Technology*, Program on Negotiation at Harvard Law School (Cambridge, MA, 1996). I've added several details based on further conversations and similar examples from informants.

11. Howard Gadlin, "Conflict Resolution, Cultural Differences, and the Culture of Racism," *Negotiation Journal* 10 (1994): 33–47.

12. This list of criteria is adapted from Mary Gentile, "Ann Livingston and Power Max Systems," teaching note 9-395-069 (Boston: Harvard Business School, 1994).

13. Gamson, Fireman, and Rytina, *Encounters with Unjust Authorities*.

14. Joanne Martin, "Deconstructing Organizational Taboos: The Suppression of Gender Conflict in Organizations," *Organization Science* 1 (1990): 339–359. Also see Deborah M. Kolb and Jean M. Bartunek, ed., *Hidden Conflict in Organizations: Uncovering Behind-the-Scenes Disputes* (Thousand Oaks, CA: Sage,1992).

Chapter 5

1. Deborah Kolb and Anne Donnellon, "Constructive Conflict for All: Dispute Resolution and Diversity in Organizations," *Journal of Social Issues*

(Sept.–Oct. 1994): 124–136. Kolb and Donnellon point out that the ideology of individualism reinforces the interpretation that individuals are the problem. Even individuals who are systematically penalized in organizations buy into this explanation and interpret their problems in terms of their own deficiencies. Such explanations preclude exploration of more systematic dynamics and, most important, examination of the various interests and groups who benefit from the status quo. More to the point, this explanation serves to keep conflicts underground.

2. Lotte Bailyn, *Breaking the Mold: Women, Men and Time in the New Corporate World* (New York: Free Press, 1993).

3. In a discussion with a litigator for the ACLU whose work focuses on racial profiling, I learned that the issue is fundamentally different in England than in the United States. This stems from several factors, most notably that racial profiling has become so commonplace in the United States that people, including the victims, have become numb to this institutionalized form of discrimination. In England, citizens are less accustomed to this practice and have been much more outraged by these incidents. Moreover, the relationship between the British police and the citizens they protect is less antagonistic than what is typical in the United States. As one indicator, police still do not carry guns in many communities in Britain. Thus it is not at all clear whether Cathy would have acted in the same way or been as openly received in the United States given the nature of public relations.

4. In subsequent conversations with Cathy (pseudonyms) she explained that part of her capacity to make this shift may not just be attitudinal. Cathy is a well-educated, professional woman who speaks in "the Queen's English" and is married to a white man. Not all black people would have had the same legitimacy or opportunity to make this shift, even if they were psychologically prepared to do so. Even so, her process points to possibility and alternative courses of response other than revenge or complacency.

5. Ronald Heifetz, *Leadership Without Easy Answers* (Cambridge, MA: Harvard University Press, 1994). It is akin to what Harvard lecturer Heifetz prescribes in his popular course on leadership when he urges people to stand "on the balcony."

6. Barry Staw, Lloyd Sandelands, and Jane Dutton, "Threat-Rigidity Effects in Organizations: A Multi-level Analysis," *Administrative Science Quarterly* 26 (1981): 501–524.

7. Michael White and David Epston, *Narrative Means to Therapeutic Ends* (New York: Norton, 1990), 38–75. See also David Barry, "Telling Changes: From Narrative Family Therapy to Organizational Change and Development," *Journal of Organizational Change Management* 7 (1997): 32–48.

8. Erving Goffman, in *Asylums: Essays in the Social Situation of Mental Patients*

and Other Inmates (New York: Doubleday, 1961), pointed to the notion of developing alternative outcomes to move people out of "normal."

9. Hazel Marcus and Paula Nurius, "Possible Selves," *American Psychologist* 41 (1986): 954–969. These psychologist make a compelling case for how imagined possible selves can be powerful sources of motivation and identity: "Possible selves represent individuals' ideas of what they would like to become, and what they are afraid of becoming, and thus provide a conceptual link between cognition and motivation. . . . Possible selves are important, first, because they function as incentives for future behavior (i.e., they are selves to be approached or avoided)." (954)

10. Shelley Taylor, *Positive Illusions: Creative Self-deception and the Healthy Mind* (New York: Basic Books, 1989). Taylor has shown how imagined outcomes have had remarkable effects with cancer patients who, once they imagined positive outcomes, felt a sense of control and took it upon themselves to heal. Many of them actually did heal, despite physicians' predictions about their likely mortality. An enhanced sense of mastery among these patients resulted in objectively greater recovery rates

11. White and Epston, *Narrative Means*.

12. Peter Senge, *The Fifth Discipline* (New York: Currency, 1993). Personal mastery is one of the key disciplines of creating learning in organizations. Senge also emphasizes the importance of seeing the bigger picture as a cornerstone of learning and system thinking.

13. In their highly effective personal leadership seminars, the organization "Learning as Leadership" pushes people to develop concrete goals that anchor them to desires outside their own "ego-driven" impulses. These goals enable people to act with more choice and agency.

14. Rosabeth Moss Kanter, *The Change Masters* (New York: Simon and Schuster, 1983), 209–240.

15. The notion of facing your fears and anxieties is one of the cornerstones of leadership emphasized by the program "Learning as Leadership."

16. This is a fundamental principle of negotiation, discussed in any solid negotiation text. See, for example, Max Bazerman and Margaret Neale, *Negotiating Rationally* (New York: Free Press, 1993). People often get so caught up in making a deal or resolving a conflict that they risk making a bad deal or they rush to resolve a conflict in a way that undermines their own interests.

17. Alan Cohen and David Bradford, *Influence Without Authority* (New York: Wiley, 1989). Some people object to the notion of currency on the grounds that not every conflict lends itself to this kind of transactional metaphor. Still, I find the notion useful because it encourages us to think in terms of relative values rather than absolute values and also emphasizes the multiplicity of things that can be of value. It also allows for people placing different values

on different factors. When we think this expansively, we create opportunity for developing mutually beneficial exchanges.

18. Deborah Kolb, *The Mediators* (Cambridge, MA: MIT Press, 1983).

19. See Edgar Schein, *Process Consultation* (Reading, MA: Addison-Wesley, 1969), on the importance of creating safety to enable adaptation at the system level. Karl Weick has consistently emphasized the way anxiety and stress limit cognitive functioning such that when people are overly stressed, they resort to overlearned behaviors or habits and shut down their capacity to think creatively. This becomes problematic in crisis situations when sometimes creative solutions and heightened mindfulness are called for. See Karl Weick, "The Collapse of Sense-making in Organizations: The Mann Gulch Disaster," *Administrative Science Quarterly* 38 (1993): 628–652.

20. Kurt Lewin, *Field Theory in Social Science* (New York: Harper & Row, 1951) on the importance of working with factors that contribute to resistance.

21. Francis Conley described how she used an informal group of trusted colleagues as her advisors during a heated time when she accused members of her department at Stanford Medical School of ongoing sexual harassment and later resigned from her department. She received national attention for this dramatic move because she was at the pinnacle of her profession and one of very few women to have achieved this status. In *Walking Out on the Boys* (New York: Farrar, Straus and Giroux, 1998), she describes in detail her traumatic encounter with the sexist medical and academic establishment. She described her reliance on her "kitchen cabinet" in a talk she gave in Jeffrey Pfeffer's class on Power and Politics at Stanford Business School, winter 2000.

Chapter 6

1. Quote from Karl Weick's class notes. This definition is very close to the one offered in Karl Weick, "Wisdom in the 90's: Adaptations Through Small Wins" (Hale Lecture #4, University of Michigan, 30 December 1991).

2. The head of product, while not the CEO, was still a main board director.

3. Albert Bandura, *Social Foundations of Thought as Action* (Englewood Cliffs, NJ: Prentice-Hall, 1986).

4. Saul D. Alinsky, *Rules for Radicals: A Pragmatic Primer for Realistic Radicals* (New York: Vintage Books, 1971).

5. Karl E. Weick, "Small Wins: A Pragmatic Primer for Realistic Radicals," *American Psychologist* 39, no. 1 (1984): 40–49.

6. Kurt Lewin, *Field Theory in Social Science* (New York: Harper & Row, 1951). See also Sim Sitkin, "Learning Through Failure: The Strategy of Small Losses," in *Research in Organizational Behavior* 14, ed. Barry Staw and Lloyd Cummings (Greenwich, CT: JAI, 1992), 231–266.

7. Karl E. Weick, e-mail to author, 28 January 2000.

8. Alinsky, *Rules for Radicals*, 75. See also Eric Eisenberg, "Ambiguity as Strategy in Organizational Communication," *Communication Monographs* 51 (1984): 227–242. I have argued elsewhere that visions of equity may, by necessity, be no more concrete than a process of continually moving toward a more equitable state. Envisioning equitable gender relations, for example, requires moving outside of the current system of gender, which is currently constructed as an unequal power relation. See Robin Ely and Debra Meyerson, "Theories of Gender in Organizations: A New Approach to Organizational Analysis and Change" in *Research in Organizational Behavior*, ed. Barry Staw and Robert Sutton (Greenwich, CT: JAI, 2000), 103–151.

9. Weick, "Wisdom in the 90's."

10. Karl E. Weick and Robert E. Quinn, "Organizational Change and Development," *Annual Review of Psychology* 50 (1999): 361–386.

11. We made a similar argument in Ely and Meyerson, "Theories of Gender in Organizations."

12. Kenneth Gergen and Mary Gergen, "The Social Construction of Narrative Accounts," in *Historical Social Psychology*, ed. Kenneth J. Gergen and Mary M. Gergen (Hillsdale, N.J.: Erlbaum, 1984), 173–189. See also the work of Ellen O'Conner, "The Plot Thickens: Past, Present, and Future Approaches to Narrative Studies in Organization Studies," talk given at SCANCOR, Samples of the Future, Stanford University, Stanford, CA, September 1998.

13. Joanne Martin, *Cultures in Organizations: Three Perspectives* (New York: Oxford University Press, 1992).

14. Patricia Ewick and Susan Silbey, in "Subversive Stories and Hegemonic Tales: Toward a Sociology of Narrative," *Law and Society Review* 29 (1995): 197–226, describe how dominant narratives keep in place existing realities that preserve interests of those in power. Subversive narratives attempt to undermine them.

15. Different cultures have their own stories that explain who gets ahead in that society. These are similarly based on the specific culture's values and beliefs. Within those contexts, these stories would be seen as "true." In India, for example, stories that explain and justify opportunity based on caste may be equally transparent and uncontestable within that culture.

16. This example was borrowed from Debra E. Meyerson and Joyce K. Fletcher, "A Modest Manifesto for Shattering the Glass Ceiling," *Harvard Business Review*, January/February 2000.

17. Barbara Czarniawska, *Narrating the Organization: Dramas of Institutional Identity* (Chicago: University of Chicago Press, 1997). James March and Herbert Simon, in *Organizations* (New York: Wiley, 1958), called attention to the pivotal role language plays in shaping perceptions and made it central to their analysis of

communication in organizations. Louis Pondy and Ian Mitroff later explored language and its role in organizational behavior. They pointed to four functions of language: (1) to control perceptions, (2) to define the meaning of experiences by categorizing events, (3) to influence the ease of communication (because one cannot exchange ideas except as language permits), and (4) to provides channels of social influence. Their research appears in "Beyond Open System Models of Organizations," *Research in Organizational Behavior* 1, ed. Barry Starry (Greenwich, CT: JAI, 1979), 3–40.

18. Carol Cohen, "Sex and Death in the Rational World of Defense Intellectuals," *Journal of Women, Culture, and Society* 12, no. 4 (1987): 687–718.

19. Ely and Meyerson, "Theories of Gender in Organizations."

20. Debra Meyerson and Maureen Scully, "Tempered Radicalism and the Politics of Ambivalence and Change," *Organizational Science* 6, no. 5 (1995): 585–601.

21. Ruth Fainsod Katzenstein, *Faithful and Fearless: Moving Feminist Protest Inside the Church and Military* (Princeton, NJ: Princeton University Press, 1998), 7–8. In contrast to feminists in the Church who rely on these discursive means of protest, feminists in the Military rely on activism that focuses on common interests and has a basis in claims for "rights."

22. Ibid.

Chapter 7

1. David (pseudonym) was enrolled in the New Academy of Business's Masters in Social Responsibility, which is a jointly administered program with the School of Management, Bath University, U.K.

2. Joanne Martin and Debra Meyerson, "Women and Power: Conformity, Resistance, and Disorganized Coation," in *Power and Influence in Organizations*, ed. Roderick Kramer and Margaret Neale (Thousand Oaks, CA: Sage, 1998), 311–348.

3. Mayer Zald and M. Berger, "Social Movements in Organizations: Coup d'etat, Insurgency, and Mass Movements," *American Journal of Sociology* 83 (1978): 823–861.

4. Doug McAdam, John McCarthy, and Mayer Zald, ed., *Comparative Perspectives on Social Movements: Political Opportunities, Mobilizing Structures, and Cultural Framings* (New York: Cambridge University Press, 1996).

5. John McCarthy and Mayer Zald, "Resource Mobilization and Social Movements: A Partial Theory," *American Journal of Sociology* 82 (1977): 1212–1241.

6. William Gamson, "The Social Psychology of Collective Action," in *Frontiers in Social Movement Theory*, ed. A. Morris and C. M. Mueller (New Haven, CT: Yale University Press, 1992), 53–76.

7. The formation of the GLB group at Atlas in response to the impending legislation is an example of what some researchers have called micromobilization contexts: "small group settings in which process of attribution are combined with rudimentary forms of organization to produce mobilization for collective action." Doug McAdams, "Micromobilization Contexts and Recruitment to Activism," in *From Structure to Action: Comparing Social Movement Research Across Cultures*, ed. Bert Kandermans, Hanspeter Kriesi, and Sidney Tarrow (Greenwich, CT: JAI, 1988), 134.

8. I thank Professor Nancy Hopkins for providing a detailed account of her experiences. See Nancy Hopkins, speech delivered to the "Women in the Chemical Workforce" national research workshop, National Academy of Sciences, Washington, D.C., 4 May 2000. And I thank MIT Professor Lotte Bailyn, both for her account of this in a personal communication (August 2000) and in a speech, "Under and Over the Radar: The Effect of the Report on Women Faculty in the School of Science on Gender Awareness at MIT" (presented at the Annual Meetings of the Academy of Management, Toronto, August, 2000). At the time the story broke to the public, Professor Bailyn was chair of the MIT faculty. I also thank her for introducing me to Professor Hopkins. Bailyn's and Hopkinss' accounts match identically, in both the facts of the case and in their emphasis on why events transpired as they did.

9. Hopkins, "Women in the Chemical Workforce" speech.

10. Bailyn, personal correspondence and "Under and Over the Radar." Hopkins also detailed this information in personal correspondence (August 2000).

11. Saul D. Alinsky, *Rules for Radicals: A Pragmatic Primer for Realistic Radicals* (New York: Vintage Books, 1971).

12. Maureen Scully and Amy Segal, "Passion with an Umbrella: Grassroots Activists in the Workplace" (unpublished paper, MIT, 1999).

13. William Gamson, "Hiroshima, the Holocaust, and the Politics of Exclusion: 1994 Presidential Address," *American Sociological Review* 60 (1995): 1–20.

14. bell hooks, *Talking Back: Thinking Feminist, Thinking Black* (Boston: South End Press, 1989), 75. hooks describes the exclusion of women of color when feminist politics take on this lowest-common-denominator approach to feminism. The inextricable relationship between various aspects of one's identity is less salient for people who belong to dominant groups. To many white women, for example, race does not figure consciously into their identity as women, whereas for a black woman, being a woman is inseparable from being a black woman.

15. Karen Proudford, "Notes on the Intra-Group Origins of Inter-Group Conflict in Organizations: Black-White Relations as an Exemplar," *Journal of Labor and Employment Law* 1 (Fall 1998): 615–637. Proudford provides a case example of intragroup conflict within white and black women's collectives.

Some of these conflicts got expressed as conflicts between the black women and the white women to allow for continued solidarity within groups.

16. This prescription is an adaptation of recommendations offered by Sharon Kurtz, "All Kinds of Justice: Labor and Identity Politics" (Ph.D. dissertation, Department of Sociology, Boston College, 1994).

17. Scully and Segal, "Passion with an Umbrella." As these authors discuss, the legitimacy granted to these sanctioned groups may be unique to the workplace because the groups are poised to challenge the very institution that provides the structure and grants them legitimacy in the first place.

18. Ironically, the media initially criticized the group who were advancing change for working in such cooperative way with the administration. Bailyn, personal communication (August 2000).

19. Scully and Segal, "Passion with an Umbrella."

20. Though they did not support employee groups at the time I conducted research, by the date of publication, Western had adopted a policy to support certain kinds of employee caucus groups.

21. McCarthy and Zald, "Resource Mobilization."

22. Doug McAdam, "Specifying the Relationship Between Social Ties and Activism," *American Journal of Sociology* 50 (1993): 640–667. As McAdam discusses, previous research has specified a number or mechanisms and types of ties that explain individuals' tendency to "join." Some ties are based on attitudinal "fit" with a cause, others posit that it is an individual's structural location relative to a movement, and still others locate the tendency to join a movement in interpersonal ties to the other people involved.

23. Alinsky, *Rules for Radicals*, 114.

Chapter 8

1. The arguments in the first two sections of this chapter are extensions of Debra Meyerson and Maureen Scully, "Tempered Radicalism and the Politics of Ambivalence and Change," *Organizational Science* 6, no. 5 (1995): 585–601.

2. For example, Sigmund Freud, "The Interpretation of Dreams," in *The Standard Edition of the Complete Psychological Works of Sigmund Freud* 10, ed. J. Strachey (London: Hogarth, 1961), 3–149, and Sigmund Freud, *Civilization and its Discontents* (New York: Norton, 1961).

3. Kenwyn Smith, Valerie Simmons, and T. Thames, "Fix the Woman: An Intervention into an Organizational Conflict Based on Parallel Process Thinking," *Journal of Applied Behavioral Sciences* 25 (1989): 11–29. The authors account for how people split off the undesirable side of their ambivalence and project it onto others who will "carry" and express their opposing feelings. This splitting and

projecting dynamic appears to be a common response to ambivalence. Because of the intimate and familial social relationships white women share with white men (as their wives, daughters, mothers, sisters), their feelings of ambivalence toward men and male institutions produce a heightened degree of anxiety, so they may be particularly driven to "split off," if not repress, their gender-based ambivalence.

4. Andrew Weigart and David Franks, "Ambivalence: A Touchstone of Modern Times," in *The Sociology of Emotions*, ed. David D. Franks and E. Doyle McCarthy (Greenwich, CT: JAI, 1989), 205–227, and Erving Goffman, *Stigma: Notes on the Management of Spoiled Identity* (Englewood Cliffs, NJ: Prentice-Hall, 1963).

5. This example was taken from Meyerson and Scully, "Tempered Radicalism."

6. Mona Harrington's depiction of the now-practicing women graduates of the Harvard Law School Class of 1960 is from her *Women Lawyers: Rewriting the Rules* (New York, Penguin 1993), 7, quoted in Mary Fainsod Katzenstein, *Faithful and Fearless: Feminist Protest in the Military and Church* (Princeton, NJ: Princeton University Press, 1998), 161. Harrington wrote: "Their sex connects them to conventional roles for women, their work to men. And in their duality, they are not part of either camp."

7. James March made the point long ago that inconsistent behavior can be a signpost of change. He argued that people should be more generous in their treatment of apparent hypocrites because their hypocrisy could be a sign of flux. People who act badly while they talk about being good, for example, may be in the midst of trying to become good. See James March, "The Technology of Foolishness," in *Ambiguity and Choice in Organizations*, ed. James G. March and Johan P. Olsen (Bergen, Norway: Universitetsforlaget, 1976), 69–81.

8. All processes that lead to conformity are not alike. People undergo many different processes of self-modification. Herbert Kelman sketched a useful typology of processes of self-change that vary in their psychological form and depth. Internalization of a value, identity, or belief is the most deeply rooted effect of social influence. If people internalize the influence of an insider group, they integrate the group's identities, personae, beliefs, and so on as their own. Once a person internalizes a belief, he or she no longer depends on the influence to act according to the belief. In contrast, identification involves a desire or need to be similar to those who influence the person. As a result, people adopt personae, behaviors, and ideas not because they believe in them or because they seem correct, but because, by adopting them, they become similar to those that influence. The shallowest form of self-modification in Kelman's typology is compliance, which refers to submission to an opinion, action, or belief upheld by a powerful person or group. The submission lasts only so long as the power to enforce it does. See Herbert Kelman, "Compliance, Identification and Interelations:

Three Processes of Attitudinal Change," *Journal of Conflict and Resolution* 2 (1964): 51–66.

9. The work of such eminent psychologists as Leon Festinger, Bibb Latane, Morten Deutsch, Stanley Milgram, and Stanley Schacter were predicated on this foundation of conformity research.

10. Solomon Asch's research laid the foundation for an important tradition of conformity research. Some of this work is found in Solomon Asch, *Social Psychology* (New York: Prentice-Hall, 1952). Also, see Solomon Asch, "Studies on Independence and Conformity: A Minority of One against a Unanimous Majority," *Psychology Monograph* 70, no. 9, (1956).

11. The original experiments were published in Stanley Milgram, *Soumission à l'Autorité* (Paris: Calmann-Levy, 1974).

12. Edwin Hollander, "Conformity, Status, and Idiosyncrasy Credits," *Psychological Review* 65 (1958): 117–127. Hollander describes idiosyncrasy credits as a tactic used by leaders in their efforts to be exemplars of the status quo and path-breakers.

13. Carol Cohen, "Sex and Death in the Rational World of Defense Intellectuals," *Journal of Women in Culture and Society* 12 (1987): 687–718.

14. Ibid.

15. Ibid., 704.

16. Ibid., 708.

17. One of the primary tactics suggested by Jane Dutton and Sue Ashford's theory of issue selling is the use of well-established and accepted language. See Jane Dutton and Susan Ashford, "Selling Issues to Top Management," *Academy of Management Review* 18 (1993): 397–428. For an empirical test of the importance of issue labels and meanings, see Susan Ashford, "Championing Charged Issues: The Case of Gender Equity within Organizations," in *Power and Influence in Organizations*, ed. Roderick Kramer and Margaret Neale (Thousand Oaks, CA: Sage, 1998), 349–380. This is also a tactic prescribed by community organizers. See Saul Alinsky, *Rules for Radicals: A Pragmatic Primer for Realistic Radicals* (New York: Vintage, 1972).

18. Erving Goffman, *The Presentation of Self in Everyday Life* (Garden City, NY: Doubleday, 1959).

19. Herminia Ibarra, "Provisional Selves: Experimenting with Image and Identity in Professional Adaptation," *Administrative Science Quarterly* (December 1999): 764–785.

20. Rosabeth Moss Kanter, *Men and Women of the Corporation* (New York: Basic Books, 1977).

21. Stephen Carter, "The Black Table, the Empty Seat, and the Tie," in *Lure and Loathing*, ed. Gerald Early (New York: Penguin, 1993), 55–79.

22. Aida Hurtado, "Relating to Privilege: Seduction and Rejection in the Subordination of White Women and Women of Color," *Journal of Women, Culture, and Society* 14 (1989): 833–855.

23. This theme of women upholding traditional expectations of gender roles—and gaining favor for doing so—has been played over and over throughout history and has surfaced in the stories of history's most accomplished women. When historian Jill Ker Conway examined the autobiographies of influential women in history, she found that even powerful, achievement-oriented white women, such as Jane Adams, depicted themselves in ways consistent with traditional gender roles and notions of (white) womanhood. Jill K. Conway, *In Her Own Words* (New York: Vintage Books, 1998).

24. Hurtado, "Relating to Privilege."

25. Ashford, "Championing Charged Issues."

26. Joanne Martin and Debra Meyerson, "Executive Women at Link.com," Teaching Case OB 33 (Stanford, CA: Graduate School of Business, Stanford University, 1997).

27. Joanne Martin, "Swimming against the Tide: Aligning Values and Work," in *Renewing Research Practice*, ed. Ralph Stablein and Peter Frost (Thousand Oaks, CA: Sage, forthcoming).

28. Joanne Martin, *Culture in Organizations: Three Perspectives* (New York: Oxford University Press, 1992).

29. Joanne Martin and Caren Siehl, "Organizational Culture and Counterculture: An Uneasy Symbiosis," *Organizational Dynamics* (Autumn 1983): 52–64.

30. Robin Ely, "The Power in Demography: Women's Social Constructions of Gender Identity at Work," *Academy of Management Journal* 38 (1994): 589–634.

31. Susan Ashford, Jane Dutton, and Jeffrey Edwards, "Decomposing Demographic Effects: The Impact of Gender Proportions on Issue-selling Initiation" (paper presented at the National Academy of Management Meetings, Boston, 1997).

32. A few token people at the top of an organization can do more harm than good if those holding these positions succeed by passively conforming, or worse, by actively demonstrating their loyalty to the majority while distancing themselves from their own identity groups. The success of a few token minorities, for example, can create the appearance that boundaries have been obliterated and that dynamics of exclusion no longer exist—that anyone with the "right stuff" can make it if they just work hard enough. Conservatives who are also minorities, such as Ward Connerly, often receive tremendous visibility and legitimacy because they support majority viewpoints and, most important, support the notion that the world is fair—that people are where they deserve to

be in society and that policy intervention into the natural ordering of society does more harm than good. Of course, these people are typically at the top of their social spheres, so their arguments justify their own positions. Their assertions of meritocracy may in fact do more harm than good for others who are "different." In a similar way, the claims by women at the top of their fields that systemic inequities do not exist carry a lot of social clout because they themselves have made it. Their testimony that the system is fair undermines efforts to try to eradicate systemic obstacles.

33. Maureen Scully and Amy Segal, "Passion with an Umbrella: Grassroots Activism in the Workplace," (unpublished manuscript, MIT, 1999).

34. Ashford, "Championing Charged Issues."

35. Susan Ashford, Nancy Rothbard, Sandy Piderit, and Jane Dutton, "Out on a Limb: The Role of Context and Impression Management in Selling Gender Equity Issues," *Administrative Science Quarterly* 23 (1998): 23–57.

36. Ibid. See also Dutton and Ashford, "Selling Issues to Top Management." On the importance of available structures, see Doug McAdam, John McCarthy, and Mayer Zald, ed., *Comparative Perspectives on Social Movements: Political Opportunities, Mobilizing Structures, and Cultural Framings* (New York: Cambridge University Press, 1996).

37. One factor that I have not discussed, but have suggested throughout the book, is the general climate for learning, experimentation, and change. In particular, organizations that view diversity as a mechanism of learning rather than strictly the fair or "right" thing to do, will tend to foster conditions that enable diverse viewpoints, styles, and understandings to emerge. See David A. Thomas and Robin Ely, "Making Differences Matter: A New Paradigm for Managing Diversity," *Harvard Business Review*, September/October 1996, 79–90, for a detailed elaboration of this argument. Organizations that take this stance try to connect diverse viewpoints to the work itself, foster experimentation with different ways to do work, and lower the negative consequences of experimentation. The important point here is that some organizations and groups within organizations are more conducive to variation and experimentation, and some of these link diversity as a source of positive variation. These conditions should nurture tempered radicals. It is beyond the scope of this chapter to explore these mechanisms in detail, however.

38. Edgar Schein, *Process Consultation* (Reading, MA: Addison-Wesley, 1969), has argued that change can take place only when people feel safe. Managers' ability to create a sense of physical and psychological safety for employees enables employees to take risks and learn from one another's trials.

39. Thomas and Ely, "Making Differences Matter," 79–90.

40. Martin, "Swimming Against the Tide."

Chapter 9

1. Karl Weick, "Wisdom in the 90's: Adaptations Through Small Wins" (Hale Lecture #4, University of Michigan, 30 December 1991).

2. Jerry Sternin and Robert Choo, "The Power of Positive Deviancy," *Harvard Business Review*, January–February 2000.

3. Peter Senge, *The Fifth Discipline* (New York: Currency, 1993).

4. Karl E. Weick, *The Social Psychology of Organizing*, 2nd ed. (New York: Random House, 1979). See also Sternin and Choo, "The Power of Positive Deviancy."

5. Ronald Heifetz, *Leadership Without Easy Answers* (Cambridge, MA: Harvard University Press, 1994).

6. Ibid.

7. Saul D. Alinsky, *Rules for Radicals: A Pragmatic Primer for Realistic Radicals* (New York: Vintage Books, 1971), 114.

8. Karl E. Weick, *Sensemaking in Organizations* (Thousand Oaks, CA: Sage, 1995).

9. Debra Meyerson and Joanne Martin, "Cultural Change: An Integration of Three Different Views," *Journal of Management Studies* 24, no. 6 (1987): 623–647.

10. Weick, *Sensemaking in Organizations*.

11. Joanne Martin, "Swimming against the Tide: Aligning Values and Work," in *Renewing Research Practice*, ed. Ralph Stablein and Peter Frost (Thousand Oaks, CA: Sage, forthcoming).

Appendix A

1. The team included Deborah Kolb (my co-principal investigator), Robin Ely, Gil Coleman, Ann Rippin, Maureen Harvey, and Rhona Rappaport.

Index

About the Author

Debra E. Meyerson is Visiting Professor of Organizational Behavior at Stanford University's Graduate School of Business and at the Center for Work, Technology, and Organization within Stanford's School of Engineering. She is also affiliated faculty at Stanford's Center for Social Innovation and Center for Comparative Study of Race and Ethnicity and at the Center for Gender in Organizations at the Simmons Graduate School of Management. She received her Ph.D. from Stanford University and her B.S. and M.S. degrees from MIT, and was previously on the faculty at the University of Michigan Business School.

Meyerson has given seminars for companies and not-for-profit organizations throughout the world and currently serves on the faculty of UCLA's Women's Leadership Institute, Stanford's Project Management Program, and Stanford's Executive Program for Nonprofit Leaders. She is currently on the editorial board of *Organization* and has been advisor or director on the boards of Pacific Crest Outward Bound School, Women of Silicon Valley, 20% by 2020, and East Palo Alto Young Women's Entrepreneurship Project. She was selected as one of the Bay Area's "seventy-five most influential women in business" by the *San Francisco Business Times* and has been the recipient of a number of awards and research grants, most recently from the Ford Foundation. She has published more than thirty articles and chapters in scholarly and applied publications.

Meyerson lives in Northern California with her husband and three children.

DATE DUE